Phipson on Evidence

VOLUMES IN THE COMMON LAW LIBRARY

Arlidge, Eady & Smith on Contempt
Benjamin's Sale of Goods
Bowstead & Reynolds on Agency
Bullen & Leake & Jacob's Precedents of Pleadings
Charlesworth & Percy on Negligence
Chitty on Contracts
Clerk & Lindsell on Torts
Gatley on Libel and Slander
Goff & Jones on Unjust Enrichment
Jackson & Powell on Professional Liability
McGregor on Damages
Phipson on Evidence

THE COMMON LAW LIBRARY

PHIPSON ON EVIDENCE

FIRST SUPPLEMENT TO THE TWENTIETH EDITION

Up to date to 31 August 2023

GENERAL EDITOR

HODGE M. MALEK KC, B.C.L., M.A. (OXON.)

One of His Majesty's Counsel
A Bencher of Gray's Inn
A Deputy High Court Judge
A Recorder of the Crown Court
Chairman of the Competition Appeal Tribunal
A Deemster in the Isle of Man
Chairman of the Human Fertilisation and Embryology Authority Appeals Committee

SWEET & MAXWELL

THOMSON REUTERS

Published in 2023 by Thomson Reuters, trading as Sweet & Maxwell.
Thomson Reuters is registered in England & Wales,
Company number 1679046.
Registered office: 5 Canada Square, Canary Wharf, London E14 5AQ.

For further information on our products and services, visit *http:// www.sweetandmaxwell.co.uk.*

Computerset by Sweet & Maxwell.
Printed and bound in Great Britain by
CPI Group (UK) Ltd, Croydon, CR0 4YY.
A CIP catalogue record of this book is available from the British Library.

ISBN (print): 978-0-414-11749-5

ISBN (e-book): 978-0-414-11751-8

ISBN (print and e-book): 978-0-414-11750-1

ISBN (mainwork print and e-book set): 978-0-414-11752-5

ISBN (Proview mainwork and supplement): 978-0-414-11753-2

FSC
www.fsc.org
MIX
Paper | Supporting
responsible forestry
FSC® C013604

Editors

First Edition	(1892)	Sidney L. Phipson
Second Edition	(1898)	Sidney L. Phipson
Third Edition	(1902)	Sidney L. Phipson
Fourth Edition	(1907)	Sidney L. Phipson
Fifth Edition	(1911)	Sidney L. Phipson
Sixth Edition	(1921)	Sidney L. Phipson
Seventh Edition	(1930)	Roland Burrows
Eighth Edition	(1942)	Roland Burrows, K.C.
Ninth Edition	(1952)	Sir Roland Burrows
Second Impression	(1959)	Sir Roland Burrows
Tenth Edition	(1963)	Michael V. Argyle, Q.C.
Eleventh Edition	(1970)	John Buzzard, Roy Amlot, Stephen Mitchell
Twelfth Edition	(1976)	John Buzzard, Richard May, M. N. Howard
Thirteenth Edition	(1982)	John Buzzard, Richard May, M. N. Howard
Fourteenth Edition	(1990)	M. N. Howard, Q.C,. Peter Crane, Daniel Hochberg
Fifteenth Edition	(2000)	M. N. Howard, Q.C. and Specialist Editors
Sixteenth Edition	(2005)	Hodge M. Malek Q.C. and Specialist Editors
Seventeenth Edition	(2010)	Hodge M. Malek Q.C. and Specialist Editors
Eighteenth Edition	(2013)	Hodge M. Malek Q.C. and Specialist Editors
Nineteenth Edition	(2018)	Hodge M. Malek Q.C. and Specialist Editors
First Supplement to the Nineteenth Edition	(2019)	Hodge M. Malek Q.C. and Specialist Editors
Second Supplement to the Nineteenth Edition	(2020)	Hodge M. Malek Q.C. and Specialist Editors
Twentieth Edition	(2022)	Hodge M. Malek K.C. and Specialist Editors
First Supplement to the Twentieth Edition	(2023)	Hodge M. Malek K.C. and Specialist Editors

HOW TO USE THIS SUPPLEMENT

This is the First Supplement to the Twentieth Edition of *Phipson on Evidence* and has been compiled according to the structure of the main volume.

At the beginning of each chapter of this Supplement, a mini table of contents of the sections in the main volume has been included. Where a heading in this table of contents has been marked with a square pointer ■, this indicates that there is relevant information in this Supplement to which the reader should refer.

Within each chapter, updating information is referenced to the relevant paragraph in the main volume.

TABLE OF CONTENTS

CONTENTS

CONTENTS

TABLE OF CASES

R. v McGowan (Owen), sub nom. R. v Backhouse (Nyle); R. v Baker (Bradley); R. v
Dawuda-Wodu (Emeka) [2023] EWCA Crim 247; [2023] 2 WLUK 494 CA (Crim Div) 19-25
R. v McKenna (Gerard) [2023] NICA 12; [2023] 2 WLUK 452 CA (NI) 9-11
R. v McKenzie (Mark Anthony) [2008] EWCA Crim 758; [2008] 4 WLUK 316; (2008)
172 J.P. 377; [2008] R.T.R. 22; (2008) 172 J.P.N. 559 CA (Crim Div) 19-02, 19-60
R. v McMinn (Saul) [2007] EWCA Crim 3024; [2007] 11 WLUK 652 CA (Crim Div) 19-02
R. v McNally (Wayne) [2020] EWCA Crim 333; [2020] 2 WLUK 538 CA (Crim Div) 19-39
R. v McNeill (Tracy) [2007] EWCA Crim 2927; [2007] 11 WLUK 96; (2008) 172 J.P. 50;
(2008) 172 J.P.N. 257 CA (Crim Div) 19-25
R. v McPherson (Franklin Rupert) [1957] 1 WLUK 371; (1957) 41 Cr. App. R. 213 CCA . . . 6-16
R. v McPherson (Milton) [2010] EWCA Crim 2906; [2010] 11 WLUK 267 CA (Crim Div) . . 19-25
R. v Mentor (Steven) [2004] EWCA Crim 3104; [2004] 12 WLUK 81; [2005] 2 Cr. App.
R. (S.) 33; [2005] Crim. L.R. 472 CA (Crim Div) 18-18
R. v Metzger 2023 SCC 5 15-33
R. v MH [2012] EWCA Crim 2725; [2012] 12 WLUK 464; [2013] Crim. L.R. 849 CA
(Crim Div) 9-11
R. v Miles (George James) (1890) 24 Q.B.D. 423; [1890] 2 WLUK 28 Crown Cases
Reserved 43-24
R. v Millar (Lee), sub nom. R v Smith (Carl Anthony); joined case(s) R v Smith (Carl
Anthony) [2017] EWCA Crim 639; [2017] 5 WLUK 67 CA (Crim Div). 30-34, 30-35
R. v Milligan [1989] 2 WLUK 29; *Times*, March 11, 1989 CA (Crim Div) 6-09
R. v Mills (Clifford Ernest); joined case(s) R. v Rose (Peter Samuel) [1962] 1 W.L.R. 1152;
[1962] 3 All E.R. 298; [1962] 7 WLUK 33; (1962) 46 Cr. App. R. 336; (1962) 126 J.P.
506; (1962) 106 S.J. 593 CCA 41-01
R. v Milne (Andrew); joined case(s) R. v Barnard (Jacob Damon) [2022] EWCA Crim 753;
[2022] 5 WLUK 448 CA (Crim Div) 31-03
R. v Minors (Craig); joined case(s) R. v Harper (Giselle Gaile) [1989] 1 W.L.R. 441;
[1989] 2 All E.R. 208; [1988] 12 WLUK 161; (1989) 89 Cr. App. R. 102; [1989] Crim.
L.R. 360; (1989) 133 S.J. 420 CA (Crim Div) 30-101
R. v Mitchell [1892] 1 WLUK 23; (1892) 17 Cox C.C. 508 Assizes 37-07
R. v Mitchell (Angeline) [2016] UKSC 55; [2017] A.C. 571; [2016] 3 W.L.R. 1405; [2017]
1 All E.R. 1037; [2017] N.I. 108; [2016] 10 WLUK 414; [2017] 1 Cr. App. R. 9; (2017)
181 J.P. 77; [2017] Crim. L.R. 310; *Times*, October 27, 2016 SC (NI) 19-35
R. v M'Naghten, sub nom. M'Naghten Rules; McNaghten or McNaughton's Case;
McNaughten Rules; R. v McNaghten 8 E.R. 718; (1843) 10 Cl. & F. 200; [1843] 6
WLUK 145 HL 6-12
R. v Mockble (Lee David) [2010] EWCA Crim 2540 CA (Crim Div) 19-39
R. v Mohammad (Naif); joined case(s) R. v Mohammed (Manzoor) [2022] EWCA Crim
380; [2022] 3 WLUK 639; [2022] Crim. L.R. 856 CA (Crim Div) 6-53
R. v Mohammed (Hassan) [2020] EWCA Crim 761; [2020] 5 WLUK 497 CA (Crim Div) . . . 19-02
R. v Mohammedzai (Ibrahim) [2022] EWCA Crim 162; [2022] 2 WLUK 476 CA (Crim
Div) 21-07
R. v Molliere (Pascal) [2023] EWCA Crim 228; [2023] 1 WLUK 506 CA (Crim Div) . 20-12, 20-31
R. v Moody (Macaulay) [2019] EWCA Crim 1222; [2019] 7 WLUK 256; [2019] Crim.
L.R. 975 CA (Crim Div) 22-46
R. v Morgans [2010] EWCA Crim 3089 19-51
R. v Mullings (Tyler Joel) [2010] EWCA Crim 2820; [2010] 12 WLUK 3; [2011] 2 Cr.
App. R. 2 CA (Crim Div) 19-25
R. v Murphy (John) [2021] NICA 16; [2021] 2 WLUK 672 CA (NI) 15-33
R. v Murphy (William Francis) [1980] Q.B. 434; [1980] 2 W.L.R. 743; [1980] 2 All E.R.
325; [1980] 3 WLUK 64; (1980) 71 Cr. App. R. 33; [1980] R.T.R. 145; [1980] Crim.
L.R. 309; (1980) 124 S.J. 189 CA (Crim Div) 33-78
R. v Murray (Jack Leigh) [2016] EWCA Crim 278; [2016] 2 WLUK 832 CA (Crim Div) . . . 19-02
R. v Murray (Marc Jason) [2019] EWCA Crim 1535; [2019] 8 WLUK 222 CA (Crim Div) . . 19-25
R. v Murray (Robert John) [2016] EWCA Crim 1051; [2016] 4 W.L.R. 142; [2016] 7
WLUK 822; [2016] 2 Cr. App. R. 31; [2016] Crim. L.R. 935 CA (Crim Div) 36-38
R. v Musharraf (Sana) [2022] EWCA Crim 678; [2022] 5 WLUK 197; [2022] Crim. L.R.
987 CA (Crim Div) 11-30
R. v Musone (Ibrahim) [2007] EWCA Crim 1237; [2007] 1 W.L.R. 2467; [2007] 5 WLUK
592; [2007] 2 Cr. App. R. 29; (2007) 171 J.P. 425; [2007] Crim. L.R. 972; (2007) 171
J.P.N. 689; (2007) 151 S.J.L.B. 709; *Times*, June 11, 2007 CA (Crim Div) 30-53
R. v Mussell (Barry Charles); joined case(s) R. v Dalton [1995] 2 WLUK 423; [1995]
Crim. L.R. 887 CA (Crim Div) 15-03

TABLE OF STATUTES

TABLE OF CIVIL PROCEDURE RULES

TABLE OF STATUTORY INSTRUMENTS

CHAPTER 1

INTRODUCTION

7.   IMPACT OF THE HUMAN RIGHTS ACT

(a)   General principles

(ii)   The Convention and rules of evidence

Replace footnote 267 with:

²⁶⁷ e.g. *Schenk v Switzerland* (1988) 13 E.H.R.R. 313 at [74]; *Kostovski v Netherlands* (1989) 13   **1-47**
E.H.R.R. 491; *Edwards v United Kingdom* (1993) 15 E.H.R.R. 417 at [47], and more recently *Vidgen v Netherlands* (68328/17) (2019) 69 E.H.R.R. SE3 at [40].

CHAPTER 2

THE DEFINING OF THE ISSUES

2. STATEMENTS OF CASE AND PLEADINGS

(a) Civil cases

Replace footnote 9 with:

2-02 [9] See *Forrest Fresh Foods Ltd v Coca-Cola European Partners Great Britain Ltd* [2021] CAT 29 at [26]–[27] where the Competition Appeals Tribunal emphasised the importance of a properly particularised competition law claim, citing with approval the summary provided by the Court in *King v Stiefel* [2021] EWHC 1045 (Comm) at [145]–[149], as to what constitutes a properly pleaded claim. A trial judge should not decide a case in one party's favour on the basis of a theory not relied upon by either party either in the pleadings or in argument: *Al-Medenni v Mars UK Ltd* [2005] EWCA Civ 1041 at [21]; *Satyan Enterprises Ltd v Burton* [2021] EWCA Civ 287; [2021] B.C.C. 640 at [35]–[38]; *Ali v Dinc* [2022] EWCA Civ 34.

3. VARIANCE AND AMENDMENT

(a) Civil cases

Replace the first paragraph with:

2-07 The court has a wide power to permit amendment of the statements of case of the parties.[53] A party may amend his statement of case at any time before it has been served on any other party. If it has been served he may amend only with the consent of all the other parties or with permission of the court.[54] Even in cases where permission of the court is not required, it may still disallow the amendment.[55] This power to amend is not so wide to enable one form of procedure to be transformed at a later date into another.[56] The court should only deal with permission to amend on the basis of a formal application.[57] Whether to permit an amendment is governed by the overriding objective to deal with cases justly. It must be shown that any amendment has a real prospect of success and it must be sufficiently pleaded.[58] The overriding principle, regardless of the degree of lateness, is that the amendments must have a real, as opposed to fanciful, prospect of success which is one that is more than merely arguable and carries some degree of conviction.[58a] The pleading must be coherent and properly particularised.[58b] The pleading must be supported by evidence which establishes a factual basis which meets the merits test.[58c] Leave to amend is readily granted where it has the effect of narrowing or clarifying the issues between the parties. Even extensive amendments may be permitted (including amendments inconsistent with the case already pleaded)[59] where any prejudice to the other parties may be capable of being remedied in costs.[60] Where there is real prejudice which cannot be compensated in costs, then the amendment may be refused.[61] However, even where costs will not adequately compensate the other side, it is still open to the court to permit the amendment if it is required in the interests of justice.[62] Even where prejudice to the other party may be capable of being compensated in costs, it is still open to the court to refuse an amendment on case management grounds taking into account the overriding objective in the CPR where all the circumstances may be taken into account.[63] However, amendments are more carefully scrutinised the nearer a case is to trial, and if the effect of an amendment may prejudice the ability of the other parties to prepare for trial, or even necessitate the adjournment of the trial if granted, then permission to amend may be refused.[64] Whilst some authorities refer to a heavy onus on a party seeking a late amendment,[65] such an additional requirement has been doubted.[66] Whether or not to allow an amendment at any time will often require the court to undertake a balancing exercise and the later the amendment may make it more likely that a respondent will in fact be prejudiced. The utility in characterising an amendment as late comes from focusing attention to any prejudice caused by the timing, and the need for explanation.[66a] Thus whether or not one puts it in terms of a heavy onus for late amendments, in practical terms a late application must be capable of being justified and this may involve a heavy onus. In striking a fair balance, a number of considerations come into play including the overriding objective of dealing with cases justly and in a proportionate way. The factors are likely to include the following:

(1) the history as regards the amendment and the explanation as to why it is being made late;
(2) the prejudice which will be caused to the applicant if the amendment is refused;
(3) the prejudice which will be caused to the resisting party if the amendment is allowed;
(4) whether the amendment has a real prospect of success;
(5) whether the text of the amendment is satisfactory in terms of clarity and particularity.[67]

These factors are to be balanced in the light of the overriding objective.

[53] CPR Pt 17; cf. formerly RSC Ord.20 r.5, and CCR Ord.15. Any amendments must be verified by a statement of truth unless the court otherwise directs: CPR Pt 17 PD para.1.4. In suitable cases the court may dispense with a statement of truth: *Binks v Securicor Omega Express Ltd* [2003] EWCA Civ 993; [2003] 1 W.L.R. 2557 CA.

[54] CPR r.17.1.

[55] CPR r.17.2.

[56] *Osea Road Campsites Ltd, Re* [2005] 1 W.L.R. 760 Ch D at [17].

[57] *Magdeev v Tsvetkov* [2019] EWCA Civ 1802 at [26]–[27].

[58] *CH Offshore v PDV Marina SA* [2015] EWHC 1986 (Comm) at [18].

[58a] *ED&F Man Liquid Products Ltd v Patel* [2003] EWCA Civ 472; [2003] C.P. Rep. 51; *Elite Property Holdings Ltd v Barclays Bank Plc* [2019] EWCA Civ 204 at [40]–[42]; *Duke of Sussex v News Group Newspapers Ltd* [2023] EWHC 1944 (Ch) at [59]–[63].

[58b] *Elite Property Holdings Ltd v Barclays Bank Plc* [2019] EWCA Civ 204 at [42].

[58c] *Elite Property Holdings Ltd v Barclays Bank Plc* [2019] EWCA Civ 204 at [41]; *Kawasaki Kisen*

Kaisha Ltd v James Kemball Ltd [2021] EWCA Civ 33; [2021] 1 C.L.C. 284 at [16]–[18]; *Duke of Sussex v News Group Newspapers Ltd* [2023] EWHC 1944 (Ch) at [62]–[63].

[59] *Binks v Securicor Omega Express Ltd* [2003] EWCA Civ 993; [2003] 1 W.L.R. 2557.

[60] *Cobbold v Greenwich LBC* unreported 9 August 1999 CA; *Morris v Bank of America & NTSA* [2002] EWCA Civ 425; [2003] 3 C.P.L.R. 251 (successful appeal against decision refusing permission to re-amend points of claim and reply); *Deutsche Bank v Unitech Global* [2016] EWCA Civ 119 at [14]. This was also the practice under the RSC: e.g. *Clarapede v Commercial Union Assn* (1883) 32 W.R. 262; *Cropper v Smith* (1883) 26 Ch. D. 700 at 710–711 (Bowen LJ); *NML Capital Ltd v Republic of Argentina* [2011] UKSC 31; [2011] 2 A.C. 495 at [75].

[61] As to what may constitute prejudice, see *P and O Nedlloyd BV v Arab Metals* [2006] EWCA Civ 1300; [2007] 1 W.L.R. 2483 at [22]–[23].

[62] *Gabriel v Hayward* [2004] EWHC 2363 (TCC).

[63] *Savings and Investment Bank Ltd v Fincken* [2003] EWCA Civ 1630; [2004] 1 W.L.R. 667; *CIP Properties (AIPT) Ltd v Galliford Try Infrastructure Ltd* [2015] EWHC 1345 (TCC) at [15] to the effect that approach in *Cobbold v Greenwich LBC* 9 August 1999 CA is no longer the starting point.

[64] *Woods v Chaleff* [1999] EWCA Civ 1522; *The Times,* 28 May 1999 CA; *Morris v Bank of America* [2002] EWCA Civ 425; *Savings and Investment Bank v Fincken* [2003] EWCA Civ 1630 (last minute amendments will not be readily allowed under CPR, especially where there is a risk of losing the trial date); cf. *Electronic Data Systems Ltd v National Air Traffic Services* [2002] EWCA Civ 13 (late amendment allowed); *Archlane Ltd v Johnson Controls Ltd* [2012] EWHC B12 (TCC): *Bourke v Favre* [2015] EWHC 277 (Ch); *Patel v National Westminster Bank Plc* [2015] EWCA Civ 332; *Su-Ling v Goldman Sachs International* [2015] EWHC 759 (Comm); *Wani LLP v Royal Bank of Scotland* [2015] EWHC 1181 (Ch); *Willmott Dixon Construction Ltd v Robert West Consulting Ltd* [2016] EWHC 3291 (TCC). For a useful summary of the authorities and principles in dealing with late amendments see *CIP Properties (AIPT) Ltd v Gulliford Try* [2015] EWHC 1345 (TCC) at [19], per Coulson J; *Ventra Investments Ltd v Bank of Scotland Plc* [2019] EWHC 2058 (Comm) at [42]–[46]; *Scipion Active Trading Fund v Vallis Group Ltd* [2020] EWHC 795 (Comm) (amendment to reply allowed a trial setting out propositions of law); *The New York Laser Clinic Ltd v Naturastudios Ltd* [2019] EWCA Civ 421 (late amendment to substitute claim for breach of warranty in place of negligent misstatement).

[65] *Swain-Mason v Mills & Reeve* [2011] EWCA Civ 14; [2011] 1 W.L.R. 2735 at [70] (late amendment at trial should have been disallowed); following *Worldwide Corp Ltd v GPT Ltd* [1998] EWCA Civ 1894; *Hayer v Hayer* [2012] EWCA Civ 257; *CIP Properties (AIPT) v Galliford Try Infrastructure Ltd* [2015] EWHC 1345 (TCC) at [19] (summary of approach to late amendments); *Duke of Sussex v News Group Newspapers Ltd* [2023] EWHC 1944 (Ch) at [64]–[66]; *ABP Technology Ltd v Voyetra Turtle Beach Inc* [2022] EWCA Civ 594; [2022] E.T.M.R. 33 at [21]–[25], [30].

[66] *JW Spear & Sons Ltd v Zynga Inc* [2013] EWHC 1640 (Ch) at [59]–[66].

[66a] *ABP Technology Ltd v Voyetra Turtle Beach Inc* [2022] EWCA Civ 594; [2022] E.T.M.R. 33 at [30] (no explanation given for late application, so judge ought to have refused it).

[67] *Brown v Innovatorone Plc* [2011] EWHC 3221 (Comm) at [14]; *PJSC Tatneft v Bogolyubov* [2020] EWHC 623 (Comm) at [15]; *Berkeley Square Holdings Ltd v Lancer Property Asset Management Ltd* [2021] EWHC 750 (Ch) at [11]–[20].

CHAPTER 3

JUDICIAL NOTICE

8. NOTORIOUS FACTS

Replace the second paragraph with:

Examples of where judicial notice has been given are: ordinary course of nature; **3-17** the standards of weight and measure[160]; the public coin and currency,[161] and its difference of value in early and modern times[162]; invariable banking and accounting practice as to the debiting of bank accounts[163]; the course of post such that letters sent by first class post do not invariably arrive on the following day,[164] the stamps of post offices on letters, and the fact that postcards are unclosed documents whose contents are visible to those dealing with them, and so have been read and published[165]; the fact that cocaine hydrochloride is a form of cocaine, which is a controlled drug[166]; the meaning of common words and phrases, e.g. of "nominal rent" in a modern statute,[167] or that beans are a species of pulse[168]; the existence of the Universities of Oxford and Cambridge, and the fact that they are national institutions for the advancement of learning and religion[169]; the difference of time in places east and west of Greenwich[170]; and the almanac annexed to the Common Prayer Book being part of the law of the land[171]—e.g. the number of days in a given month or that a certain day of a month was a Sunday,[172] though not, it has been said, matters therein contained—e.g. the time of sunset or sunrise on a particular day,[173] but an almanac is prima facie evidence of the time of the moon's rising.[174] Nowadays, however, courts in referring to the almanac have as little thought of any particular edition as in referring to the Bible or Aesop's Fables. Nonetheless, a modern court has refused to rely on Whitaker's Almanack for the purposes of proving the time of sunset.[175] This was probably because the Almanack gave the time of sunset at Greenwich, and the distance between Greenwich and the place where the offence (assault on a gamekeeper) was alleged to have taken place might have been crucial.[176] Under the Definition of Time Act 1880, expressions of time in legal docu-

[5]

ments are to be construed with reference to Greenwich mean time, but by the Summer Time Acts 1922 to 1925, during the period of "summer time" they are to be construed with reference to that time. The courts have also noticed that the streets of London are crowded and dangerous[177]; that boys are naturally reckless and mischievous[178]; that the life of a criminal is not a happy one[179]; that many cars bought on hire purchase are wrongfully disposed of[180]; that the purpose of tachographs is to reduce the hours lorry drivers spend at the wheel and that lorry drivers frequently take steps to frustrate this purpose[181]; the fact that the NHS uses "first responder" vehicles to arrive at an emergency ahead of the ambulance team[182]; that cats are ordinarily kept for domestic purposes[183]; that people who go to hotels do not like having their nights disturbed[184]; that venereal disease may lie dormant for a long time[185]; that gestation ordinarily lasts for particular periods, but not what are the limits for extraordinary periods of gestation[186]; that a person's genetic make up could be related to the incidence and course of a medical disorder[187]; that television was a common feature of domestic life and almost entirely for recreational purposes[188]; that social networking sites, Twitter and the internet, generally now provide an alternative means of publication to traditional newspapers[189]; that notice can be taken as to certain facts as to the history of the IRA in deciding whether certain organisations were proscribed by the Terrorism Act 2000[190]; that there is a NATO-led security mission in Afghanistan engaged in extensive peace enforcement measures[191]; that High Court judges have a good understanding of international cases, so in an appropriate case are able to take judicial notice of international situations[192]; that persons who operate a cash business (such as taxi drivers) do not always declare their full income to the Revenue;[193] that women bear the greater burden of childcare responsibilities than men, and that can limit their ability to work hours is a fact that has been noticed for many years.[193a]

[160] *Hockin v Cooke* (1791) 4 T.R. 314.

[161] But not of Irish money: *Kearney v King* 2 B. & Ald. 301.

[162] *Bryant v Foot* (1868) L.R. 3 Q.B. 497.

[163] *Holmes, Re* [2005] 1 Cr. App. R. 16.

[164] *Heron Bros Ltd v Central Bedfordshire Council* [2015] EWHC 604 (TCC) at [42].

[165] *Robinson v Jones* (1879) L.R. 4 Ir. 391; *Huth v Huth* [1915] 3 K.B. 32 CA at 39.

[166] AG for the *Cayman Islands v Roberts* [2002] 2 Cr. App. R. 28 PC; cf. *Hydes v R.* [1980–1983] C.I.L.R. 335. See also *Ringstaad v Butler* [1978] 1 N.S.W.L.R. 754 ("grass" may mean Indian hemp).

[167] *Camden v IRC* [1914] 1 K.B. 641 CA, expert evidence as to the meaning of ordinary English words under modern Acts of Parliament being inadmissible.

[168] *R. v Woodward* (1831) 1 Moo. C.C. 323.

[169] *Oxford Poor Rate Case, Re* (1857) 8 E. & B. 184.

[170] *Curtis v March* (1858) 3 H. & N. 866.

[171] *Collier v Nokes* (1849) 2 C. & K. 1012; *Tutton v Darke* (1860) 5 H. & N. 647.

[172] *Hanson v Shackleton* (1835) 4 Dowl. 48.

[173] *Collier v Nokes* (1849) 2 C. & K. 1012; and *Tutton v Darke* (1860) 5 H. & N. 647.

[174] *R. v Hillier & Harnham* (1840) 4 J.P. 155.

[175] *R. v Crush* [1978] Crim. L.R. 357.

[176] See also *Dugas v Reclair* (1962) 32 D.L.R. (2d) 459; *Freeman v Griffiths* (1976) 13 S.A.S.R. 494.

[177] *Dennis v White* [1916] 2 K.B. 1, 6.

[178] *Clayton v Hardwick Colliery Co* (1916) 32 T.L.R. 159 HL; *Williams v Eady* (1893) 10 T.L.R. 41; *Robinson v WH Smith & Son* (1900) 17 T.L.R. 235 at 423.

[179] *Burns v Edman* [1970] 2 Q.B. 541.

[180] *Royscott Trust v Rogerson* [1991] 2 Q.B. 297 CA.

[181] *Vehicle Inspectorate v Nuttall* [1999] 1 W.L.R. 629 HL. See also *Kahn v Newberry* [1959] 2 Q.B. 1; judicial notice taken that a costermonger's barrow moves; *Poole v Smith's Car Sales (Balham) Ltd* [1962] 1 W.L.R. 744; judicial notice taken of seasonal decline in second-hand car market.

[182] *DPP v Issler* [2014] EWHC 669 (Admin); [2014] 1 W.L.R. 3686 at [34].

[183] *Nye v Niblett* [1918] 1 K.B. 23.

[184] *Andreae v Selfridge* [1938] Ch. 1 at 8.

[185] *Glenister v Glenister* [1945] P. 30 at 36.

[186] *Preston-Jones v Preston-Jones* [1951] A.C. 391 at 401; *R. v Luffe* (1807) 8 East 193 (fortnight too short for human gestation); *Cavanett v Chambers* [1968] S.A.S.R. 97 at 100 (will not take notice of limits of abnormal periods of gestation); cf. *Flaherty v Piva* [1960] Qd. R. 53 at 59–60.

[187] *F (A Minor), Re* [1993] Fam. 375 CA.

[188] *Bridlington Relay Ltd v Yorkshire Electricity Board* [1965] Ch. 436 (though quaere whether the second part of this proposition remains true today).

[189] *Robinson v Sunday Newspapers Ltd* [2011] NICA 13 at [24]. As to Twitter and the limits as to the extent to which judicial notice may be given as to how it works, see *Monroe v Katie* [2017] EWHC 433 (QB) at [5].

[190] *R. v Z* [2005] UKHL 35; [2005] 2 A.C. 645 HL; cf. *Thomas v Mowbray* [2007] HCA 33 High Ct of Australia.

[191] *B. v Refugee Appeals Tribunal* [2011] IEHC 198 HC (Ireland); cf. *R. v Ahmed (Rangzieb)* [2011] EWCA Crim 184 at [58] (time not yet come to give judicial notice about generally accepted facts about Al Qaeda).

[192] *Re H* [2014] EWCA Civ 989 at [15].

[193] *R. v Panesar* [2008] EWCA Crim 1643 CA.

[193a] *Dobson v North Cumbria Integrated Care NHS Foundation Trust* [2021] I.C.R. 1699 at [46].

Replace paragraph with:

Judicial notice may, however, be taken of the fact that the standard form of **3-18** Lloyd's S.G. Policy, with appropriate Institute Warranties attached, is used all over the world[194]; that outside members of Lloyd's have little or no knowledge of how business is conducted on their behalf.[195] Lay justices are not entitled to accept the evidence of one who is not an expert that new tyres are less adhesive than tyres which have been driven several hundred miles.[196] Judicial notice will, however, be taken of the fact that a flick-knife is an offensive weapon,[197] and the same is true of a butterfly knife,[198] but not that a sheath-knife or a "Rambo knife" is one, for this is a question of fact in each case.[199]

[194] *Amin Rasheed Shipping Corp v Kuwait Insurance Co* [1984] A.C. 50 HL at 64–65, per Lord Diplock.

[195] *PCW Syndicates v PCW Reinsurers* [1996] 1 W.L.R. 1136 CA at 1141. See also *Sedgwick v PT Reasuransi* [1990] 2 Lloyd's Rep. 334 at 339 (judicial notice taken of state of insurance market).

[196] *Gubby v Littman* [1976] R.T.R. 470 DC.

[197] *Gibson v Wales* [1983] 1 W.L.R. 393 DC; *R. v Simpson* [1983] 1 W.L.R. 1494 CA.

[198] *DPP v Hynde* [1998] 1 W.L.R. 1222 DC.

[199] *R. v Williamson* (1977) 67 Cr. App. R. 35 CA; *R v STC Ltd* [2021] EWCA Crim 1237; [2021] 4 W.L.R. 131 at [31] (judge wrong to direct jury that a "Rambo knife" is an offensive weapon).

CHAPTER 4

ADMISSIONS

2. FORMAL ADMISSIONS FOR PURPOSES OF TRIAL

(a) Civil cases

(2) By an admission made after the commencement of proceedings

Replace the first paragraph with:

4-06   Under CPR r.14.1 any party to civil proceedings may admit the truth of the whole or any part of another party's case[28] by giving notice in writing, such as in a statement of case or by letter.[29] Where the defendant makes such an admission,[30] the claimant may then apply for judgment on the admission.[31] The purpose of CPR Pt 14 admissions was set out by Nugee J in *Lufthansa Technik AG v Astronics Advanced Electronic Systems*[32]:

> "...the purpose of what the CPR says about admissions is that, if an admission is made, the opponent can proceed on the basis that that will not be something in issue. Whether it is an admission of fact or an admission of law, it will not be necessary to devote any resources or energy or thoughts to that part of a case, because it is not one of the matters that will be in issue. That, of course, is subject to the powers of the court to allow the admission to be withdrawn in rule 14.1(5), and everybody who faces an admission knows that there is always a possibility that an admission may be withdrawn.
>
> However, I agree ... that litigation should be capable of being conducted on the basis that admissions mean what they say and that, if a party whose case has been admitted by the other side is facing an application to withdraw the admission, it is relevant to consider whether they will now be put in a worse position – not in a worse position than they would have been had the admission not been made in the first place, but in a worse position than they are with the admission."

[28] CPR r.14.1(1).

[29] CPR r.14.1(2).

[30] A formal admission must be clear and unequivocal: *Dorchester Group Ltd (t/a Dorchester Collection) v Kier Construction Ltd* [2015] EWHC 3051 (TCC). It was acknowledged in *Kulkarni v Gwent*

Holdings Ltd [2023] EWHC 484 (Ch) at [17] that whether a statement constitutes an admission for the purposes of CPR r.14.1(1) is to a significant extent a matter of impression. The "clear and everyday language" employed in the rule does not require detailed contextual or textual analysis, and should not be construed narrowly: *Sabbagh v Khoury* [2019] EWHC 3004 (Comm); [2020] 1 W.L.R. 187 at [40].

[31] CPR r.14.4; *Lancashire Welders v Harland and Wolff* [1950] 2 All E.R. 1096; *Sabbagh v Khoury* [2019] EWHC 3004 (Comm); [2020] 1 W.L.R. 187 at [41].

[32] *Lufthansa Technik AG v Astronics Advanced Electronic Systems* [2020] EWHC 83 (Pat); [2020] F.S.R. 18 at [22]–[23]; *J v South Wales Local Authority* [2021] EWCA Civ 1102.

(b)   Criminal cases

After the second paragraph, add new paragraph:

A formal admission made pursuant to s.10 should be distinguished from a writ-   **4-09**
ten statement adduced under s.9 of the Criminal Justice Act. As the Court of Appeal in *R. v Drummond* stated,[81a] an admission under s.10 is conclusive of the matter stated and it is not open to the court to reject that fact. The account of a witness read to the jury under s.9 is evidence read by agreement, not agreed evidence, and it is treated no differently than if the account were given from the witness box. The tribunal of fact is therefore entitled to accept or reject the account as it sees fit. Making wilfully false allegations in a s.9 statement, as in *R. v Cordingly*,[81b] may result in a prosecution for doing an act tending and intended to pervert the course of public justice.

[81a] *R. v Drummond* [2020] EWCA Crim 267 at [58]–[59].

[81b] *R. v Cordingly* [2022] EWCA Crim 505.

CHAPTER 5

ESTOPPELS

TABLE OF CONTENTS

1. INTRODUCTORY

(c) Restrictions on estoppels

Replace footnote 34 with:

5-03 ³⁴ Lord Walker of Gestingthorpe. The principles applicable to proprietary estoppel, and the approach to remedies in particular, have recently been reviewed by the Supreme Court in the case of *Guest v Guest* [2022] UKSC 27; [2022] 3 W.L.R. 911. Neither of the more recent decisions of the House of Lords, *Cobbe v Yeoman's Row Management Ltd*, nor *Thorner v Major* [2009] UKHL 18; [2009] 1 W.L.R. 776, had provided a detailed consideration of the appropriate relief to satisfy the equity once established.

Replace footnote 77 with:

5-04 ⁷⁷ *Janred Properties Ltd v ENIT* [1989] 2 All E.R. 444 CA.

(d) Classifications and possible underlying principles

Replace footnote 99 with:

5-06 ⁹⁹ Particularly in the High Court of Australia; see *Waltons Stores (Interstate) Ltd v Maher* (1988) 164 C.L.R. 387; *Commonwealth of Australia v Verwayen* (1990) 170 at 444–446, per Deane J (see also 411–413, per Mason CJ (dissenting)), considered by the Supreme Court in *Guest v Guest* [2022] UKSC 27; [2022] 3 W.L.R. 911. See also Priestley JA (an Australian judge writing extra-judicially) in Waters (ed.), *Equity Fiduciaries and Trusts* (Toronto: Carswell, 1993), pp.273–296; Spence, *Protecting Reliance, The Emergent Doctrine of Equitable Estoppel* (Oxford: Hart Publishing, 1999). See also *Tipperary Developments Pty Ltd v The State of Western Australia* [2009] WASCA 126.

2. LEGAL ESTOPPELS

(d) Estoppels in pais (or by conduct)

(iii) By representation

The first requirement in detail

Replace footnote 275 with:

5-30 ²⁷⁵ *Lipkin Gorman v Karpnale Ltd* [1991] 2 A.C. 548 at 577–580, per Lord Goff. The precise details of this defence are still being worked out. Many of the outstanding issues are discussed in G. Jones, *Goff*

& *Jones on Unjust Enrichment*, 10th edn (London: Sweet & Maxwell, 2022), Ch. 27; and in S. Hedley and M. Halliwell (eds), *The Law of Restitution* (London: Butterworths, 2002), Ch.21. See also P.B.H. Birks, "Change of Position: The Nature of the Defence and its Relationship to Other Restitutionary Defences" in M. McInnes (ed.), *Restitution: Developments in Unjust Enrichment* (Sydney: 1996, Lawbook Co). In the Canadian Supreme Court case of *BMP Global Distribution Inc v Bank of Nova Scotia* [2009] 1 S.C.R. 504; 2009 SCC 15, where a cheque from one bank was deposited into an account held at another bank and it was later found that the cheque was forged, the principle of unjust enrichment in a three party situation envisaged by the House of Lords in *Kipkin* was not applied.

(iv)   From silence, omission or acquiescence

Replace footnote 291 with:

[291] *Berkeley Square Holdings v Lancer Property Asset Management Ltd* [2020] EWHC 1015 (Ch) at [62]; upheld on appeal: [2021] EWCA Civ 551. For the exceptions to the without prejudice rule, see *Oceanbulk Shipping SA v TMT Ltd* [2010] UKSC 44; *Unilever Plc v Proctor & Gamble Co* [2000] 1 W.L.R. 2436; [2001] 1 All E.R. 783.

5-31

3.   EQUITABLE ESTOPPELS

(b)   Equitable proprietary estoppel

After "… of the law made by the Court of Appeal).", add new footnote 320a:

[320a] In *Guest v Guest* [2022] UKSC 27; [2022] 3 W.L.R. 911, the Supreme Court considered the principles that apply in respect of remedies, where the principle of proprietary estoppel is found to apply.

5-36

Replace footnote 347 with:

[347] *Andrew Guest v (1) David Guest (2) Joseph Guest* [2019] EWHC 869 (Ch); decision upheld by the Court of Appeal, [2020] EWCA 387. However, the Supreme Court allowed an appeal by a majority: [2022] UKSC 27; [2022] 3 W.L.R. 911, holding that the equity would be satisfied by alternate remedies of either putting the farm into trust in favour of the son and his siblings or paying compensation to the son now, but with a reduction properly to reflect his earlier-than-anticipated receipt. The parents were to be entitled to choose between these options. The minority would have calculated the son's detriment and awarded financial compensation. This decision provides a reasoned understanding of the principles governing the identification of appropriate relief to satisfy the equity once established.

5-41

CHAPTER 6

BURDEN AND STANDARD OF PROOF

1. CONCEPTS

(a) Distinction between burden and standard of proof

To the end of the paragraph, add:

6-01   The standard of proof in civil cases is "on the balance of probabilities" or "more likely than not"; with some exceptions (discussed below) in criminal cases it is "beyond reasonable doubt", or so that jury or other tribunal of fact is "sure" of the matter in dispute.

(b) Persuasive and evidential burden

After "In criminal cases, or in civil jury cases", delete "such as libel cases" and add new footnote 3a:

6-02   ³ᵃ Civil cases that may be tried by a jury include those for malicious prosecution, false imprisonment, fraud or defamation—see s.69 of the Senior Courts Act 1981 and s.66 of the County Courts Act 1984, as amended by s.11 of the Defamation Act 2013.

(c) Burden and standard of proof as to admissibility of evidence

Replace footnote 10 with:

6-04   ¹⁰ *R. v Boyes* (1861) 1 B. & S. 311; 121 E.R. 730; approved in *Phillips v News Group Newspapers Ltd* [2012] UKSC 28; [2013] 1 A.C. 1 at [15]; *Gold Nuts Ltd v Revenue and Customs Commissioners* [2016] UKFTT 82 (TC); [2016] Lloyd's Rep. F.C. 249 at [223].

3. BURDEN OF PROOF IN CRIMINAL CASES

(a) General rule

Replace the first paragraph with:

The burden is upon the prosecution to prove a defendant's guilt. This includes **6-09** negative as well as positive allegations, although there is a limit to what can reasonably be required of the prosecution when seeking to prove a negative.[57a] It also includes allegations where there is an evidential burden on the defendant: once that evidential burden has been satisfied, it is for the prosecution to prove its case beyond reasonable doubt. If on the whole case the jury have such a doubt, the defendant is entitled to be acquitted.[58] So the prosecution must prove absence of consent on a rape charge,[59] and if capacity to consent is in issue then the prosecution bears the burden of proving incapacity.[60] It is fundamental to any summing up that the jury must be instructed as to the burden of proof.[61]

[57a] *R. Mandry* [1973] 1 W.L.R. 1232; [1973] 3 All E.R. 996.

[58] *Mancini v DPP* [1942] A.C. 1; *Woolmington v DPP* [1935] A.C. 462; *Chan Kau v R.* [1955] A.C. 206; *R. v Lobell* [1957] 1 Q.B. 547; *Mckenzie v HM Advocate* [1960] Crim. L.R. 273; *R. v Bentley* [1960] Crim. L.R. 777. The topic is reviewed in *R. v Hunt* [1987] A.C. 352.

[59] *R. v Horn* (1912) 7 Cr. App. R. 200; *R. v Donovan* [1934] 2 K.B. 498; cf. *R. v Thomas* (1982) 77 Cr. App. R. 63 at 65; *R. v Gardiner* [1994] Crim. L.R. 455.

[60] *R v A* [2014] EWCA Crim 299; [2014] 1 W.L.R. 2469.

[61] And at the outset of the summing up: *R. v Ching* (1976) 63 Cr. App. R. 7; *R. v Milligan, The Times,* 11 March 1989. However, no particular "incantation" is needed. Thus, a submission that a direction was defective because the judge did not say that the burden was on the prosecution "throughout the trial" was described as "legalistic nonsense": *R. v Lock* [1975] Crim. L.R. 35. The formulation that the jury must be sure of guilt is now more common: see para.6-51.

(b) Criminal defences and insanity

Replace the fourth paragraph with:

Where the accused raises insanity as a defence, he bears the persuasive burden **6-12** of proving it on a balance of probabilities.[79a] Where the prosecution raises the issue of insanity, the prosecution must prove it beyond reasonable doubt.[80] In rare and exceptional cases, the judge may of his or her own motion raise the issue and leave it to the jury.[80a]

[79a] *R. v Podola* [1960] 1 Q.B. 325; [1959] 3 W.L.R. 718.

[80] *McNaghten's Case* (1843) 4 St. Tr. (N.S.) 847; *Woolmington v DPP* [1935] A.C. 462 at 475; *Sodeman v R.* [1936] 2 All E.R. 1138. See *R. v Carr-Briant* [1943] K.B. 607. Insanity may, of course, be only one of the defences raised.

[80a] *R. v Thomas* (1996) 29 B.M.L.R. 120; [1995] Crim. L.R. 314.

(c) Statutory reverse burdens

Replace footnote 83 with:

[83] Prevention of Crime Act 1953 s.1(1); *R. v Petrie* [1961] 1 W.L.R. 358; *Davis v Alexander* (1970) 54 **6-13** Cr. App. R. 398; *R. v Brown (DW)* (1971) 55 Cr. App. R. 478.

(d)   Satisfying the evidential burden

Replace footnote 98 with:

6-16   [98] The relevant authorities are as follows.

(i)   Non-insane automatism: *Bratty v Att.-Gen. (Northern Ireland)* [1963] A.C. 386; *Hill v Baxter* [1958] 1 Q.B. 277; *R. v Dervish* [1968] Crim. L.R. 37; *Cook v Atchinson* [1968] Crim. L.R. 266 DC; *Bensley v Smith* [1972] R.T.R. 221 DC; *Moses v Winder* [1981] R.T.R. 37; *R. v Cottle* [1958] N.Z.L.R. 999; *R. v Stripp* (1978) 69 Cr. App. R. 318.

(ii)   Loss of control: s.54(5) of the Coroners and Justice Act 2009; *R. v Martin* [2017] EWCA Crim 1359; [2018] Crim. L.R. 340; *R. v Goodwin* [2018] EWCA Crim 2287; [2018] 4 W.L.R. 165; *R. v Clinton* [2012] EWCA Crim 2; [2013] Q.B. 1 at [45]–[47]. For the old cases applicable to provocation see: *Mancini v DPP* [1942] A.C. 1; *R. v Rossiter* [1994] 2 All E.R. 752; *R. v Cambridge* [1994] 2 All E.R. 760; *R. v Stewart* [1995] 4 All E.R. 999; cf. *R. v Walch* [1993] Crim. L.R. 714; *R. v Wellington* [1993] Crim. L.R. 616 and *R. v Cox* [1995] 2 Cr. App. R. 513; *R. v Gauthier* (1943) 29 Cr. App. R. 113; *R. v Holmes* [1946] A.C. 588; *Chan Kau v R.* [1955] A.C. 206; *Bullard v R.* [1957] A.C. 635; *R. v McPherson* (1957) 41 Cr. App. R. 213; *R. v Wheeler* (1968) 52 Cr. App. R. 28; *R. v Cascoe* (1970) 54 Cr. App. R. 401; *Culmer v The Queen* [1997] 1 W.L.R. 1296 PC.

(iii)   Self-defence: *R. v Lobell* [1957] 1 Q.B. 547; *Chan Kau* [1955] A.C. 206: *R. v Wheeler* (1968) 52 Cr. App. R. 28; *Palmer v R.* [1971] 1 All E.R. 1077 PC; *R. v Abraham* [1973] 1 W.L.R. 1270 CA; *R. v Folley* [1978] Crim. L.R. 556; *Irvine v Heywood* 2003 S.L.T. 1193; 2003 S.C.C.R. 561, High Court of Justiciary; *Steel v The State of Western Australia* [2010] WASCA 118.

(iv)   Duress: *R. v Gill* (1963) 47 Cr. App. R. 166; *R. v Bone* (1968) 52 Cr. App. R. 546 CA; *R. v Steane* [1947] K.B. 997. Cf. *R. v Hasan (Aytach)* [2005] UKHL 22; [2005] 2 A.C. 467 at [20] for potential future reform. For similar principles relating to duress in civil contempt proceedings, see *Coca-Cola Co v Aytacli* [2003] EWHC 91 (Ch); (2003) 26(3) I.P.D. 26016.

(v)   Mechanical defect: *R. v Spurge* [1961] 2 Q.B. 205; *R. v Atkinson* [1970] Crim. L.R. 405.

(vi)   Intoxication: *Kennedy v HM Advocate* 1944 J.C. 171; 1945 S.L.T. 11; *R. v Foote* [1964] Crim. L.R. 405; *R. v Groark* [1999] Crim. L.R. 669, *R. v Hatton* [2005] EWCA Crim 2951; [2006] 1 Cr. App. R. 16.

(vii)   Alibi: *R. v Johnson* [1961] 1 W.L.R. 1478; *R. v Denney* [1963] Crim. L.R. 191; *R. v Wood* (1968) 52 Cr. App. R. 74. Note that a defendant is now under a statutory obligation to give the prosecution notice of an alibi defence and to provide certain details of that defence— see Criminal Procedure and Investigations Act 1996 s.6A, inserted by the Criminal Justice Act 2003 s.33.

(viii) Road Traffic Act 1988 ss.6, 7 (failure without reasonable excuse to provide a specimen of breath or a sample): see per Geoffrey Lane J in *R. v Clarke* [1969] 1 W.L.R. 1109 at 1113; *Roland v Thorpe* [1970] 3 All E.R. 195; *R. v Harling* [1970] R.T.R. 441.

(ix)   Impossibility in cases of common law conspiracy: the Court of Appeal gave the following guidance relating to the evidence and burden of proof in such cases. The burden of proof is on the prosecution. If the prosecution have evidence available showing that at the time the agreement was made, the carrying out of it was impossible, they must call the evidence or make it available to the defence. If there was no such evidence, the evidential burden of proving "impossibility" shifts to the defence. The probative burden remains with the prosecution, and if there is some evidence of "impossibility" it should be left to the jury with the appropriate directions. If there is no evidence of impossibility the judge need not direct the jury about it: *R. v Bennett, Wilfred and West* (1979) 68 Cr. App. R. 168 at 177. These guidelines are laid down for dealing with cases such as *DPP v Nock* [1979] 3 W.L.R. 57. There, the House of Lords held that an agreement of producing cocaine or a particular powder was not criminal where the powder was not capable of producing cocaine, for the carrying out of the agreement would not result in the commission of the offence. In *Bennett*, above, the court held that there was no evidence which made it the judge's duty to direct the jury on the question of impossibility.

(x)   Belief in lawful authority: *R. v Gannon* (1988) 87 Cr. App. R. 254 CA (taking motor vehicle without authority).

4.   PRESUMPTIONS

(d)   Examples of presumptions of law

(ix)   Due performance of public or official acts

Replace footnote 152 with:

152 *Tingle Jacobs & Co v Kennedy* [1964] 1 W.L.R. 638n; *DPP v Marrable* [2020] EWHC 566 (Admin); [2020] Crim. L.R. 966; *Ali v DPP* [2020] EWHC 2864 (Admin); [2021] R.T.R. 14.   **6-30**

5.   IMPACT OF THE HUMAN RIGHTS ACT ON REVERSE BURDENS AND PRESUMPTIONS

(a)   General principles

Replace footnote 198 with:

198 *Coca-Cola Co v Aytacli* [2003] EWHC 91 (Ch); (2003) 26(3) I.P.D. 26016. Although the strength of this authority has been criticsed in *Truell v Zalinska* [2021] EWHC 1877 (Ch) at [37].   **6-40**

(b)   Specific categories of cases

(iii)   Reverse burdens as to other factual issues (not states of mind)

After the fourth paragraph, add new paragraph:

In *DPP v Barker*[250a] it was held that where a defendant relies on s.37(3) of the Road Traffic Offenders Act 1988, the burden is on the defendant to show that, at the relevant time, he had a provisional license and was driving in accordance with its conditions.   **6-47**

250a *DPP v Barker* [2004] EWHC 2502 (Admin); [2006] Crim. L.R. 140.

6.   STANDARD OF PROOF: CRIMINAL CASES

(b)   Meaning of "beyond reasonable doubt"

After the fifth paragraph, add new paragraph:

In *R. v Mohammad*,[291a] the jury sent a note to the judge: "We are directed to be 'sure' of guilt. How sure do we have to be? Do we have to be 100% with no doubt? Would 99% be acceptable for example?" In his response, the judge said: "…you are not required to be 100% sure with no doubt. The courts do not place percentages on the word 'sure' …you should use 'sure' in your deliberations as you would in your day-to-day lives, when making decisions in matters of importance in your own affairs, in your own lives or those of your loved ones". The Court of Appeal upheld this direction and held that a report prepared by expert forensic linguists to the effect that the law on the standard of proof was unsatisfactory and that there were major problems with use of the word "sure" was unsuitable for admission as evidence before the Court of Appeal.   **6-53**

291a *R. v Mohammad* [2022] EWCA Crim 380; [2022] Crim. L.R. 856.

7. STANDARD OF PROOF: CIVIL CASES

(b) Serious or criminal allegations and quasi-criminal proceedings

Replace the fifth paragraph with:

6-58   The approach in *B* has been applied in a variety of civil contexts,[327] e.g. in *Aspinalls Club Ltd v Lester Hui Chun Mo*.[327a]*Aspinalls* (at [125]–[135]) contains a helpful and detailed review of the relevant authorities (including *B*).

[327] e.g. *Bank St Petersburg PJSC v Arkhangelsky* [2020] EWCA Civ 408; [2020] 4 W.L.R. 55; *Singh v Singh Jhutti* [2021] EWHC 2272 (Ch) at [114]–[118].

[327a] *Aspinalls Club Ltd v Lester Hui Chun Mo* [2023] EWHC 2036 (KB), which cited para.6-57 of the 20th edition of this work and applied its analysis of the authorities cited herein.

CHAPTER 7

RELEVANCE, ADMISSIBILITY AND WEIGHT: PREVIOUS AND SUBSEQUENT EXISTENCE OF FACTS: THE BEST EVIDENCE RULE

4. RELEVANCE AND ADMISSIBILITY

(c) Relevance: tests and scope

(iii) Narrative relevance

Replace footnote 28 with:

[28] *Old Chief v United States*, 519 U.S. 172 (1997) at 188, citing Stephen A. Saltzburg, "A Special Aspect of Relevance: Countering Negative Inferences Associated with the Absence of Evidence" (1978) 66 Calif. L. Rev. 1011. In *Hewey v The Queen* [2022] UKPC 12 PC (Ber), the Privy Council held that prosecution evidence of the finding of particles containing one or two of the metals associated with gun-shot residue was admissible to counter the forensic point that no scientific evidence had been found to link the accused to a shooting, despite the fact that it is only particles with the correct morphology and containing three metals (lead, antimony and barium) that are properly described as "characteristic" of gun-shot residue; in the event, although the evidence was admissible, the trial judge had fallen into error by overstating the significance of the evidence.

7-10

5. WEIGHT OF EVIDENCE

Replace the first paragraph with:

Questions of the admissibility of evidence belong, as we have seen, to the judge; those of its weight, credibility and sufficiency, to the jury[58] (or, if there is no jury, to the judge[59]). Unlike admissibility, the weight of evidence cannot be determined by fixed rules, since it depends mainly on common sense, logic and experience.

7-17

"For weighing evidence and drawing inferences from it, there can be no canon. Each case presents its own peculiarities and in each common sense and shrewdness must be brought to bear upon the facts elicited."[60]

"The weight of evidence depends on rules of common sense."[61]

[58] See Ch.1.

[59] Where a judge must decide on the admissibility of evidence and assess its weight, as is the case in most civil trials, it is not mandatory for him or her to settle the question of the admissibility of an item of evidence before considering its weight: *Shagang Shipping Co Ltd v HNA Group Co Ltd* [2020] UKSC 34; [2020] 1 W.L.R. 3549 at [57]–[59].

[60] *R. v Madhub Chunder* (1874) 21 W.R. Cr. 13 at 19 (Ind), per Birch J. In *Muyepa v Ministry of Defence* [2022] EWHC 2648 (KB) (helpfully glossed by A. Keane [2023] Crim. L.R. 235), Cotter J provided a useful summary of his approach to the evaluation of lay witness evidence, at [11]–[21].

[61] *Lord Advocate v Blantyre* (1879) 4 App. Cas. 770 at 792, per Lord Blackburn; *Sofaer v Sofaer* [1960] 1 W.L.R. 1173. In *Deng v Zheng* [2022] NZSC 76; [2022] 1 N.Z.L.R. 151 (Supreme Court of New Zealand), the court addressed the question how a court should deal with a situation where the rules of thumb that might usually be applied in order to assess the credibility of a witness and the plausibility of their testimony depended on "normal practice" specific to a culture not shared by the parties (such as what sorts of contracts might normally be reduced to writing). The court held, at [79], that a witness can always seek to explain their conduct by reference to their own social and cultural background, and that in some circumstances expert evidence of cultural practices might be appropriate, particularly when seeking to explain another's behaviour: but care must be taken to avoid any type of stereotyping.

9.   THE BEST EVIDENCE RULE

(c)   The remaining instance

Replace footnote 190 with:

7-44

[190] On the facts of the case Marcus Smith J held that the judge's assessment of whether to exclude a heavily redacted deed of assignment as evidence of an assignment was unacceptably flawed, and that the redacted version should have been excluded in light of the questions which the other evidence in the case raised, the insufficiency of the reasons given for redaction and the procedural history. (Though he subsequently held that the claimants could rely on a different route to proving their title: [2020] EWHC 563 (Ch).) The Court of Appeal, however, held that Marcus Smith J was wrong to have overturned the judge's decision to admit and give weight to the redacted deed: *Promontoria (Oak) Ltd v Emanuel* [2021] EWCA Civ 1682; [2022] 1 W.L.R. 2004 at [85]–[87]. Where the issue to which a document is relevant is relatively simple, such as whether it assigns a debt or not, there is no absolute rule that the whole document must be disclosed, since parts of a document dealing with a range of transactions may obviously be entirely irrelevant to that limited issue: "The ultimate question is always whether it is possible for the court to reach a safe conclusion on the effect of the document: if it cannot, it would be unfair to the other party for the court to proceed on the basis that the document had a particular effect, but if it can, there is no reason why it should not do so, and it would be unfair on the party relying on the document to refuse to do so", at [46]. In reaching this conclusion, the Court of Appeal confirmed that "the best evidence rule" is "now defunct", at [80]. (The Supreme Court refused the debtor's application for permission to appeal: [2022] 1 W.L.R. 4592.)

CHAPTER 8

ATTENDANCE OF WITNESSES

2.   ATTENDANCE OF WITNESSES IN CIVIL CASES

(g)   Inferior courts and tribunals

Replace footnote 90 with:

[90] e.g. Solicitors Act 1974 s.46(11); Medical Act 1983 Sch.4 para.2(1); The Armed Forces (Summary Appeal Court) Rules 2009 Pt 10; Inquiries Act 2005 s.21; *R. (Cabinet Office) v Chair of the UK Covid-19 Inquiry* [2023] EWHC 1702 (Admin).   **8-20**

(h)   Responding to and challenging witness summons

Replace footnote 97 with:

[97] *Harmony Shipping v Saudi Europe Line* [1979] 1 W.L.R. 1380; *Boeing Co v PPG Industries Inc* [1988] 3 All E.R. 839 at 842; cf. *Jonal Properties Pty Ltd v Ms McLeod Holdings Ltd* [1994] SASC 4380 Supreme Court of South Australia (in general no locus standi in opposing party to apply to set aside subpoena). See also, Justice Su Tiang Joo, "Is There Any Property in a Witness: Can the Truth Be Owned By Any Party?" (2023) Jul *Journal of the Malaysian Judiciary* 74, for an illuminating analysis of the position under the law in Malaysia.   **8-21**

6.   EVIDENCE IN THE JURISDICTION FOR FOREIGN CIVIL PROCEEDINGS

(e)   Applying for an order

Replace paragraph with:

The procedure appears from CPR Pt 34[258] and PD 34 r.6. The application for an order pursuant to letters of request should be made pursuant to a Pt 8 claim form and supported by evidence containing the letter of request, a statement of the issues relevant to the proceedings, a list of questions or the subject-matter of ques-   **8-52** tions to be put to the proposed deponent, and a draft order.[259] Where the examination is for oral testimony, the order should include, or have appended to it, a list of topics and may even include specific questions to be covered by the witness, and the examiner will be astute to ensure that the questioning does not go beyond the scope of the order. Where there are specific questions this should not prevent follow up questions as long as they fall within the scope of the topics provided.[259a] Usually the application is made without notice to a King's Bench Division master, although in practice the applicant will often contact the witness in advance of taking out of the application and may be criticised for not doing so where the court considers that it should have done so.[260] As with any without notice application, there is a duty of full and frank disclosure, which if breached may have the consequences of the order for examination being set aside or the court may decide to impose a lesser sanction such as in costs depending on what is reasonable and proportionate.[261] The order may be set aside on an application. In addition to the witness, a party in the foreign proceedings[262] and the person to whom the documents belong or who has rights to confidentiality in them have the standing to challenge an order.[263]

[258] Previously set out in Ord.70.

[259] CPR Pt 34 PD "Depositions and Court Attendance by Witnesses", para.6.3; CPR r.34.17. An application may be made by the Treasury Solicitor.

[259a] *Microtechnologies LLC v Autonomy Inc* [2017] EWHC 613 (QB) at [10]–[20].

[260] *Productivity-Quality Systems Inc v Cybermetrics Corporation* [2019] EWHC 2518 (QB) at [21].

[261] *Compagnie des Grandes Hotels d'Afrique SA v Purdy* [2021] EWHC 1031 (QB) (serious non-disclosure, appropriate costs sanction without order being set aside); *Productivity-Quality Systems Inc v Cybermetrics Corporation* [2019] EWHC 2518 (QB) at [34] (applicant ordered to pay cost of dealing with a limited non-disclosure).

[262] *Boeing v PPG Industries Ltd* [1988] 3 All E.R. 839 CA.

[263] *Nationwide Mutual Insurance Co v Home Insurance Co* unreported 20 October 1998, Sachs J.

(f) Conduct of the examination

Replace paragraph with:

8-53   The rules follow the rules for depositions under CPR Pt 34 and PD 34, "Depositions and Court Attendance by Witnesses". The examination is before an examiner of the court, appointed under CPR r.34.15.[264] In practice it is usual for the witness to be supplied with a bundle of the documents which are to be put to them at the examination, and the court may give directions as to service of such a bundle.[264a] The evidence must be taken "in the English mode", either in accordance with English rules or in a manner which is not inconsistent with English law and procedure.[265] Therefore examination usually follows the practice in English proceedings, but if a foreign court requests a particular manner for taking depositions, the English court has a discretion to follow the request, unless it is so contrary to English procedures that it ought not be adopted.[266] Thus a request for oral evidence to be taken from a company rather than a stated individual is not permissible.[267] Under English rules a person who is called as a witness may not be cross-examined by the person calling them, unless it is permitted on the basis that they are found to be a hostile witness. Where cross-examination is permitted under the rules of the foreign requesting state, then the request may seek cross-examination and the English court may permit such cross-examination.[267a] The court has the power to give directions for the purposes of the examination.[268] To the extent known, the examination will follow the rules of evidence of the foreign court. The examiner has no powers to compel the witness to do anything; he can merely give his opinion.[269] Thus, if the witness fails to attend, refuses to be sworn or to answer questions, an application may be made to the English court to compel him.[270] This is a cumbersome process. If there is still non-compliance, proceedings may be taken for contempt.[271] It is debatable whether or not there is an implied restriction on collateral use of the evidence provided other than the proceedings for which the request has been made. In principle this should be the case, but the proposition has been doubted. The court has the power to provide an express restriction on use in the order for the examination, or it may leave it to the foreign court to deal with restrictions.[271a]

[264] Often the parties agree an examiner.

[264a] *Microtechnologies LLC v Autonomy Inc* [2017] EWHC 613 (QB) at [6]–[9].

[265] *Desilla v Fells* (1879) 40 L.T. 423 at 424 (Cockburn CJ).

[266] *J Barker & Sons v Lloyd's Underwriters* [1987] Q.B. 103; *R. v Horseferry Road Magistrates Court, Ex p. Bennett (No.3), The Times,* 14 January 1994 (videotaping for foreign court was permitted as not inconsistent with English procedure).

[267] *Penn-Texas Co v Murat Anstalt* [1964] 1 Q.B. 40 at 57; [1963] 2 W.L.R. 111. However, the company can be required by its proper officer to produce specified documents, *Penn-Texas Co v Murat Anstalt,* ibid.; *Panthalu v Ramnord Research Laboratories* [1966] 2 Q.B. 173; [1965] 3 W.L.R. 682.

[267a] *Microtechnologies LLC v Autonomy Inc* [2017] EWHC 613 (QB) at [21]–[29].

[268] *USA v Philip Morris Inc* [2004] EWCA Civ 330.

[269] CPR Pt 34 PD "Depositions and Court Attendance by Witnesses", para.4.5.

[270] CPR r.34.10; see generally *R. v Rathbone, Ex p. Dikko* [1985] Q.B. 630 at 648.

[271] Curiously, the remedy under CPR r.34.10(4) is stated to be merely a costs sanction. The contempt provision is found at Pt 34 PD "Depositions and Court Attendance by Witnesses", para.4.11.

[271a] *Microtechnologies LLC v Autonomy Inc* [2017] EWHC 613 (QB) at [34].

CHAPTER 9

COMPETENCE AND COMPELLABILITY, OATH AND AFFIRMATION

TABLE OF CONTENTS

1. COMPETENCE

(e) Infancy

Replace the seventh paragraph with:

9-11   Child witnesses are not to be treated as if they are miniature adults. Allowance must be made for the fact that they may well have difficulties such as placing things in the correct chronological order, but that does not render their evidence unreliable and it does not turn them into an incompetent witness.[62] However, the passage of time between the events that the witness gives evidence about and their giving evidence about those events, may render incompetent an otherwise competent child witness; the issue for the court to determine is whether the length of time involved has left the child unable to give intelligible and reliable answers to questions about the incident.[62a]

[62] *R. v Krezolek* [2014] EWCA Crim 2782; [2015] 2 Cr. App. R. (S) 2 at [45]; and *R v. McKenna* [2023] NICA 12 at [48].

[62a] *R v MH* [2012] EWCA Crim 2725; [2013] Crim. L.R. 849.

After the seventh paragraph, add new paragraph:

The court should be careful in dealing with the cross-examination of children and other vulnerable witnesses, and appropriate measures and restrictions may be necessary to prevent undue distress and avoid oppression.[63]

[63] For a summary, see *The Crown Court Compendium (June 2023): Part 1*, section 10-5; paras 11-35 to 11-47.

CHAPTER 10

EVIDENCE TAKEN OR SERVED BEFORE TRIAL: DUTY TO DISCLOSE EVIDENCE

TABLE OF CONTENTS

1. CIVIL CASES

(a) Evidence taken before trial

(ii) Depositions

Replace footnote 17 with:

¹⁷ CPR r.32.3. See *Deutsche Bank AG v Sebastian Holdings Inc* [2023] EWHC 2234 (Comm) at [44]–[60] for the principles that apply when the court is asked to exercise its discretion to allow a witness to give evidence by video link.

10-04

(iii) Witness statements and affidavits as evidence

Replace footnote 24 with:

²⁴ CPR r.32.14. It is not clear why it was thought necessary to retain the two tier system with affidavits and witness statements, as one no longer has any discernible advantage over the other given the Statement of Truth. On 1 October 2020 a new CPR Pt 81 was introduced which sets out the procedure to be followed for contempt proceedings. See *Deutsche Bank AG v Sebastian Holdings Inc* [2022] EWHC 2057 (Comm), for the principles that apply when considering the appropriate sentence for contempt. (For the principles that applied with respect to permission to bring proceedings for contempt of court under the former procedural rules under CPR r.32.14(2)(b)see *Kirk v Walton* [2008] EWHC 1780 (QB); [2009] 1 All E.R. 257. See also *Barnes (t/a Pool Motors) v Seabrook* [2010] EWHC 1849 (Admin); [2010] C.P. Rep. 42; [2010] A.C.D. 87.)

10-06

Replace footnote 27 with:

²⁷ See the former Ord.26; Matthews and Malek, *Disclosure*, 5th edn (London: Sweet & Maxwell, 2016), Ch.20.

2. CRIMINAL CASES

(d) The duty to disclose evidence

(i) Historical background

Replace the third paragraph with:

There is in fact an extensive Code of Practice under Pt II of the 1996 Act, which

10-44

[23]

sets out the manner in which police officers are to record, retain and reveal to the prosecutor material obtained in a "criminal investigation"[127] and which may be relevant to the investigation, and related matters. It is supplemented by the CPS Disclosure Manual, the CPS Guidance for Experts on Disclosure, Unused Material and Case Management and the Attorney General's December 2020 Guidelines on Disclosure for investigators, prosecutors and defence practitioners.[128]

[127] *DPP v Metten* unreported 22 January 1999 DC.

[128] See *HM Advocate v Murtagh* [2009] UKPC 36 for discussion on the duty on the prosecution to disclose previous convictions of its witnesses. See also *Fraser (Nat Gordon) v HM Advocate* [2011] UKSC 24.

CHAPTER 11

RULES OF EVIDENCE RELATING TO THE COURSE OF A TRIAL: GENERAL

TABLE OF CONTENTS

1. CIVIL CASES

(a) Modern civil trials and the Civil Procedure Rules (CPR)

After "; to the much wider approach of the Civil Evidence Act 1995,", replace "giving carte blanche to the use of hearsay evidence at trial," with:
    which provides that evidence shall not be excluded in civil proceedings on the ground that it is hearsay with   **11-01**

Replace the third paragraph with:
    Most of the rules in Pts 32 and 33 of the CPR (which the civil part of this chapter is primarily concerned with) do not apply to cases proceeding on the small claims track.[2]

[2] CPR r.27.2(1)(c). CPR r.32.1 still applies to cases on the small claims track.

(b) Control of evidence and case management

Replace the first paragraph with:
    The CPR gives courts a general power to control evidence by giving directions as to: (a) the issues on which it requires evidence; (b) the nature of the evidence which it requires for each issue; and (c) the way in which evidence is to be placed before it.[2a] Specifically, as to the evidence of witnesses, the court may give directions identifying or limiting: (a) the issues to which evidence may be directed; (b) the witnesses who may be called or whose evidence may be read; and (c) the length or format of witness statements.[3] The court's case management control over the issues and evidence to be adduced may be particularly strict when dealing with trials of preliminary issues.[4]   **11-02**

[2a] CPR r.32.1(1).

[3] CPR r.32.2(3).

[4] E.g., the debate over whether, and to what extent, qualified privilege and malice should be tried as preliminary issues in libel claims. See *GKR Karate (UK) Ltd v Yorkshire Post Newspapers Ltd (No.1)* [2000] 1 W.L.R. 2571 CA (upheld judge's decision to do so); *Macintyre v Phillips* [2002] EWCA Civ 1087; [2003] E.M.L.R. 9 CA (no rule of practice dictating holding of preliminary issues here); *Jameel*

v Wall Street Journal Europe SPRL (No.1) [2003] EWCA Civ 1694; [2004] E.M.L.R. 6 CA (distinguished *Yorkshire Post*).

Replace the third paragraph with:

As decisions on the admission and use of evidence form part of the court's wider case management role, such decisions may involve wider considerations beyond simply determining whether evidence is admissible under the main exclusionary rules of evidence. For example, a court may direct that, because a party has failed to comply with orders for service of pleadings or evidence,[9a] the trial will be restricted to issues and/or evidence as already served by a particular date.[10]

[9a] CPR r.32.10 provides that if a witness statement or witness summary for use at trial is not served in respect of an intended witness within the time specified by the court, then the witness may not be called to give oral evidence unless the court gives permission. The prohibition imposed by CPR r.32.10 amounts to a sanction in terms of CPR r.3.8(1). The defaulting party applying for permission under CPR r.32.10 must also apply for relief from sanctions as provided for in CPR r.3.8 and r.3.9, per the test in *Denton v TH White Ltd* [2014] EWCA Civ 906; [2014] 1 W.L.R. 3926.

[10] E.g. as in *Stockman v Payne* [2000] C.P. Rep. 50 QBD, Buckley J; *Walsh v Misseldine* [2000] C.P. Rep. 74; [2000] C.P.L.R. 201 CA; *Price v Price (Trading as Poppyland Headware)* [2003] EWCA Civ 888; [2003] All E.R. (D) 340 (Jun) CA. See also *Harland & Wolff Pensions Trustees Ltd v AON Consulting Financial Services Ltd* [2009] EWHC 1557 (Ch) where the Court permitted the appellant to amend its claim under CPR r.17.1 to introduce a new claim as a further head of loss and damage flowing from the original breach. See also *Interflora Inc v Marks & Spencer Plc* [2012] EWCA Civ 1501; [2013] 2 All E.R. 663 where the court conducted a balancing exercise when deciding whether to admit evidence of witnesses who had responded to an online survey.

(c) Exclusion of relevant and otherwise admissible evidence

Replace the first paragraph with:

11-03   The CPR expressly empowers courts to exclude evidence which would otherwise be admissible.[11] It is said that the courts' power to control evidence pursuant to CPR Pt 32 is, in effect, the power to restrict evidence which would otherwise be admissible rather than the power to receive evidence which would otherwise be inadmissible.[11a] Prior to the introduction of the CPR, a judge in a civil case had been unable to exclude evidence even where the prejudice resulting from its admission would outweigh its value in proving a litigant's claim. This position is now reversed by the CPR r.32.1(2).[12]

[11] CPR r.32.1(2). Also see *O'Brien v Chief Constable of South Wales Police* [2005] UKHL 26; [2005] 2 W.L.R. 1038 HL.

[11a] In *Ras Al Khaimah Investment Authority v Azima* [2021] EWCA Civ 349; [2021] 1 C.L.C. 715 at [43], the court emphasised the discretionary nature of the power by stating that power under CPR r.32.1 "is, of course, a power rather than a duty".

[12] *Grobbelaar v Sun Newspapers Ltd, The Times,* 12 August 1999, CA.

Replace the second paragraph with:

There are no criteria given in the CPR as to when otherwise admissible evidence may be excluded pursuant to CPR r.32.1(2). The starting position must be that parties may adduce all evidence that is relevant and not excluded pursuant to any exclusionary rule of evidence, unless there is good reason for excluding such otherwise admissible evidence. The reason may relate to the inappropriateness of adducing any evidence on a particular issue with which the evidence deals, or to the inappropriateness of the particular item of evidence in issue. Where it is claimed by a party that evidence ought to be excluded under an established exclusionary rule of evidence (e.g. on the grounds of communications being caught under the "without prejudice" rule), the source of the court's power to exclude the evidence is not found in CPR Pt 32; however, it is common for such applications to nonetheless be predicated on CPR Pt 32.

Replace the third paragraph with:

There is no general power available to the court to exclude relevant and admissible evidence. Thus, where the court exercises its powers under CPR r.32.1(2), it is necessarily exercising its power to exclude evidence that is otherwise admissible. As such, the power in CPR r.32.1(2) to exclude evidence ought to be used exceptionally.[13] The discretion must be exercised fairly and in accordance with the overriding objective of dealing with cases justly. It must now also be exercised with regard to proportionality of costs.[14] The stronger the probative force of the evidence, the more willing the court should be to admit it; however whilst the court should lean toward excluding evidence which would tend to lengthen the proceedings, unless there are strong countervailing arguments.[15] Although the Rules would not allow the court to stop a litigant advancing a point vital to his defence, the court would hold some control over the way in which the point was presented in the interest of saving costs.[16]

[13] *National Crime Agency v Amir Azam* [2014] EWHC 4742 (QB) at [48].

[14] CPR r.1.1(1).

[15] *O'Brien v Chief Constable of South Wales* [2003] EWCA Civ 1085; [2004] C.P. Rep. 5 CA, applied by the Court of Appeal in *JP Morgan Chase Bank v Springwell Navigation Corp* [2005] EWCA Civ 1602 at [67]–[69].

[16] *McPhilemy v Times Newspapers Ltd (Re-amendment: Justification)* [1999] 3 All E.R. 775; *Grobbelaar v Sun Newspapers Ltd, The Times,* 12 August 1999, CA.

Replace the fourth paragraph with:

The ability of a third party to apply to a court to protect his interests (in that case by seeking to have allegations about him in a witness statement struck out) was considered in *Various v News Group Newspapers Ltd.*[17] The court, however, did not determine whether it did in fact have such jurisdiction in relation to a witness statement, proceeding instead on assumption that, in some circumstances (including in that case), jurisdiction did exist.[18]

[17] *Various v News Group Newspapers Ltd* [2019] EWHC 1969 (Ch).

[18] The court dismissed the application on the basis that upon the material facts, it would require a mini-trial, which would not be appropriate on an application.

Replace footnote 20 with:

[20] E.g. *Barclay v Barclay* [2020] EWHC 1179 (QB); *Mustard v Flower* [2019] EWHC 2623 (QB); *B (A Child) (Family Proceedings: Judicial Guidance), Re* [2017] EWCA Civ 1579; [2017] 4 W.L.R. 202. See also *Ras Al Khaimah Investment Authority v Azima* [2021] EWCA Civ 349; [2021] 1 C.L.C. 715 at [41], where the Court of Appeal stated: "Cases of evidence procured by torture aside, the general rule of English law is that evidence is admissible if it is relevant to the matters in issue. If it is, it is admissible and the court is not concerned with how the evidence was obtained."

Replace the sixth paragraph with:

CPR r.32.1(2) may also be a means for excluding similar fact evidence in civil proceedings. In *O'Brien v Chief Constable of South Wales*,[21] the House of Lords held that the test of relevance was the correct test for admissibility of similar fact evidence in a civil suit, and there was no warrant for the automatic application of the test from criminal proceedings. The test for admissibility of similar fact evidence is a two-stage test: (i) whether the material was potentially probative of an issue in the case; and (ii) whether as a matter of case management and proportionality the material should be admitted.[21a] The CPR's power to exclude otherwise admissible evidence would not necessarily cause unfair prejudice, though it might carry such a risk.[22]

[21] *O'Brien v Chief Constable of South Wales* [2005] UKHL 26; [2005] W.L.R. 1038. See also *R v P (Children: Similar Fact Evidence)* [2020] EWCA Civ 1088; [2020] 4 W.L.R. 132 for its application in family proceedings. The Court of Appeal confirmed that the analysis in *O'Brien* was to be applied in family proceedings.

[21a] *JP Morgan Chase Bank v Springwell Navigation Corp* [2005] EWCA Civ 1602 at [67]; *BGC Brokers LP v Tradition (UK) Ltd v Bell* [2019] EWHC 3588 (QB) at [49].

[22] The relevance test laid down by the House of Lords in *O'Brien* has been followed in a number of High Court decisions, e.g. *Gulati v MGN Ltd* [2013] EWHC 3392 (Ch); *Mitchell v News Group Newspapers Ltd* [2014] EWHC 3590 (QB); *Kimathi v Foreign and Commonwealth Office* [2015] EWHC 3432 (QB); *Signia Wealth Ltd v Marlborough Trust Co Ltd* [2017] EWHC 363 (Ch) (in the context of amending a claim); *R. (on the application of Khaled) v Secretary of State for Foreign and Commonwealth Affairs* [2019] EWHC 2383 (QB) (in the context of resolving disclosure issues, although unlike in *O'Brien*, this case was not concerned with balancing probative cogency against the risk of causing unfair prejudice to the defendants); *BGC Brokers LP v Tradition (UK) Ltd v Bell* [2019] EWHC 3588 (QB).

Replace the seventh paragraph with:

CPR r.32.1(3) specifically provides that the court may limit cross-examination.[23] As with the court's general power to control evidence, in exercising the power to limit cross-examination, or declining to do so, the court is required to give effect to the overriding objective of dealing with cases justly.[23a] In practice, the court is likely to limit cross-examination in two ways: (i) limiting the issues to be considered both at trial and in cross-examination;[23b] and (ii) limiting the time available during the trial for cross-examination of witnesses.[23c]

[23] *GKR Karate (UK) Ltd v Yorkshire Post Newspapers Ltd* [2000] 1 W.L.R. 2571 CA (cross-examination may be limited where it is disproportionately expensive or time consuming); *Watson v Chief Constable of Cleveland Police* [2001] EWCA Civ 1547 CA (decision to limit cross-examination to some, but not all, previous convictions of claimant); *Hayes v Transco Plc* [2003] EWCA Civ 1261; (2003) 147 S.J.L.B. 1089.

[23a] *Three Rivers DC v Bank of England* [2005] EWCA Civ 889; [2005] C.P. Rep. 46 at [1].

[23b] E.g., *Watson v Chief Constable of Cleveland* [2001] EWCA Civ 1547 (the trial judge had not erred in restricting cross-examination to matters going to the credibility of a witness).

[23c] E.g., *Hayes v Transco Plc* [2003] EWCA Civ 1261, where the Court of Appeal inter alia found that there was a serious procedural irregularity where the trial judge curtailed the cross-examination of a witness, particularly when no notice had been provided that this was to be the case. The Court of Appeal also noted: "Nothing in this judgment is intended to fetter in any way the useful power which judges have to control cross-examination, which can often be unnecessarily prolix or even unnecessary altogether. All depends upon the facts of the particular case. The facts of this case do, however, point perhaps to the importance of giving reasonable notice of an intention to curtail cross-examination."

(d)   The general approach to evidence under the CPR

Replace the first paragraph with:

11-04   The general rule is that facts which need to be proved by the evidence of witnesses should be proved at trial by oral evidence given in public.[24] At hearings other than trials, the general rule is that evidence is to be proved in writing.[25] This should be read with CPR r.32.6, which provides that, in hearings other than trials, evidence is to be by witness statement, and in some circumstances parties can rely on facts stated in statements of case or application notices insofar as they are verified by a statement of truth. These rules are subject to provisions to the contrary in the CPR or elsewhere, or to any order of the court.[26]

[24] CPR r.32.2(1)(a).

[25] CPR r.32.2(1)(b). A party may nonetheless apply for permission to cross-examine the person giving evidence pursuant to CPR r.32.7(1).

[26] CPR r.32.2(2).

Replace list item "statements contained in statements of case and application notices that are verified by a statement of truth;" with:

- statements contained in statements of case and application notices that are verified by a statement of truth[28a]; **11-05**

[28a] Pursuant to CPR r.32.6(2), this is restricted for use at hearings other than the trial. A statement of case is not to be treated as evidence in a trial, even though verified by a statement of truth: see *Kimathi v Foreign and Commonwealth Office* [2018] EWHC 2066 (QB) at [35]. The court in *Aegean Baltic Bank SA v Renzlor Shipping Ltd* [2020] EWHC 2851 (Comm) at [28]–[29] considered that the principle stated in *Kimathi* was right as a matter of application of the general rule; however, it also considered that a pleading with an appropriate statement of truth could constitute hearsay evidence in accordance with CPR r.33.2, and be subject to questions of weight in the event that it is incapable of being challenged in cross-examination.

(e) Witness statements and summaries

Replace footnote 37 with: "The CPR draws a clear distinction between witness "statements" and "summaries". A witness statement is, in effect, a full proof of evidence (albeit the court can issue directions limiting the issues to be covered). A witness summary merely identifies the witness and indicates the issues with which their evidence will deal. See also, Matthews and Malek, *Disclosure*, 6th edn (London: Sweet & Maxwell, 2023), paras 21.14 to 21.37." **11-06**

Replace the first paragraph with:

The court will allow a party to serve on the other parties any written statement signed by a person which contains the evidence that person would be allowed to give orally, and serve all such evidence which the party intends to rely on in relation to any issues of fact to be decided at trial.[38] Trial witness statements, in particular, are important for informing the parties and the court of the evidence a party intends to rely on at trial. The use of witness statements at trial promote the overriding objective by helping the court to deal with cases justly, efficiently and at proportionate cost, including by helping to put parties on an equal footing, saving time at trial and promoting settlement in advance of trial.[38a]

[38] CPR r.32.4. As to the preparation of witness statements and their form and content, see Practice Direction to Pt 32 paras 17–23; Chancery Guide (2022, amended June 2023), Ch.8; Commercial Court Guide, 11th edn (2022), section H; King's Bench Guide (2023), para.10.57–10.64. In *GG v YY* [2014] EWHC 1627 (QB), Tugendhat J used the power under CPR r.3.1(2)(m) to strike out entire witness statements on the grounds that they were irrelevant, an abuse of the court's process and likely to obstruct the just disposal of the proceedings. In *Lachaux v Independent Plant* [2015] EWHC 2242 (QB) at [170]–[184], the authorities and principles on the striking out of irrelevant parts of witness statements were considered. In that case rather than striking out irrelevant and inadmissible passages in witnesses' statements, the judge directed that only edited versions of the statements should be made available to the public and an order was made under CPR r.32.13(2). The judge decided it was not necessary to go so far as to strike out the passages as they might become relevant in future.

[38a] CPR PD 57AC, para.2.2.

Replace the second paragraph with:

Witness statements must not take the form of a repetition or paragraph-by-paragraph affirmations of a party's statement of case. That is particularly so in complex litigation, where such an approach would place an unreasonable burden on the other parties, requiring them to have to reconstruct the evidence by matching it up with the relevant statement of case.[39] Witness statements are to be in the form stipulated by CPR r.32.8. A witness statement should be in the witness' own words and should be restricted to matters to which the witness could readily speak if cross-examined.[39a]

[39] *ACL Netherlands BV (As Successor to Autonomy Corp Ltd) v Lynch* [2018] EWHC 2105 (Ch).

[39a] *Alex Lawrie Factors Ltd v Morgan* [2001] C.P. Rep. 2 CA.

After the second paragraph, add new paragraphs:

Witness statements for use at trials taking place in the Business and Property Courts of England and Wales[39b] must comply with requirements provided for in CPR PD 57AC.[39c]

[39b] In *Nieman v Withers LLP* [2022] EWHC 2237 (QB) at [124], the judge stated that while PD 57AC did not apply in that case, he considered para.2.1 of PD 57AC to be a truism not limited to that of the Business and Property Courts.

[39c] The purpose and requirement of CPR PD 57AC has been considered in a number of cases, including *Mansion Place v Fox Industrial Services Ltd* [2021] EWHC 2747 (TCC) at [37]–[38]; *Blue Manchester Ltd v BUG-Alu Technic GmbH* [2021] EWHC 3095 (TCC) at [40]–[41]; *Primavera Associates Ltd v Hertsmere BC* [2022] EWHC 1240 (Ch) at [61]–[62]; *McKinney Plant & Safety Ltd v Construction Industry Training Board* [2022] EWHC 2361 (Ch) at [20]–[21]. See also Matthews and Malek, *Disclosure* (2023), paras 21.19 to 21.26.

They should be prepared in accordance with: (i) the Statement of Best Practice contained in the Appendix to Practice Direction 57AC[39d]; and (ii) any relevant court guide.[39e] A trial witness statement in the Business and Property Courts must be endorsed with a certificate of compliance with PD 57AC.[39f] CPR PD 57AC was introduced in the light of consistent failure by parties in the Business and Property Courts to prepare trial statements that contained only the evidence that the witness would be able and allowed to give orally.[39g] If a party fails to comply with any part of PD 57AC,[39h] the court may, upon the application by any other party or of its own motion, do one or more of the following: (1) refuse to give or withdraw permission to rely on, or strike out, part or all of a trial witness statement; (2) order that a trial witness statement be re-drafted in accordance with PD 57AC or as may be directed by the court; (3) make an adverse costs order against the non-complying party; and/or (4) order a witness to give some or all of their evidence in chief orally.[39i] Although PD 57AC now relates to trial witness statements in proceedings pending in the Business and Property Courts, it is clear that it has not changed the law concerning the admissibility of witness statement; it only prescribes the contents of witness statements and seeks to eradicate the improper use of witness statements as vehicles for narrative, commentary and argument.[39j]

[39d] Even prior to the introduction of PD 57AC, a proper approach to preparation of a trial witness statement would result in compliance with the Statement of Best Practice: *Mansion Place Ltd v Fox Industrial Services Ltd* [2021] EWHC 2747 (TCC); [2022] C.L.Y. 431 at [45].

[39e] CPR PD 57AC, para 3.4.

[39f] CPR PD 57AC, para 4.4.

[39g] *Greencastle MM LLP v Payne* [2022] EWHC 438 (IPEC) at [22]; see also *Adams v FS Capital Ltd* [2023] EWHC 1649 (Ch) at [51], where the court said that the "key purpose of the provisions of PD 57AC is to ensure that the evidence of a witness is confined only to matters of fact of which that witness has personal knowledge and recollection".

[39h] The courts have considered numerous applications in relation to witness statements said to not

comply with PD 57AC. The courts tend to take a pragmatic approach to such applications taking into account the overriding objective, what is proportionate and the nature and extent of the non-compliance. For a discussion of these cases, see Matthews and Malek, *Disclosure* (2023), para.21.26.

[39i] CPR PD 57AC, para 5.2. Although in *Cumbria Zoo Co Ltd v The Zoo Investment Co Ltd* [2022] EWHC 3379 (Ch) at [52]–[53], following the approach identified in *Lifestyle Equities CV v Royal County of Berkshire Polo Club Ltd* [2022] EWHC 1244 (Ch) at [98], the court stated that parties should be careful about the proportionality of taking objection to minor non-compliance with PD 57AC.

[39j] *Mad Atelier International BV v Manes* [2021] EWHC 3335 (Comm) at [9]; *Polypipe Ltd v Davidson* [2023] EWHC 1681 (Comm) at [18].

Replace the first paragraph with:

If a party is unable to obtain a witness statement from a witness he intends to call, **11-07** the party may instead seek to serve a witness summary.[50] Witness summaries are to be in the form stipulated by CPR r.32.9. The assertion that a party has been "unable to obtain" a witness statement requires proof.[51] A witness summary is a summary of the evidence which could otherwise be included in the witness statement or (if the evidence is not known) the matters about which the party calling the witness proposes to question the witness.[52] The witness summary must include the name and address of the intended witness.

[50] CPR r.32.9. The difference between witness summaries and witness statements is explained in *Otuo v Watch Tower Bible and Tract Society of Britain* [2019] EWHC 346 (QB). Also see *Morley (t/a Morley Estates) v Royal Bank of Scotland Plc* [2019] EWHC 2865 (Ch); [2019] 4 W.L.R. 152.

[51] *Otuo v Watch Tower Bible and Tract Society of Britain* [2019] EWHC 346 (QB).

[52] CPR r.32.9(2).

(f) Disclosure of identity of parties or witnesses

After "… considers non-disclosure necessary", replace "in order to protect the interests of that party or" with:

to secure the proper administration of justice and in order to protect the interests **11-09** of that

(g) Proceedings in open court and in private

Replace the first paragraph with:

As with criminal trials, the general rule is that a hearing is to be in public.[73] Any **11-10** derogation from the general rule will only be justified if one or more of the limited matters provided for in CPR r.39.2(3) apply and it that is necessary for a hearing to be in private to secure the proper administration of justice.[74] A hearing will not be heard in private simply because the parties all agree that a hearing should be held in private, nor will the parties' consent be a sufficient reason in itself for the judge to hold the hearing in private. The parties cannot waive the rights of the public.[74a] Where a court has sat in private without justification, the decision made by the court will be unlawful.[75] The authorities prior to the CPR stress the exceptional nature of the decision to sit in private.[76] Domestic courts have frequently stressed the importance of the public interest in hearings being open,[77] which "trumps" any statutory provision which provides for confidentiality in the context of the conduct of regulatory investigations.[78]

[73] CPR r.39.2(1). See generally the authorities cited in respect of the criminal section at para.11-24. Many of those are civil cases. The leading authorities as to the general principles are *Scott v Scott* [1913] A.C. 417; and *Att.-Gen. v Leveller Magazine* [1979] A.C. 440. Also see *Cliberry v Allan* [2002] Fam. 261 CA (Civ Div); *Cherney v Deripaska* [2012] EWHC 1781 (Comm); *Cape Intermediate Holdings Ltd v Dring* [2018] EWCA Civ 1795; [2019] 1 W.L.R. 479.

[74] *Att.-Gen. v Leveller Magazine* [1979] A.C. 440 at 450, per Lord Diplock.

[74a] *JIH v News Group Newspapers Ltd* [2011] EWCA Civ 42; [2011] 1 W.L.R. 1645 at [21].

[75] *Storer v British Gas Plc* [2000] 1 W.L.R. 1237; *R. (on the application of O'Connor) v Aldershot Magistrates' Court* [2016] EWHC 2792 (Admin); [2017] 1 W.L.R. 2833.

[76] *R. v Reigate Justices, Ex p. Argus Newspapers Ltd* (1983) 147 J.P. 385; *R. v Malvern Justices, Ex p. Evans* [1988] 2 W.L.R. 218; *London and Norwich Investment Services* [1988] B.C.L.C. 226, Browne-Wilkinson VC; *Crook, The Times, 13 November 1989.*

[77] e.g. *DE v AB (Permission Hearing: Publicity Protection)* [2014] EWCA Civ 1064; [2015] 1 F.L.R. 1119, where this was held to be the case despite the fact that one of the parties' interests in the litigation was primarily to publicly embarrass the other. It was, however, appropriate to take other steps including the making of an anonymity order.

[78] *T, R. (On Application of) v Financial Conduct Authority* [2021] EWHC 396 at [15]–[17]; [2021] 1 W.L.R. 3246.

Replace the second paragraph with:

Except where the CPR or other legislation provides otherwise, the general rule is that all courts have an inherent jurisdiction to determine what the principle of open justice requires in terms of access to documents or information placed before the court. In *Cape Intermediate Holdings Ltd v Dring*,[79] the Supreme Court found that, unless inconsistent with statute or rules of court, all courts and tribunals had an inherent jurisdiction to determine what the constitutional principle of open justice required in terms of access to documents or other information placed before the court or tribunal in question and that the default position is that the public should be allowed access, not only to the parties' written submissions, but also to the documents placed before the court and referred to during a hearing. This is not limited by what the judge has chosen to read or has said he has read.[80] However, the Supreme Court also stated that, although the court has the power to allow access, the applicant has no right to be granted it (save to the extent that the rules grant such a right). It is for the person seeking access to explain why he seeks it and how granting him access will advance the open justice principle. In considering such applications, the court much carry out a fact-specific balancing exercise between: (i) the purpose of the open justice principle and the potential value of the information in question in advancing that purpose; and (ii) any risk of harm which disclosure may cause to the maintenance of an effective judicial process or the legitimate interests of others.[80a]

[79] *Cape Intermediate Holdings Ltd v Dring* [2019] UKSC 38; [2020] A.C. 629.

[80] See also *R. (on the application of Guardian News and Media Ltd) v City of Westminster Magistrates' Court* [2012] EWCA Civ 420; [2013] Q.B. 618 (the *Guardian* was entitled to inspect and have disclosure of court documents which had been referred to in an open court at an extradition hearing. The default position was that access should be permitted on grounds of open justice). On access to documents filed in court, see CPR r.5.4C.

[80a] *Cape Intermediate Holdings Ltd v Dring* [2019] UKSC 38; [2020] A.C. 629 at [45]–[46]. See also *Goodley v The Hut Group Ltd* [2021] EWHC 1193 (Comm); *Re Port Finance Investment Ltd* [2021] EWHC 454 (Ch).

Replace the third paragraph with:

Where proceedings are held in public, the court must take reasonable steps to ensure that the hearing is of an open and public character.[81] Courts have wide powers to facilitate the principle of open justice, including transmission of proceedings to another court to enable a greater number of people to follow the proceeding live, applications to live tweet the proceedings can be made, daily transcripts of the proceedings can be ordered, and can be made accessible on the web as soon as available. However, the live streaming of court proceedings will not generally be permitted.[82]

[81] CPR r.39.2(2A).

[82] *R. (Spurrier) v Secretary of State for Transport* [2019] EWHC 528 (Admin); [2021] 4 W.L.R. 33.

Replace the fourth paragraph with:
CPR r.39.2(3) provides that a hearing, or any part of it, may be in private if publicity would defeat the object of the hearing; if it involves matters relating to national security; if it involves confidential information (including information relating to personal financial matters) and publicity would damage that confidentiality; if a private hearing is necessary to protect the interests of any child or protected party; if it is a hearing of an application made without notice and it would be unjust to any respondent for there to be a public hearing; if it involves uncontentious matters arising in the administration of trusts or in the administration of a deceased person's estate; or if the court for any other reason considers this to be necessary to secure the proper administration of justice. An order for a hearing to take place in private under CPR r.39.2(3) does not automatically render secret the information in those proceedings. The giving of a press interview about elements of a hearing does not amount to a contempt of court unless there is also an express order made under s.12(1)(e) of the Administration of Justice Act 1960 forbidding such publication; or alternatively if the proceeding falls within one of the four exceptional categories in s.12(a)–(d).[83]

[83] *AF Noonan (Architectural Practice) Ltd v Bournemouth and Boscombe Athletic Community Football Club Ltd* [2007] EWCA Civ 848; [2007] 1 W.L.R. 2614 CA. See also *Al Rawi v The Security Service* [2009] EWHC 2959 (QB) (Special Advocate procedure even in a civil case).

After "In the past, most interlocutory hearings in the", replace "Queen's" with:
King's   **11-11**

(h)   Evidence by video link and other means

Replace the second paragraph with:
There is now detailed guidance issued by UK courts on the conduct of remote   **11-12**
hearings. There is guidance issued (26 March 2020) jointly by the Master of the Rolls, the President of the Queen's (now King's) Bench Division, the Chancellor of the High Court, the Senior Presiding Judge, and the Deputy Head of Civil Justice, titled "Protocol Regarding Remote Hearings".[93] This applies to civil hearings of all kinds in the County Court, High Court and Court of Appeal (Civil Division), including the Business and Property Courts. The guidance addresses issues such as the privacy and public nature of remote hearings, recording of hearings, the mechanics of such hearings, and various procedural issues.

[93] *https://www.judiciary.uk/wp-content/uploads/2020/03/Remote-hearings.Protocol.Civil_.Generally ApplicableVersion.f-amend-26_03_20-1-1.pdf* [Accessed 29 September 2021].

Delete the third paragraph.

After "The norm is still for witnesses to give evidence in person", add new footnote 95a:
[95a] CPR PD 32, Annex 3, para.2 provides that "VCF may be a convenient way of dealing with any part of proceedings: it can involve considerable savings in time and cost. Its use for the taking of evidence from overseas witnesses will, in particular, be likely to achieve a material saving of costs, and such savings may also be achieved by its use for taking domestic evidence. It is, inevitably not as idea as having the witness physically present in court. Its convenience should not therefore be allowed to dictate its use."

Replace footnote 97 with:
[97] CPR Pt 32 PD "Evidence", Annex 3 paras 19-21; Practice Note to CPR Pt 32; also see Chancery

Guide (2022, amended June 2023), para.31-29; King's Bench Guide (2023), paras 9.91–9.94, 14.27 and 20.12; Commercial Court Guide, 11th edn (2022), section H.4.

(i)   Presence of witnesses in court

Replace the first paragraph with:

11-13   In civil cases, the usual practice is to permit witnesses to remain in court during the evidence. Sometimes the judge accedes to a request that the witnesses remain outside court until they are to give evidence, particularly when there is a risk that the witnesses may alter their evidence in accordance with that which has already been given.[100] In *Luckwell v Limata*,[100a] the court stated that there can be no rational grounds for distinction between civil and family cases, and the approach should be that if a court is sitting in public and if an application is made to exclude a witness or witnesses, then the court may exclude them if it is satisfied, on the facts and in the circumstances of the particular situation, that it would, for good reason, be an appropriate step to take. The threshold is not a high one and the reason may not need to be a very cogent one; however, it needs to be a good enough reason to depart from the general rule that no one who wishes to be present in a public hearing, including witnesses, should be excluded.

[100] See, in the context of proceedings in the magistrates' court, *Tomlinson v Tomlinson* [1980] 1 W.L.R. 322 at 326. But it is a matter of practice not law: *R. v Kingston* [1980] R.T.R. 51 DC at 53; cf. *Luckwell v Limata* [2014] EWHC 536 (Fam); [2014] 2 F.L.R. 1252.

[100a] *Luckwell v Limata* [2014] EWHC 536 (Fam); [2014] 2 F.L.R. 1252 at [16].

(k)   The right and obligation to call witnesses

After "unless the intention to call the witness has been notified", add:

11-15   , within the time specified by the court,

Replace the second paragraph with:

In civil litigation, the starting position is that a court has no general power to order one party to call, as a witness on the substantive issues, a person whom that party does not wish to call. This derives from the principle that party autonomy is paramount.[109] Thus, if a party does not wish to call a witness, the court cannot compel that party to do otherwise, although that may have adverse consequences for the party in question, including that the court may draw an adverse inference against a party who fails to call a witness to deal with certain evidence.[110] No such adverse inference will be drawn where it is not reasonable to expect the witness to be called, for example where there is no case to answer.[111] An entirely different situation arises if a party has provided a witness statement from a witness but does not wish to tender that witness for cross-examination. In those circumstances, if the court takes the view that the evidence of the witness is important and cannot be dealt with satisfactorily other than by way of oral evidence, then the court may order that that witness be tendered for cross-examination.[111a] Where one party chooses not to call a witness but the other side considers that the evidence of the witness is crucial, it can issue a witness summons pursuant to CPR Pt 34; however, this may not always be a safe course because the party calling the witness by a summons cannot cross-examine the witness, rather the evidence would have to be adduced by way of examination-in-chief. This may be part of the reason CPR Pt 34 is often not utilised in such circumstances, but rather the other party will ask the court to draw adverse inferences.[111b] Where a party proposes to rely on a witness statement as hearsay evidence and does not propose to call the person who made the original statement to give oral evidence, the court may, on the application of the other party, permit that party to call the maker of the statement to be cross-examine on the contents of that statement.[111c]

[109] *QX v Secretary of State for the Home Department* [2022] EWCA Civ 1541; [2023] 2 W.L.R. 1103 at [133]; *Jaffray v Society of Lloyd's* [2002] EWCA Civ 1101; (2002) 146 S.J.L.B. 214.

[110] *Jaffray v Society of Lloyd's* [2002] EWCA Civ 1101; (2002) 146 S.J.L.B. 214 applying the principles in *Wisniewski v Central Manchester Health Authority* [1998] P.I.Q.R. 324. See also *R. (Stapleton) v Revenue and Customs Prosecution Office* [2008] EWHC 1968 (QB) at [36]–[39].

[111] *Polarpark Enterprises Inc v Allason* [2007] EWHC 22 (Ch); [2007] All E.R. (D) 130 (Jan).

[111a] *R. (on the application of G) v Ealing LBC (No.2)* [2002] EWHC 250 (Admin); [2002] M.H.L.R. 140 at [20]; *QX v Secretary of State for the Home Department* [2022] EWCA Civ 1541; [2023] 2 W.L.R. 1103 at [137].

[111b] *QX v Secretary of State for the Home Department* [2022] EWCA Civ 1541; [2023] 2 W.L.R. 1103 at [136].

[111c] CPR r.33.4(2). See also *Douglas v Hello! Ltd (No.5)* [2003] EWCA Civ 332; [2003] C.P. Rep. 42 (CA); *Electromagnetic Geoservices ASA v Petroleum Geo-Services ASA* [2016] EWHC 27 (Pat); [2016] 1 W.L.R. 2353.

(l)   Order of proceedings: the right to begin

Replace footnote 113 with:

[113] Such a discretion is implicit in CPR r.32.1, thus there would be nothing wrong in the judge deciding that in the particular circumstances it would be convenient to hear the defendant's witnesses first. The King's Bench Guide (2023), para.14.21 provides that the claimant's advocate will normally begin the trial with a short opening speech, and the judge may then allow the other party to make a short speech. See also CPR r.3.1(2)(j); CPR r.3.1(2)(m).   **11-16**

Replace footnote 116 with:

[116] See in particular the Commercial Court Guide, 11th edn (2022), para.J8.1.

(o)   Documents and exhibits as evidence

Replace footnote 124 with:

[124] CPR r.32.19. See also, the Commercial Court Guide, 11th edn (2022), para.J8.5.   **11-19**

(q)   Closing speeches

Replace paragraph with:

The order of closing speeches is ultimately a matter for the discretion of the judge. The traditional order of closing speeches was defendant first and claimant last. There is an increasing tendency to alter this, particularly where the court has not needed to hear more than a relatively short oral opening from the claimant.[133] The practice is often now: closing by claimant-closing by defendant-reply by claimant.[134] Increasingly, the court will often require, at least, written outlines of closing submissions to be submitted to the court in advance of oral closing speeches.[134a]   **11-21**

[133] See para.11-16.

[134] See, for example, the Commercial Court Guide, 11th edn (2022), para.J11.2.

[134a] See, for example, the Commercial Court Guide, 11th edn (2022), paras J10.1 and J11.1.

2. CRIMINAL CASES

(b) Proceedings in open court

Replace footnote 144 with:

11-23 [144] The Court of Appeal has repeatedly made clear that the circumstances in which counsel should see the judge privately in his room are very limited (see particularly *R. v Turner* [1970] 2 Q.B. 321), and that there should be a shorthand note or other record of such discussions (see, e.g. *R. v Smith (TC)* (1990) 90 Cr. App. R. 413). See also *Att.-Gen.'s Reference (No.44 of 2000) (R. v Peverett)* [2001] 1 Cr. App. R. 27; and *Att.-Gen.'s Guidelines on the Acceptance of Pleas* (21 October 2005, revised 1st December 2009), Archbold 2023 Supplement (A-276).

After the third paragraph, add new paragraph:

Section 85A of the Courts Act 2003 makes provision for the remote observation of hearings.[144a]

[144a] Inserted by Police, Crime, Sentencing and Courts Act 2022. The governing regulations are the Remote Observation and Recording (Courts and Tribunals) Regulations 2022 (SI 2022/705). Practice guidance has been issued in *Practice Guidance (Open Justice: Remote Observation of Hearings)* [2022] 1 W.L.R. 3538.

(c) Hearing cases in camera, in chambers or in private

Replace footnote 146 with:

11-24 [146] The Criminal Procedure Rules 2020 (SI 2020/759) came into force on 5 October 2020. A full version of the rules containing current amendments can be found at *https://www.legislation.gov.uk/uksi/2020/759/contents/made*.

(i) Reporting restrictions

Replace the first paragraph with:

11-30 Although there is a general right to publish reports of legal proceedings,[173] there are exceptions[174]:

(1) a court has power to prevent publication of matters withheld from the public in the proceedings[175];

(2) a court has power to order the postponement of any report of the proceedings or other pending proceedings, where it is necessary to avoid a substantial risk of prejudice to the administration of justice[176];

(3) a court has power to prohibit the identification in reports of persons, including witnesses and victims, under 18 and of adult witnesses eligible for protection[177] and of a defendant where either the administration of justice requires it or there is a real and immediate threat to the life of the defendant were the order not made[178];

(4) a court has power to restrict reporting special measures directions and orders protecting witnesses from cross-examination by defendants acting in person[179];

(5) applications to dismiss a charge transferred to the Crown Court under the Criminal Justice Act 1991 s.53 (cases involving child witnesses), and under the Crime and Disorder Act 1998 s.51, may not be reported, unless the judge permits reporting[180];

(6) applications to dismiss a charge transferred to the Crown Court under the Criminal Justice Act 1987 (serious or complex fraud) and preparatory hearings in such cases may not be reported, unless the judge permits reporting[181]; similar provisions apply to preparatory hearings in other long and

complex cases[182] and pre-trial hearings[183];

(7) a court has power to prohibit the reporting of derogatory assertions made in a speech of mitigation[184];

(8) complainants in rape and other sexual cases may not be identified in reports unless the judge permits such reporting[185];

(9) unless the court orders otherwise there can be no publication of special measures directions made under the Youth Justice and Criminal Evidence Act 1999 s.19, or of a direction prohibiting an accused from cross-examining a witness under s.36 of the same Act.[186]

Reporting restrictions may have to be imposed to protect a witness's Convention right to respect for private life.[187] In *Clibbery v Allan*,[188] Munby J said that a balance must be struck between the private and public interest in preserving an individual's privacy and the private and public interest in enabling a party who wishes to do so to publicise the proceedings. A balance must also be struck between the public interest in maintaining the privacy of proceedings in order to enable justice to be done and the public interest in the publicity of proceedings to ensure public confidence in the administration of justice:

> "Those balances could very well be required to be struck in such a way as would justify ... the restraint of the publication of certain types of personal information of a genuinely confidential or sensitive nature notwithstanding that such material had been deployed in the course of judicial proceedings. Equally those balances could well require to be struck in such a way as to justify restraining in the same way the publication of materials disclosed under judicial compulsion." (*Clibbery v Allan* at 970.)

[173] Contempt of Court Act 1981 s.4(1). For an order made under the Contempt of Court Act 1981 and Senior Courts Act 1981 s.45(4) which gives the Crown Court the powers of the High Court in relation to contempt of court, where media organisations were ordered not to report the trial on Facebook and to disable the ability of readers to post comments on any report of the trial, see *R. v F* [2016] EWCA Crim 12; [2016] 2 Cr. App. R. 13.

[174] See the restrictions listed in the Criminal Procedure Rules 2020 Pt 6. There is a discretion to permit representations by the press about the making of an order restricting reporting: *R. v Beck, Ex p. Daily Telegraph* (1992) 94 Cr. App. R. 376 CA at 31–32; *R. v Clerkenwell Metropolitan Stipendiary Magistrate, Ex p. The Telegraph Plc* (1933) 97 Cr. App. R. 18 DC; *R. v CCC, Ex p. Crook* [1995] 2 Cr. App. R. 212 CA.

[175] Contempt of Court Act 1981 s.11. For a review of the principles of open justice and the circumstances in which it can be departed from see *A v BBC* [2014] UKSC 25; [2015] A.C. 588; considered in *M v Times Newspapers Ltd* [2015] 1 Cr. App. R. 1. See also the guide "*Reporting Restrictions in the Criminal Courts*" published by the Judicial College (April 2015, revised May 2016).

[176] Contempt of Court Act 1981 s.4(2).

[177] Youth Justice and Criminal Evidence Act 1999 ss.44–46. A child or young person is not "concerned in the proceedings" unless a victim of the alleged offence, a defendant or a witness; being generally affected is insufficient, see *R. v Jolleys, Ex p. Press Association* [2013] EWCA Crim 1135; [2014] 1 Cr. App. R. 15. The same principles and practice can be applied to applications under the Youth Justice and Criminal Evidence Act 1999 s.45 as were applied to applications under the Children and Young Persons Act 1933 s.39 which was replaced by s.45 of the 1999 Act from 3 April 2015; see *R v H* [2016] 1 Cr. App. R.(S.) 94(13).

[178] *Times Newspapers Ltd, The Times, 31 October 2008*. As to the balance between a defendant's art.8 rights (right to privacy) and art.10 rights (freedom of expression) see *BBC; Att.-Gen.'s Reference (No. 3 of 1999), The Times*, 18 June 2009. Section 45A of the Youth Justice and Criminal Evidence Act 1999 provides power to restrict reporting of criminal proceedings for the lifetime of witnesses and victims under 18 and has not ousted the court's jurisdiction to make anonymity for life in respect of defendants ("Venables" or "Mary Bell" orders) but such orders are exceptional, see *RXG v MoJ* [2019] EWHC 2026 (QB); [2019] A.C.D. 114 DC; and *R. v Aziz* [2019] EWCA Crim 1568; [2020] Crim. L.R. 356 DC & CA where the lifting of reporting restrictions in relation to a 17-year-old convicted of rape and murder

was upheld. See also *A LBC v B* [2022] EWHC 320 (Fam); [2023] 1 F.L.R. 93, Fam D where an application to prohibit reporting the names of the parents and the child they murdered was refused.

[179] Youth Justice and Criminal Evidence Act 1999 s.47; Crim. PR 2015 Pt 23.

[180] Criminal Justice Act 1991 Sch.6 para.6. See para.9-21. Crime and Disorder Act 1998 Sch.3 para.3.

[181] Criminal Justice Act 1987 s.11. The section also covers interlocutory appeals under that Act.

[182] Criminal Procedure and Investigations Act 1996 s.37.

[183] Criminal Procedure and Investigations Act 1996 s.41.

[184] Criminal Procedure and Investigations Act 1996 s.58.

[185] Sexual Offences (Amendment) Act 1992. The right to anonymity does not apply to the reporting of a trial or appeal where the complaint of a sexual offence is not the subject of the charges before the court, see *R. v Musharraf* [2022] EWCA Crim 678; [2022] Crim. L.R. 987. For the position in extradition cases see *Bullman v High Court in Dublin (Ireland)* [2022] EWHC 194 (Admin); CLW/22/08/1.

[186] Youth Justice and Criminal Evidence Act 1999 s.47.

[187] See, e.g. *Z v Finland* (1988) 25 E.H.R.R. 371; cf. B. Emmerson and A. Ashworth, *Human Rights and Criminal Justice* (London: Sweet & Maxwell, 2001), para.18-63. The High Court has jurisdiction to impose reporting restrictions on the identity of complainants in the requesting state in extradition proceedings, see *Short v Falkland Islands (No. 2)* [2020] EWHC 439 (Admin); [2020] 4 W.L.R. 68 DC.

[188] *Clibbery v Allan* [2002] 2 F.L.R. 819; [2001] 2 F.C.R. 577.

(n) Vulnerable and intimidated witnesses

Replace footnote 223 with:

11-35 [223] See *Criminal Practice Directions 2023* Pt 6, which came into force on 29 May 2023 and can be found at *https://www.judiciary.uk/wp-content/uploads/2023/04/Criminal-Practice-Directions-2023-1.pdf*. The 2015 Directions have been revoked (apart from some sections which are no relevant for present purposes) and extensively rewritten. See also the guidance in *R. v Lubemba* [2014] EWCA Crim 2064; referred to in *R. v RK* [2018] EWCA Crim 603; [2019] Crim. L.R. 439; *R. v Jonas* [2015] EWCA Crim 562; [2015] Crim L.R. 742. For a case where breach of the ground rules in relation to the cross-examination of a vulnerable witness leading to her failure to return to court to continues being cross-examined did not render the trial unfair see *R. v RT and Stuchfield* [2020] EWCA Crim 155; [2020] Crim. L.R. 1168 CA. Crim P R [2020] Pt. 3 r. 3.9 contains provisions requiring a pre-trial case management hearing to discuss and set ground rules and directions in relation to the questioning of a witness or defendant.

(o) The available special measures

(ii) Live link

Replace the first paragraph with:

11-37 Under s.24 of the 1999 Act, a special measures direction may provide for a witness to give evidence by means of a live link, which means a live television link or other arrangement (but not by a telephone link[231] even where the parties consent,[232] save in respect of the exercise of the court's pre-trial case management functions)[233] whereby a witness, where absent from the court room or other place where the proceedings are being held, is able to see and hear a person there and to be seen and heard by the judge, the jury, legal representatives and any interpreter or other person appointed to assist the witness.[234] Where the witness is outside the UK and if the foreign state has no objection, a video link via WhatsApp can amount to another arrangement.[234a] Once such a direction has been made, the witness may not give evidence in any other way without permission of the court.[235] Such permission may be given if it is in the interests of justice to do so and may be given of the court's own motion or, if there has been a material change of circumstances since the direction or last application for a direction was made, on application by a party.[236] Where a direction is made in proceedings in a magistrates' court but facilities do not exist at that court for evidence to be given by live link, the court may sit at a place where such facilities are available.[237]

[231] See *R. v Diane (Hammala)* [2009] EWCA Crim 1494; [2010] 2 Cr. App. R. 1.

[232] *R. v Hampson* [2014] 1 Cr. App. R. 4. *Criminal Practice Directions 2023.* The Live Link in Criminal Courts Guidance issued by the Lord Chief Justice must be complied with (available at *https://www.judiciary.uk*).

[233] Criminal Procedure Rules 3.5(2)(d); *Criminal Practice Directions 2023* Pt 63N.

[234] Youth Justice and Criminal Evidence Act 1999 s.24(8).

[234a] See *R. v Kadir* [2022] EWCA Crim 1244; [2023] 1 W.L.R. 532 where the judge refused the application; and see the commentary CLW 22/35/2.

[235] Youth Justice and Criminal Evidence Act 1999 s.24(2).

[236] Youth Justice and Criminal Evidence Act 1999 s.24(3).

[237] Youth Justice and Criminal Evidence Act 1999 s.24(5).

(v) Video-recorded evidence-in-chief

Replace the third paragraph with:

11-40

Part 18 of the Criminal Procedure Rules 2020 sets out the procedure to be followed on making an application to admit a video recording in evidence under s.27(1) of the Act of 1999.

Replace footnote 264 with:

11-42

[264] *Rawlings and Broadbent* [1995] 2 Cr. App. R. 222, considered in *R. v VJW* [2022] EWCA Crim 164; [2022] Cr. App. R. 5.

(vi) Video-recorded cross-examination or re-examination

Replace paragraph with:

11-43

Where a special measures direction provides for evidence-in-chief to be admitted by way of video recording under s.27 of the 1999 Act, s.28 will permit the direction to provide for the cross-examination and re-examination to be video recorded. At the date of publication the majority of Crown Court locations have been authorised to take advantage of these provisions.[266] Regard must be had to the eligibility of the witness, see *R. v A* [2022] EWCA Crim 988; [2022] 1 W.L.R. 4283 where the judge erred in permitting pre-recorded cross examination of a complainant in a sexual assault case who was 18 at the date of the application.

[266] Most recently in the Youth Justice and Criminal Evidence Act 1999 (Commencement No. 29) Order 2022 (SI 2022/992). Rules and directions covering cases under s.28 can be found in Crim. P.R. 2020 Pt 18 and *Criminal Practice Directions 2023* Pt 6; for a discussion of the practice surrounding the use of s.28 see *R. v PMH* [2018] EWCA Crim 2452; [2019] 1 W.L.R. 3243; and *R. v YGM* [2018] EWCA Crim 2458; [2019] 2 Cr. App. R. 5.

(vii) Examination of witness through intermediary

Replace paragraph with:

11-44

A special measures direction may provide for the examination of the witness to be conducted through an interpreter or other person approved by the court, whose function is to communicate questions put to the witness and the witness's answers to the person asking the questions, and to explain such questions or answers so far as necessary to enable them to be understood by the witness or person in question. Although s.33BA of the Youth Justice and Criminal Evidence Act 1999, which provides for the appointment of intermediaries for defendants, is not yet in force, there is nevertheless an inherent common law power for courts to appoint intermediaries for defendants.[268] This power has now been formalised in the Criminal Procedure Rules and Criminal Practice Directions 2023[269] and provides for the appointment of a registered intermediary throughout the trial.[270] The appointment of an intermediary is a question for the judge assisted by experts' reports but which are not themselves determinative of the issue.[271]

[268] *R. (on the application of S) v Waltham Forrest Youth Court* [2004] 2 Cr. App. R. 21; *C v Sevenoaks Youth Court* [2009] EWHC 3088 (Admin); *R. v Cox* [2012] EWCA Crim 549. And see also the former *Criminal Practice Directions 2015* [2015] EWCA Crim 1567, Part 3F; considered in *R. v Thomas (Dean)* [2020] EWCA Crim 117; [2020] 4 W.L.R. 66 CA; and *TI v Bromley Youth Court* [2020] EWHC 1204 (Admin).

[269] See *Criminal Practice Directions 2023* Pt 6.2.4. The procedure for the appointment of intermediaries to assist defendants is now set out in the Criminal Procedure Rules 2020 r.18.23.

[270] *R. (on the application of OP) v Secretary of State for Justice* [2014] EWHC 1944 (Admin); [2015] 1 Cr. App. R. 7; *R. v Rashid* [2017] 1 W.L.R. 2449; [2017] Cr. App. R. 25. For a case where the failure to appoint an intermediary to assist the defendant in giving evidence resulted in such unfairness as to render the conviction unsafe see *R. v Pringle* [2019] EWCA Crim 1722; [2020] Crim. L.R. 347 CA.

[271] See *R. v Thomas (Dean)* [2020] EWCA Crim 117; [2020] 4 W.L.R. 66 CA. For a case where the absence of an intermediary did not render the trial unfair or affect the safety of the conviction see *R. v Malik* [2023] EWCA Crim 311; [2023] Archbold review 1, CA.

(s)   Anonymity of witnesses

Replace the fourth paragraph with:

11-49   The procedure to be followed on making an application for an anonymity order under the Act is set out in the *Criminal Practice Directions 2023*[288] Pt 6.6 and Criminal Procedure Rules 2020 Pt 18 r.18.18. Practical arrangements to ensure that the witness's anonymity is not compromised should be put in place.[289]

[288] *Criminal Practice Directions 2023* Pt 6.6.

[289] *Criminal Practice Directions 2023* Pt 6.6.9.

Replace footnote 290 with:

[290] *Archbold 2023 Supplement* App., A-291, p.331.

Replace the seventh paragraph with:

The power under the 2008 Act to make anonymity orders expired on 31 December 2009,[297] when it was replaced by the Coroners and Justice Act 2009 ss.86–93.

[297] Criminal Evidence (Witness Anonymity) Act 2008 s.14.

(t)   Absence of the defendant

Replace the fourth paragraph with:

11-50   Where a defendant on bail does not appear for trial the judge has a discretion to commence the trial in the defendant's absence.[306] The leading case is now *R. v Jones (Anthony)*.[307] The defendant was bailed to appear for trial on charges of conspiracy to rob. He did not surrender for trial. A warrant was issued for his arrest, but he was not arrested by the time of the trial date. His legal representatives had withdrawn and he was therefore both absent and unrepresented at the trial. The trial judge took the view that the defendant had deliberately sought to frustrate his own prosecution, and ordered the trial to begin. He was convicted and sentenced to prison. The House of Lords held that the judge had a discretion to commence a trial in the defendant's absence, and that in the circumstances the trial did not contravene art.6 of the ECHR.[308] Their Lordships took into account the avenues for appeal open to the defendant and the considerable inconvenience in postponing a trial for which 25 witnesses had attended court. On balance the trial had been fair. Their Lordships emphasised that this discretion is to be exercised sparingly and approved the Court of Appeal's checklist of matters (save one) relevant to exercise of the discretion.[309] The judge must have regard to all the circumstances of the case, including, in particular:

(i)   the nature and circumstances of the defendant's behaviour in absenting himself from the trial or disrupting it, as the case may be and, in particular, whether his behaviour was deliberate, voluntary and such as plainly waived his right to appear;

(ii)   whether an adjournment might result in the defendant being caught or attending voluntarily and/or not disrupting the proceedings;

(iii)   the likely length of such an adjournment;

(iv)   whether the defendant, though absent, is, or wishes to be, legally represented at the trial or has, by his conduct, waived his right to representation;

(v)   whether an absent defendant's legal representatives are able to receive instructions from him during the trial and the extent to which they are able to present his defence;

(vi)   the extent of the disadvantage to the defendant in not being able to give his account of events, having regard to the nature of the evidence against him;

(vii)   the risk of the jury reaching an improper conclusion about the absence of the defendant;

(viii) the general public interest and the particular interest of victims and witnesses that a trial should take place within a reasonable time of the events to which it relates;

(ix)   the effect of delay on the memories of witnesses;

(x)   where there is more than one defendant and not all have absconded, the undesirability of separate trials, and the prospects of a fair trial for the defendants who are present.[310]

[306] If a judge cannot be sure that a defendant has deliberately absented himself or fails to consider the possibility that the defendant was unaware that his trial was to take place he should issue a specific warning that the trial will take place in his absence if he does not attend, see *R. v Amrouchi* unreported 22 November 2007 CA.

[307] *R. v Jones (Anthony)* [2002] UKHL 5; [2003] A.C. 1 HL (considered in *R. v Rymarz* [2022] EWCA Crim 773; [2022] Archbold Review 2, CA). For comment on the case, see *P.W. Ferguson* [2002] Crim. L.R. 554. See also *R. (on the application of R) v Thames Youth Court* [2002] EWHC 1670 Admin; [2002] Crim. L.R. 977 DC, where it was held that a district judge had erred in law in deciding that the trial ought to proceed on the basis that the defendant, a juvenile, was absent for reasons over which he had control when he had been arrested and detained on another matter. The principles set out in *R. v Jones (Anthony)* [2003] 1 A.C. 1 apply to proceedings in the magistrates' court and to a decision under s.142(1) of the Magistrates' Courts Act 1980 whether to rescind a defendant's conviction obtained in his absence, see *R. (on the application of Morsby) v Tower Bridge Magistrates' Court* unreported 31 October 2007 DC.

[308] For a discussion of the relevant European Convention law, see Emmerson, Ashworth and McDonald, *Human Rights and Criminal Justice* (London: Sweet & Maxwell, 2007), paras 14-145 et seq.

[309] Sub nom. *R. v Hayward* [2001] Q.B. 862; [2001] 3 W.L.R. 125.

[310] In the light of *R. v Jones (Anthony)* [2003] 1 A.C. 1 the court must exercise its discretion to proceed in the absence of the defendant in accordance with *Criminal Practice Directions 2023* Pt 5.4. For proof

that a defendant has waived his right to be present at his trial, see *R. v O'Hare* [2006] Crim. L.R. 950; [2006] EWCA Crim 2963.

(y)   Offering no evidence

Replace footnote 342 with:

11-56   [342] Offering no evidence must be distinguished from inviting the court to order that counts should lie on the file, not to be proceeded with without the leave of the court or the Court of Appeal (Criminal Division). See generally *Archbold* 2017, para.4-159; and in particular the *Report of the Farquharson Committee on the role of prosecuting counsel* (1986), the *Code of Conduct of the Bar Council*, 8th edn (2004), and the Bar Council Guidance on the Responsibilities of Prosecuting Counsel, *Archbold 2017 Supplement*, App.C-33. See also, the Att.-Gen.'s Guidelines on the acceptance of Pleas and the Prosecutor's role in the Sentencing Exercise, *Archbold 2023 Supplement*, App.A-276.

(au)   Order of speeches

Replace footnote 496 with:

11-81   [496] See *Archbold 2023*, Ch.4, 4-419 et seq.

(ax)   Communications between judge and jury

Replace footnote 517 with:

11-84   [517] *R. v Gorman* (1987) 85 Cr. App. R. 121, approved in *R. v APJ* [2022] EWCA Crim 942; [2023] 1 Cr. App. R. 24 where the judge's failure to discuss with counsel the jury's request to see exhibits rendered the conviction for murder unsafe; *R. v Green* [1992] Crim. L.R. 292 CA. For the approach adopted in Canada when a note is received from the jury after retirement complaining of the behaviour of one juror, see *R. v Giroux* 207 C.C.C. (3d), Ontario Court of Appeal (7 April 2006). In Australia it has been held that where the jury asks a question after retirement procedural fairness requires the judge to inform the parties in open court of the precise terms of the question *R. v Black, Watts and Black* unreported 5 April 2007 Court of Appeal of Victoria.

(az)   Defendant's character and antecedents

Replace the first paragraph with:

11-86   The *Criminal Practice Directions 2023*[531] set out the information of antecedents, including details of previous convictions, required for Crown Courts and magistrates' courts. Copies are provided to the defence. It is not now the practice for this antecedent history to be produced by a witness.

[531] *Criminal Practice Directions 2023* Pt 5.3A and Criminal Procedure Rules 2020 Pt 8.

Replace footnote 544 with:

[544] See *Archbold 2023*, Ch. 5B.

CHAPTER 12

RULES OF EVIDENCE RELATING TO THE COURSE OF A TRIAL: EXAMINATION OF WITNESSES

1. CIVIL

(b) Witness statements as evidence-in-chief

Replace the first paragraph with:

Where a witness is called to give oral evidence, his witness statement stands as **12-02** his evidence-in-chief unless the court orders otherwise.[3] For this reason oral examinations-in-chief are now rare.[3a] The court still retains a discretion in this regard, and there may be circumstances where it will wish to hear the evidence of a witness viva voce, either in relation to all of that witness's evidence, or a part of it. Where there is a conflict of fact, particularly where the witness's credibility may be in issue and his evidence is contentious, it may be appropriate for the trial judge to direct that at least part of the evidence-in-chief be given orally.[4]

[3] CPR r.32.5(2). See also, for example, the Commercial Court Guide, 11th edn (2022), para.H1.3; Chancery Guide (2022, updated June 2023), para.8.11.

[3a] Although in *Brake v The Chedington Court Estate Ltd* [2021] EWHC 2882 (Ch) at [12], the judge commented that "it is common enough these days for counsel who call witnesses to be cross-examined on their witness statements first to ask permission to ask one or two supplementary questions in chief, if there are further matters that need to be brought out. Usually this is not opposed, and usually permission is granted. That is so, in my experience, even if it relates to something quite different from what is in the witness statement."

[4] *Cole v Kivells*, The Times 2 May 1997, CA; *Mercer v Chief Constable of Lancashire* [1991] 2 All E.R. 504 at 507.

Replace the third paragraph with:

The court should only give permission if there is "good reason" not to confine the evidence of the witness to the contents of his witness statement.[6] The court will wish to be given a reason why a witness should be allowed to amplify his witness statement. The court will consider the interests in having the full factual picture before it, and to this end will take into account the relative importance of the new facts sought to be canvassed. It may wish to take into account the reasons the evidence was not contained in the witness statement, and the ability of other parties to check the facts stated and respond if appropriate.[7] One example of where it may be appropriate is where relevant events occur (or have been subsequently discovered) after the date for service of witness statements; or where a witness wishes to respond to unanticipated matters in another witness statement served. The court will be careful to ensure other parties are not prejudiced by the adducing of new evidence at this time. Where an application for permission to amplify the evidence given in a witness statement is made early enough, the court may make it a condition of permission that the gist of any further evidence to be given in chief should be communicated in writing to the other party in advance and that the other party be given sufficient time to prepare their cross-examination on the new evidence properly.[7a] It is usually expected that any proposal for amplification or new evidence (to be adduced through in-chief examination) should be discussed between advocates for each party before the witness is called.[7b]

[6] CPR r.32.5(4). For an example of its application, see *Smith v Crawshay* [2019] EWHC 2507 (Ch), where the court gave permission for questions to be put in chief to the defendant on a narrow point that had arisen from documents disclosed after the witness statements had been filed and served.

[7] In *Mander v Evans* [2001] 1 W.L.R. 2378 Ch, the judge refused to permit a party to amplify a statement to remedy deficiencies.

[7a] *Rea v Rea* [2022] EWCA Civ 195 at [26].

[7b] See, for example, the Chancery Guide (2022, updated June 2023), para.8.19; the Commercial Court Guide (2022), para H1.4.

After "… after the deadline for exchange of evidence. The High Court", add:

(then the Queen's Bench Division) considered that the application had to be treated as an application for relief from sanctions and applied the factors relevant to determining whether such relief should be granted. The High Court considered that due to the lateness of the application, it was not appropriate to grant relief. However, guidance from other divisions of the High Court state that where a witness proposes materially to add to, alter, correct or retract form what is in the witness's original statement, a supplemental witness statement should be served and permission should be sought through the court, unless the content of the statement falls within the terms of any direction already given for the service or evidence in reply or all parties consent to the service of the supplemental statement.[8a]

[8a] See the Chancery Guide (2022, updated June 2023, paras 8.16–8.17; the Commercial Court Guide (2022), para.H1.4(a).

12-04   *Delete the first paragraph.*

(c)   Oral examination-in-chief

After "As noted above, lengthy oral examinations-in-chief are now rare", add:

12-05   rare in civil trials,

(h)   Application for permission to cross-examine

Replace footnote 27 with:

12-10   [27] *Polanski v Condè Nast Ltd* [2005] UKHL 10; [2005] 1 W.L.R. 637 at [36], [67], [79]. Such an exclusionary order should not be made automatically in accordance with the principle underlying the Civil Evidence Act 1995, which is to admit hearsay evidence and let the court attach to it whatever weight may be appropriate, rather than exclude it altogether.

Replace footnote 29 with:

[29] CPR r.32.7(1). In practice, orders for cross-examination prior to trial are not routinely made: see, for example, *Stokoe Partnership Solicitors v Grayson* [2021] EWCA Civ 626; [2021] 4 W.L.R. 87 at [7] and [33], where the Court of Appeal upheld the first instance court's decision refusing the claimant an

order for the cross-examination of the defendant on an affidavit that he had sworn, despite significant inconsistencies between the defendant's evidence and that of another witness. The Court of Appeal found that to permit cross-examination on the affidavit would pre-empt cross-examination at trial and therefore it cannot be just and convenient to order cross-examination on a Norwich Pharmacal affidavit sworn by a party to substantive proceedings concerning overlapping issues.

Replace footnote 31 with:

[31] *Phillips v Symes* [2003] EWCA Civ 1769; (2003) 147 S.J.L.B. 1431; though in that case the judge erred in exercising that discretion since it was wrong to blend cross-examination of the general kind with cross-examination aimed at establishing whether a breach of the conditions of a suspension or further contempt of court had occurred. Moreover, it would be wrong to submit the maker of the statement to cross-examination at that stage because he was being given the opportunity to comply finally with the undertakings. See also *Khouj v Acropolis Capital Partners Ltd* [2021] EWHC 1667 (Comm) at [45], where the court summarised the general principles when considering whether to make an order for cross-examination.

(i)   Cross-examination

(i)   Nature and scope

After "… questions of the witness, which may", add:
(and usually will) be leading questions. Such questions need not be confined to the evidence given by the witness-in-chief; but questions must be relevant to the issues in the case. The approach taken to cross-examination is a matter for the advocate asking the questions; however, in general, they must seek answers to questions of fact and should avoid asking factual witnesses for their opinion or speculation. Cross-examination which is largely repetitive in nature, or which asks several questions which are long or hypothetical, or both, is often subject to deprecation by the court.[31a] **12-11**

[31a] See, for example, *MBR Acres Ltd v McGivern* [2022] EWHC 2072 (QB) at [61], where the judge said questions of this nature were in an "objectionable form" and that questions beginning with "if" were unlikely to be helpful where such questions were only likely to elicit the witness's comment of a hypothetical scenario.

In the third paragraph, after "In", replace "general" with:
general,

(ii)   Requirement to challenge evidence

Replace footnote 36 with: "Cited with approval in *Griffiths v Tui (UK) Ltd* [2021] EWCA Civ 1442 at [87]; *MBR Acres Ltd v McGivern* [2022] EWHC 2072 (QB) at [88]." **12-12**

Replace the second paragraph with:
This rule serves the important function of giving the witness the opportunity of explaining any contradiction or alleged problem with his evidence. If a party has decided not to cross-examine on a particular important point, he will be in difficulty in submitting that the evidence should be rejected. This may be particularly so where a witness' honesty is to be challenged, it will always be best if that is explicitly put to the witness.[38a] Thus where, during trial, a witness has not been challenged as inaccurate, it was not appropriate for that evidence to then be challenged in closing speeches.[39]

[38a] *Howlett v Davies* [2017] EWCA Civ 1696; [2018] 1 W.L.R. 948 at [39]. This may also form part of an advocate's ethical obligations. For example, the Bar Standards Board (the regulatory authority for

barristers in England and Wales) provides that a barrister must not make a serious allegation against a witness whom they have had an opportunity to cross-examine unless that witness was given a chance to answer the allegation in cross-examination: see rule C7.2 of the BSB Handbook (Version 4.6, 2020).

[39] *Chen v Ng* [2017] UKPC 27; [2018] 1 P. & C.R. DG2; applied in *Royal Mail Plc v Office of Communications* [2019] CAT 19.

Replace the third paragraph with:

However, the rule is not an inflexible one.[40] It is no longer the law that every aspect of a witness' evidence needs to be challenged head-on.[40a] Thus, in practice there is bound to be at least some relaxation of the rule, which may depend on the procedures which have been adopted by the court. For example, if there is a time-limit imposed by the judge on cross-examination it may not be practicable to cross-examine on every minor point, particularly where a lengthy witness statement has been served and treated as evidence-in-chief. The issue is said to be one of fairness to the witnesses and parties. In *BPY v MXV*,[40b] the principles were summarised as: (1) the fundamental issue is one of fairness to witnesses and to the parties; (2) usually fairness will require that when a witness gives evidence as to a specific factual matter and the court will be asked to disbelieve him or her, he or she should be challenged on it so as to have an opportunity of affirming or commenting on the challenge; but (3) this is not an inflexible rule. There may be cases in which there will be no unfairness because, looked at more generally, the procedures adopted in the litigation mean that a party and the relevant witness(es) have had ample opportunity to comment on the other side's case. It may also be the case that a particular matter does not have to be specifically put to the witness because it is obvious from other evidence which he or she has given as to what his or her response will be.

[40] *Edwards Lifesciences LLC v Boston Scientific Scimed Inc* [2018] EWCA Civ 673; [2018] F.S.R. 29 at [62]–[68]; *Royal Mail Plc v Office of Communications* [2019] CAT 19; *BPY v MXV* [2023] EWHC 82 (Comm) at [33].

[40a] *Various Claimants v Giambrone & Law* [2015] EWHC 1946 (QB) at [21]; *BPY v MXV* [2023] EWHC 82 (Comm) at [68].

[40b] *BPY v MXV* [2023] EWHC 82 (Comm) at [34].

(iii)   Limiting cross-examination

Replace the first paragraph with:

12-13   The CPR provides the courts with an express power to limit cross-examination.[41] In general, cross-examination is likely be limited in two ways: (1) by the court limiting the issues to be explored in cross-examination[41a]; and (2) by the court limiting the time available for the cross-examination of witnesses at trial.[41b] Other (non-exhaustive) circumstances in which a judge could restrict cross-examination include where they consider the cross-examination to be unduly oppressive or improper,[42] or where the cross-examination is on matters about which the witness could not fairly be expected to have any knowledge.

[41] CPR r.32.1(3).

[41a] CPR r.32.1(1) confers upon the court the power to control evidence by limiting the issues on which it requires evidence. See also *Watson v Chief Constable of Cleveland* [2001] EWCA Civ 1547.

[41b] *Hayes v Transco Plc* [2003] EWCA Civ 1261; (2003) 147 S.J.L.B. 1089; *Three Rivers DC v Bank of England* [2005] EWCA Civ 889; [2005] C.P. Rep. 46.

[42] e.g. *Vernon v Bosley (No.2)* [1995] 2 F.C.R. 78.

Replace the third paragraph with:

However, undue restriction on a party's ability to cross-examine may lead to a serious procedural irregularity. For example, in *Hayes v Transco Plc*[44] a decision by the trial judge to restrict the cross-examination of a crucial witness to five more minutes was held to be wrong in principle and unfair to the other party.

[44] *Hayes v Transco Plc* [2003] EWCA Civ 1261; (2003) 147 S.J.L.B. 1089.

2. CRIMINAL

(ac) Questions by the jury

Replace footnote 181 with:

[181] *R. v Inns and Inns* [2018] EWCA Crim 1081; [2019] 1 Cr.App. R. 5. For a case where the jury notes contained comments as distinct from questions see *R. v Quasem* [2019] EWCA Crim 2245; [2022] Crim. L.R. 511 CA.

12-44

(an) Refreshing memory out of court before giving evidence

Replace footnote 265 with:

[265] See Criminal Practice Direction 2023 Pt 6.3.21.

12-55

CHAPTER 13

EVIDENCE TAKEN AFTER TRIAL

1. CIVIL CASES

(a) New evidence after judgment but before order drawn up

Replace the first paragraph with:

13-01   A judge has jurisdiction to reverse an oral or written judgment at any time until his order is perfected, which in modern times is when the order is sealed pursuant to CPR r.40.2(2)(b).[1] This is sometimes referred to as the "Barrell jurisdiction"[1a] and the exercise of the jurisdiction is not limited to exceptional circumstances.[1b] This discretion is not to be confused with the untrammelled jurisdiction of the court to amplify its reasons for a decision at any time prior to sealing of the order.[2] Accordingly a trial judge has a discretion to receive new evidence after judgment has been given but before an order has been drawn up.[3]

[1] *Barrell Enterprises* [1972] 3 All E.R. 631; [1973] 1 W.L.R. 19 CA; *Paulin v Paulin* [2009] EWCA Civ 221 CA; [2010] 1 W.L.R. 1057 at [30]–[35]; *L-B (Children) (Preliminary Finding: Power to Reverse)* [2013] UKSC 8; [2013] 1 W.L.R. 634 at [19]; *AIC Ltd v Federal Airports Authority of Nigeria* [2022] UKSC 16; [2022] 1 W.L.R. 3223.

[1a] Following the decision in *Re Barrell Enterprises* [1972] 3 All E.R. 631; [1973] 1 W.L.R. 19 CA; see also *Stewart v Engel* [2000] 1 W.L.R. 2268 CA (Civ Div) at 2274A; *L-B (Children) (Preliminary Finding: Power to Reverse)* [2013] UKSC 8; [2013] 1 W.L.R. 634.

[1b] In *L-B (Children) (Preliminary Finding: Power to Reverse)* [2013] UKSC 8; [2013] 1 W.L.R. 634, the Supreme Court disapproved of statements in *Re Barrell Enterprises* [1972] 3 All E.R. 631; [1973] 1 W.L.R. 19 CA and *Stewart v Engel* [2000] 1 W.L.R. 2268 to the effect that exceptional circumstances were required before such a jurisdiction should be exercised.

[2] *T (Contact: Alienation: Permission to Appeal)* [2002] EWCA Civ 1736; [2003] 1 F.L.R. 536 CA; *Paulin v Paulin* [2009] EWCA Civ 221; [2010] 1 W.L.R. 1057 CA.

[3] If the application is made before judgment is handed down, it is not necessary to satisfy this test: *K v K (Abduction: Hague Convention: Adjournment)* [2009] EWHC 3378; [2010] 1 F.L.R. 1310. For a case which failed to satisfy the test, see: *Sheikh v Dogan* [2009] EWHC 2935 (Ch).

Replace the second paragraph with:

In *L-B (Children) (Preliminary Finding: Power to Reverse)*[4] the Supreme Court considered the judicial power to reverse a judgment. The Supreme Court emphasised that courts have jurisdiction to reverse "up until the order is drawn up and perfected" but that "there is no jurisdiction to change one's mind thereafter unless the court has an express power to vary".[5] The Supreme Court emphasised that the overriding goal of a court deciding to exercise this jurisdiction is to deal with the case justly.[6] The Supreme Court regarded any dicta in previous cases[7] which suggested that the jurisdiction should only be used exceptionally as wrong.[8] The decision in *L-B (Children) (Preliminary Finding: Power to Reverse)* was further considered by the Supreme Court in *AIC Ltd v Federal Airports Authority of Nigeria*,[8a] where the court considered it appropriate to re-state the applicable principles more fully than in *L-B (Children) (Preliminary Finding: Power to Reverse)*, not least because the overriding objective in the CPR had been subject to change since 2013 and the overriding objective in question in *L-B (Children) (Preliminary Finding: Power to Reverse)* was in the specific context of the Family Procedural Rules. The Supreme Court held that the task of a judge faced with an application to reconsider a judgment and/or order before the order had been sealed was to do justice in accordance with the overriding objective under the relevant procedure rules.[8b]

[4] *L-B (Children) (Preliminary Finding: Power to Reverse)* [2013] UKSC 8; [2013] 1 W.L.R. 634.

[5] *L-B (Children) (Preliminary Finding: Power to Reverse)* [2013] UKSC 8; [2013] 1 W.L.R. 634 at [19].

[6] *L-B (Children) (Preliminary Finding: Power to Reverse)* [2013] UKSC 8; [2013] 1 W.L.R. 634 at [27].

[7] Such as *Barrell Enterprises, Re* [1973] 1 W.L.R. 19 CA and *Paulin v Paulin* [2009] EWCA Civ 221.

[8] See also *Thomas Cook Tour Operators Ltd v Louis Hotels* [2013] EWHC 2469 (QB); *Karunia Holdings Ltd v Creativityetc Ltd* [2021] EWHC 1864 (Ch) at [54].

[8a] *AIC Ltd v Federal Airports Authority of Nigeria* [2022] UKSC 16; [2022] 1 W.L.R 3223.

[8b] *AIC Ltd v Federal Airports Authority of Nigeria* [2022] UKSC 16; [2022] 1 W.L.R 3223 at [30].

Replace the third paragraph with:

In *Charlesworth v Relay Roads Ltd*,[9] it was held that the trial judge had the necessary jurisdiction to allow a party to amend his pleadings and to call new evidence in such circumstances. Whilst the court held that the *Ladd v Marshall* principles (considered below) should be in the forefront of the court's mind, it also expressed the view that a trial judge is entitled to be more flexible than the Court of Appeal when considering such an application to admit new evidence. There may be cases where the application should be granted even though all three *Ladd v Marshall* requirements are not fulfilled.[9a] The trial judge, having heard the case, would be in a better position to receive fresh evidence than the Court of Appeal, who would be faced with the choice of attempting to decide what effect the new evidence would have had on the trial judge or ordering a retrial. In *Navitaire Inc v Easyjet*[10] fresh evidence was not allowed at this point as the evidence could have been obtained for trial with reasonable diligence, and it would not have changed the court's view of the relevant issue. In *AR v ML*,[10a] the judge considered that it was right and proper that a due diligence requirement should be imposed in financial remedy cases where an application is made to revisit the judgment handed down on the basis of fresh evidence which was available and not placed before the court the first time around.

[9] *Charlesworth v Relay Roads Ltd* [2000] 1 W.L.R. 230, Neuberger J, as applied in *Vringo Infrastructure Inc v ZTE (UK) Ltd* [2015] EWHC 214 (Pat); [2015] R.P.C. 23.

[9a] *Karunia Holdings Ltd v Creativityetc Ltd* [2021] EWHC 1864 (Ch) at [56].

[10] *Navitaire Inc v Easyjet* [2005] EWHC 282 (Ch); followed in *Fisher v Cadman* [2005] EWHC 2424 (Ch).

[10a] *AR v ML* [2019] EWFC 56; [2020] 1 F.C.R. 1 at [21]–[22]. The judge also noted at [16] that there had never been a case where a successful challenge to a delivered judgment, prior to the ordered being

perfected, had been achieved on the basis of fresh evidence which could have been made available to the court the first time round. See also *Augousti v Matharu* [2023] EWHC 1900 (Fam) at [34].

Replace the first paragraph with:

13-02   It should be noted that in both of the cases discussed above (i.e. *Charlesworth* and *Townsend*), the *Ladd v Marshall* principles were not seen as the only relevant considerations. While they are of central importance, the court is entitled to take into account other factors in deciding whether to receive fresh evidence. In *Augousti v Matharu*,[14a] the judge said that the test from *Ladd v Marshall* should be applied with progressively increasing rigour relative to the point in time when the application is made and thus the test will be applied much more fiercely where the application is to adduce fresh evidence post judgment but prior to an order being sealed, or on an appeal, than where the application is to adduce fresh evidence at a trial after the completion of the evidence-giving phase but before the final submissions. The court, in exercising its discretion, must seek to give effect to the overriding objective as set out in CPR r.1.1. One of the matters the court now has to consider is the finite nature of court time and resources and the need to allocate these fairly between all litigants, not just those in the case in which the application is made.

[14a] *Augousti v Matharu* [2023] EWHC 1900 (Fam) at [35].

(b)   Further evidence on appeal: status of Ladd v Marshall

Replace paragraph with:

13-04   The criteria developed under the RSC were threefold, as established in *Ladd v Marshall*.[16a] Further evidence was only admissible on an appeal where the evidence: (a) could not have been obtained with reasonable diligence for use at the trial[17]; (b) is such that, if given, it would probably have an important influence on the result of the case (though it need not be decisive); and (c) is such as is presumably to be believed. It must be apparently credible, though it need not be incontrovertible.[18]

[16a] *Ladd v Marshall* [1954] 1 W.L.R. 1489 CA. The principles are sometimes collectively called "the rule in *Ladd v Marshall*". See also *Pursell v Railway Executive* [1951] 1 All E.R. 536 CA; *Herwin, Re* [1953] Ch. 701 CA; *Skone v Skone* [1971] 1 W.L.R. 812 HL.

[17] *Skone v Skone* [1971] 1 W.L.R. 812 HL.

[18] *Roe v Robert McGregor & Sons* [1968] 1 W.L.R. 925. The same general principles applied to hearings in the National Industrial Relations Court: *Bagga v Heavy Electricals (India) Ltd* (1971) 12 K.I.R. 154; *De Mars v Gurr Johns and Angier Bird* [1973] I.C.R. 35.

Replace the first paragraph with:

13-05   The Court of Appeal has confirmed that the principles established in *Ladd v Marshall* are still relevant in determining the exercise of the court's discretion to receive fresh evidence under CPR r.52.21(2).[20]

[20] See *Hertfordshire Investments v Bubb* [2000] 1 W.L.R. 2318; *Hamilton v Al Fayed (No.4)* [2001] E.M.L.R. 15; [2001] C.L.Y. 634 at [12]–[15]; *Gillingham v Gillingham* [2001] EWCA Civ 906; [2001] C.P. Rep. 89; [2001] C.P.L.R. 355 CA; *Prentice v Hereward Housing Association* [2001] EWCA Civ 437; [2001] 2 All E.R. (Comm) 900; *Shaker v Al-Bedrawi* [2002] EWCA Civ 1452; [2003] 2 W.L.R. 922 CA; *Ministere de l'Agriculture de la Foret v Bernard Matthews Plc* [2002] EWHC 190 (Ch); [2002] E.T.M.R. 90; [2003] F.S.R. 2. See also *Saluja v Gill* [2002] EWHC 1435 (Ch); *E (Children) (Reopening Findings of Fact), Re* [2019] EWCA Civ 1447; [2019] 1 W.L.R. 6765; *R. (on the application of Al-Siri) v Secretary of Statement for the Home Department* [2021] EWCA Civ 113; [2021] 1 W.L.R. 2137; *Fixsler v Manchester University NHS Foundation Trust* [2021] EWCA Civ 1018; [2021] 4 W.L.R. 123 at [52]; *Bowser v Smith* [2023] EWCA Civ 923 at [88].

Replace the fourth paragraph with:

In *Terluk v Berezovsky*,[25] the Court of Appeal stated that the primary rules for determining whether fresh evidence should be admitted were the wording of CPR r.52.11(2) and the overriding objective. While the *Ladd v Marshall* principles considered below are still relevant, courts may therefore now also have regard to wider or further considerations not previously considered under *Ladd v Marshall*, including considerations listed in the overriding objective.[26] In any event, the *Ladd v Marshall* requirements "are not to be taken as a straitjacket" and they must be applied flexibly.[27] In *Narayanasamy v Solicitors Regulation Authority*,[27a] the court said that the Ladd v Mashall principles are fundamental to legal certainty and the proper administration of justice. Far from subverting the overriding objective, they crystallise its requirements embodying the appellate court's settled attempt to strike a fair balance between the need for concluded litigation to be determinative of disputes and the desirability that the judicial process should achieve the right result.

13-05

[25] *Terluk v Berezovsky* [2011] EWCA Civ 1534. See also *Celik v Secretary of State for the Home Department* [2023] EWCA Civ 921 at [98].

[26] *Couwenbergh v Valkova* [2004] EWCA Civ 676; [2004] W.T.L.R. 937; (2004) 148 S.J.L.B. 694 CA. See also *Transview Properties Ltd v City Site Properties Ltd* [2009] EWCA Civ 1255 at [23] where it was held that applications to admit fresh evidence which would necessitate a re-trial should be approached cautiously.

[27] *Singh v Habib* [2011] EWCA Civ 599; [2011] C.P. Rep.34 at [14]. See also *St Andrew's Catholic Primary School Governing Body v Blundell* [2011] EWCA Civ 427; [2012] I.C.R. 295 at [30].

[27a] *Narayanasamy v Solicitors Regulation Authority* [2021] EWHC 2918 (Admin); [2022] A.C.D. 7 at [25].

(c) The Ladd v Marshall requirements

(iv) *Other factors not mentioned in Ladd v Marshall*

Replace the third paragraph with:

If it is alleged that a fraud has been perpetrated on the first instance court, the appellate court has two options. If evidence of the fraud is either admitted or incontrovertible, the application to adduce fresh evidence may be granted. If evidence of the fraud is contested, the appellate court may refer this dispute of fact to a judge under CPR r.52.20(2)(b).[55] A fresh action need not therefore be commenced by the party alleging fraud.

13-10

[55] *Noble v Owens* [2010] EWCA Civ 224; [2010] 1 W.L.R. 2491; *Dickinson v Tesco Plc* [2013] EWCA Civ 36; [2013] C.P. Rep. 24 at [60].

(d) Application of Ladd v Marshall in particular types of appellate hearing

Replace footnote 77 with:

[77] *Mulholland v Mitchell* [1971] A.C. 666 HL. See also *Steve Hill Ltd v Witham* [2021] EWCA Civ 1312; [2022] P.I.Q.R. P2.

13-12

After "... except that used in chambers will be admitted.[81] But in the", replace "Queen's" with:

King's

13-14

(g)   Reopening concluded appellate proceedings

Replace the first paragraph with:

13-18   The Court of Appeal retains a residual jurisdiction to reopen proceedings in order to avoid real injustice in exceptional circumstances.[89] The High Court has been found to have a similar inherent jurisdiction to set aside an otherwise final decision.[90] The respective jurisdictions are now enshrined in CPR r.52.30. In order to justify the reopening of proceedings, it must be clearly shown that it is necessary to do so in order to avoid significant injustice; that the circumstances are exceptional and make it necessary to reopen the appeal; and that there is no alternative effective remedy.[91] The applicable principles apply to final judgments and permission to appeal decisions alike.[92] Proceedings are unlikely to be reopened because of mistakes made by legal representatives, however reasonable or understandable the mistakes.[93] Furthermore, the court will not exercise its power to reopen proceedings because of a mere factual error.[94] The Court of Appeal in *UCP Plc v Nectrus Ltd*[94a] emphasised that final decisions would only be re-opened in exceptional circumstances and this is even more so, where the court is faced with a second application pursuant to CPR r.52.30. In *UCP Plc v Nectrus Ltd* the judge's decision on the first application under CPR r.52.30 was set aside for apparent bias in circumstances where the Court of Appeal found the integrity of the first application was critically undermined.

[89] *Taylor v Lawrence* [2002] EWCA Civ 90; [2003] Q.B. 528; [2002] 3 W.L.R. 640. In a criminal context see *R. v Gohil, R. v Preko* [2018] EWCA Crim 140; [2018] 1 W.L.R. 3697. The procedure is set out in CPR r.36.15 and referred to in *R. v Lowther* [2022] EWCA Crim 1807; [2023] 2 Archbold Review 2, CA.

[90] *Seray-Wurie v Hackney LBC* [2002] EWCA Civ 909; *R. (on the application of AM (Cameroon) v Asylum and Immigration Tribunal* [2008] EWCA Civ 100; [2008] All E.R. (D) 293 (Feb).

[91] *Jaffray v Society of Lloyd's* [2007] EWCA Civ 586; [2008] 1 W.L.R. 1400.

[92] *Barclays Bank Plc v Guy (No.2) (Practice Note)* [2010] EWCA Civ 1396; [2011] 1 W.L.R. 681.

[93] *R. (Nicholas) v Upper Tribunal* [2013] EWCA Civ 799 at [20].

[94] *Guy v Barclays Bank Plc* [2010] EWCA Civ 1396; [2011] 1 W.L.R. 681. The position would have been different if the factual error had been induced by fraud or bias: see paras 29-40.

[94a] *UCP Plc v Nectrus Ltd* [2022] EWCA Civ 949; [2023] 1 W.L.R. 39.

Replace the second paragraph with:

The jurisdiction exists because in certain instances where the Supreme Court (formerly House of Lords) would not grant leave to appeal, the Court of Appeal would be the only court in which an effective remedy could be provided.[95] Likewise, where no appeal lies from a decision of the High Court, a remedy against injustice does not lie elsewhere.[96] A party wishing to reopen a decision of the Court of Appeal or High Court must in all cases apply in accordance with para.7 of CPR PD52A. The application for permission must be in writing to the relevant court.[97] The application is considered on paper by a single judge and is only allowed to proceed if, following its consideration, the court so directs.[98] The court will not grant permission without directing that the other party to the original application be served with the application and be given an opportunity to respond.[99] If permission is not given there is no right to an oral hearing of the application, and no appeal lies against this decision.[100]

[95] *Barrell Enterprises, Re* [1973] 1 W.L.R. 19; *Bremer Vulkan Schiffbau und Maschinenfabrik v South India Shipping Corp Ltd* [1981] A.C. 909; *Taylor v Lawrence* [2002] EWCA Civ 90; [2003] Q.B. 528; [2002] 3 W.L.R. 640.

[96] *R. (on the application of AM (Cameroon) v Asylum and Immigration Tribunal* [2008] EWCA Civ 100; [2008] All E.R. (D) 293 (Feb) at [26], per Waller LJ.

[97] CPR r.52.17(4)

[98] See CPR Practice Direction A to Pt 52, para.7 for the procedure for a CPR r.52.30 application.

[99] CPR r.52.17(6).

[100] CPR r.52.17(5) and (7).

In the third paragraph, after "The", replace "House of Lords" with:
Supreme Court

2. CRIMINAL CASES

(b) Evidence on appeal to the Court of Appeal (Criminal Division)

Replace footnote 107 with: See generally D.R. Thompson and H. A. Wollaston, *Court of Appeal Criminal Division*; A Guide to Commencing Proceedings in the Court of Appeal Criminal Division, *Archbold 2023 Supplement*, App.J-915; Alec Samuels, "Fresh Evidence in the Court of Appeal Criminal Division" [1975] Crim. L.R. 23 (dealing with the position as it stood under the Criminal Appeal Act 1968 in its original form). See Criminal Procedure Rules 2013 Pt 65. See also R. Pattenden, *English Criminal Appeals 1844–1994* (Oxford: Oxford University Press, 1996), pp.130–140; P. Taylor (ed.), *Taylor on Criminal Appeals* (London: Sweet & Maxwell, 2000), pp.270–289. The procedural rules are set out in Criminal Procedure Rules 2020 Pt 36.

Replace the second paragraph with:
There is nothing in these provisions to prevent the admission of fresh evidence **13-20** after a conviction upon a plea of guilty. That would no doubt be rare in the case of a plea entered at or before the beginning of the hearing, but it remains technically possible, and is not infrequent where the fresh evidence discloses malpractice on the part of the prosecution which would have entitled a defendant to apply for a stay of the indictment on the basis of abuse of process[111] or where, as in *R. v BWM* it discloses a defence which would probably have succeeded if available at trial and the plea of guilty was based upon a false understanding of his true position.[111a] It is easier to envisage suitable cases where there has been a change of plea in the course of a trial following a ruling by the judge that particular evidence was admissible, and that ruling itself turns out to be based on evidence which new material shows to be substantially incomplete or misleading.[112]

[111] See *R. v Dunk* unreported 28 July 1994 CA (Crim Div); and *R. v Smith* [2004] EWCA Crim 341.

[111a] *R. v BWM* [2022] EWCA Crim 924; [2022] 4 W.L.R. 116 where a post-trial conclusive decision was made that the defendant was a victim of trafficking which afforded a good defence (the success of the appeal was also contributed to by the judge's ill-advised indication as to sentence).

[112] cf. *R. v Swain* [1986] Crim. L.R. 480 CA (where evidence was received as to the circumstances surrounding a change of plea).

CHAPTER 14

CORROBORATION, SUPPORTING EVIDENCE AND RELATED WARNINGS

TABLE OF CONTENTS

2. SITUATIONS WHERE SUPPORTING EVIDENCE IS REQUIRED BY STATUTE

(c) Criminal Procedure (Insanity and Unfitness to Plead) Act 1991 s.1

Replace footnote 28 with:

14-04   [28] Law Commission, *Unfitness to Plead*, Law Com No 364, HC 714 (2016), paras 4.43 and 4.67. Law Commission, *Annual Report 2021–22*, Law Com. No.409, HC 960, p.66, notes that the Commission was still awaiting a Government decision as to the implementation of this report.

3. SITUATIONS WHERE A WARNING MAY BE NECESSARY

(a) Types of witness

(i) *Complainants in sexual cases*

Replace footnote 34 with:

14-05   [34] *R. v Makanjuola* [1995] 1 W.L.R. 1348 at 1351F. Further examples of what will constitute an evidential basis can be gleaned from two cases where the Court of Appeal held that it had been an error not to give a warning. In *R. v Dennis W* [2002] EWCA Crim 1732, the evidential basis was provided by medical evidence suggesting that the complainant's testimony was very unlikely to be accurate with regard to two of six charges relating to that complainant. In *R. v G (Terry)* [2002] EWCA Crim 2352, the evidential basis was provided by the fact that the complainant had claimed that her siblings had witnessed events occurring to her and had themselves been abused, whilst they made no mention of either when interviewed. By contrast, in *R. v Udaykamaur Joshi* [2012] NICA 56 the Court of Appeal in Northern Ireland held that a warning was unnecessary in a case where the complainant admitted that he had previously told lies about the relevant events to a school friend and to his therapist because of the nature of the lies and the complainant's explanations for them. In *R. v Hindle* [2021] EWCA Crim 1367, the Court of Appeal went as far as to state (at [31]) that "even where a witness may be said to be unreliable, it [i.e. a *Makanjuola* direction] is a direction that is given sparingly and only in a case where it is appropriate to do so." The court treated the facts that the relevant witness's testimony was internally consistent on many points and consistent with other evidence in the case as features pointing against the necessity for a warning.

Replace footnote 37 with:

[37] Research Board of the British Psychological Society, *Guidelines on Memory and the Law* (Leicester: the British Psychological Society, 2010), p.13. Professor Adrian Keane has argued that there are compelling reasons for introducing a statutory requirement to this effect, whilst noting that what must be required must be something "other than corroboration in the strict sense, with its complex and highly technical rules": A. Keane, "The Use at Trial of Scientific Findings Relating to Human Memory" [2010] *Criminal Law Review* 19, 29–30. (The British Psychological Society no longer presents the 2010 *Guidelines* as its current "advice": see *https://www.bps.org.uk/psychologist/not-good-look* [Accessed 28 July 2023].)

Replace footnote 49 with:

[49] *The Crown Court Compendium: Part 1 – Jury and Trial Management and Summing Up* (June 2023), **14-06** p.10-7 (para.6). See also the general guidelines as to appropriate directions on p.10-8 (paras 10(3) and 10(4)): "(3) Where there is no independent supportive evidence, it may be appropriate to remind the jury of that fact, and possibly to suggest that the jury may have wished for such evidence. ... (4) In cases where there is potentially independent supportive evidence, that evidence must be identified, adding that it is for the jury to decide whether they accept that evidence and if so whether they regard it as supportive".

(ii)   Accomplices

Replace footnote 63 with:

[63] *R. v B (MT)* [2000] Crim. L.R. 181, discussed at para.14-06. An error as to what evidence is capable **14-07** of supporting the testimony of an unreliable witness may not always lead to an appeal being allowed: for example, in *Cox v The King* [2023] UKPC 4 (PC, Turks and Caicos Islands), the Judicial Committee of the Privy Council dismissed an appeal where a judge, without a jury, had convicted an accused of murder, despite making a mistake as to whether a particular independent witness had provided testimony supporting that of an accomplice with a clear incentive to provide false evidence; the Committee treated the existence of supporting testimony from a different independent witness, the intended victim, as significant.

(b)   Types of evidence

(iii)   Confessions to a cellmate

Replace footnote 93 with:

[93] *Benedetto v The Queen* [2003] 1 W.L.R. 1545 PC at [32]. See also *R. v Pollitt* (1992) 174 C.L.R. 558 **14-14** H Ct of Aus. In New Zealand, statute requires judges to consider whether to warn the jury about the need for caution in deciding whether to accept, and how to weigh, "evidence of a statement by the defendant to another person made while both the defendant and the other person were detained in prison, a Police station, or another place of detention" (Evidence Act 2006 (New Zealand) s.122(2)(d)). In *Hudson v R* [2011] NZSC 51; [2011] 3 N.Z.L.R. 289 the Supreme Court of New Zealand opined that such a warning will normally be required (at [41]), but rejected the suggestion that "evidence of admissions made by a defendant in prison to prison inmates should be treated as presumptively inadmissible." In *W v R* [2020] NZSC 93; [2020] 1 N.Z.L.R. 382, the Supreme Court of New Zealand went beyond this and held that trial judges should assess the reliability of such evidence when deciding whether it should be excluded on the basis of a balancing of its probative value against the risk of illegitimate prejudice. See further, A. High, "The Exclusion of Prison Informant Evidence for Unreliability in New Zealand" (2021) 25 *International Journal of Evidence & Proof* 217. The Supreme Court of New Zealand has granted an accused leave to appeal in a case involving *application* of its guidance on the warnings that should be given where a prison inmate testifies as to statements allegedly made by an accused whilst detained: *Tihema v R.* [2023] NZSC 37, granting leave to appeal against [2022] NZCA 444: one issue in the appeal may be when a trial judge ought to identify specific incentives that a witness may have had to provide false evidence, particularly in the absence of evidence that the witness sought or received any form of favourable treatment.

(v)   Expert evidence in cases of unexplained infant death

Replace footnote 104 with:

14-16   [104] cf. *The Crown Court Compendium: Part 1 – Jury and Trial Management and Summing Up* (June 2023), p.10-7 (para.5(6)), where it is suggested that a judge should consider giving a warning based on *Makanjuola*, see para 14-05, in such a case.

4.   WHAT CONSTITUTES SUPPORTING EVIDENCE?

Replace paragraph with:

14-17   The question of what constitutes supporting evidence[105] has lost much of its importance for three reasons. First, where judges choose to give a direction they will now often only give the simpler direction which advises the jury to be cautious, rather than a direction which requires them to identify what evidence is capable of amounting to corroboration.[106] Secondly, many of the difficult questions about whether evidence could amount to corroboration arose from whole categories of witness being identified as suspect and the consequent issue whether witnesses from the same category, for example accomplices, could corroborate each other.[107] Now that witnesses are assessed individually, rather than as members of a category, these questions should not arise.[108] Thirdly, statutory changes have ensured that certain types of evidence, if they are admissible at all, are admissible as evidence of the matters stated and not merely for more limited purposes.[109] Difficult questions may still arise concerning the extent to which evidence of lies told by the accused, refusals by the accused to answer questions or to provide samples, and the accused's previous conduct and statements, may be capable of supporting the testimony of a potentially unreliable prosecution witness (or co-defendant). The answer to many of these questions, however, will turn on whether the conditions for treating these matters as evidence against the accused have been fulfilled, and these conditions are set out and discussed elsewhere.[110] In *Ellis v R.*,[111] the Supreme Court of New Zealand considered a case where an expert witness had identified 20 behaviours that were said to be consistent with the children concerned having been sexually abused, and it had been suggested that clusters of these behaviours could support a conclusion that such abuse had taken place. The court was concerned that many of the behaviours, such as bed-wetting and difficulties in sleeping, could be explained in many other ways than as indicators of abuse, and ruled that much of the witness's evidence had been inadmissible bolstering of the witnesses rather than corroboration: the court diagnosed a form of objectionable "circularity"—the behaviours were only likely to be treated as indicators of abuse if the evidence that the child had been abused had already been accepted.

[105] Generally, supporting evidence need not support *every* element of the prosecution case: see, e.g. *R. v Doheny and Adams* [1997] 1 Cr. App. R. 369 CA at 387, where a semen stain on a cushion which yielded DNA matching the accused's was held to support the prosecution's case in a trial for buggery where the complainant had a "disturbed personality", even though the stain could have resulted from some other sexual activity, because the defendant had denied visiting the complainant's house.

[106] See, paras.14-06 and 14-07, for discussion of when, in the light of *R. v B (MT)* [2000] Crim. L.R. 181 CA, a judge might be obliged to identify what evidence is capable of amounting to supporting evidence.

[107] See, e.g. *DPP v Hester* [1973] A.C. 296 HL; *DPP v Kilbourne* [1973] A.C. 729 HL.

[108] In *R. v Stone* [2005] EWCA Crim 105; [2005] Crim. L.R. 569 at [94] the Court of Appeal seems to have regarded "supporting evidence" as being synonymous with "the other evidence which implicated" the accused.

[109] See, e.g. ss.119 and 120(2) Criminal Justice Act 2003.

[110] See para.36-37 (lies by the accused), paras 35-04 et seq. (refusals to answer), Ch.19 (accused's bad character).

[111] [2022] NZSC 115; [2022] 1 N.Z.L.R. 338 (Supreme Court of New Zealand).

CHAPTER 15

IDENTIFICATION

2. VISUAL IDENTIFICATION

(a) General principle

Replace footnote 23 with:

15-03 [23] *R. v Mussell and Dalton* [1995] Crim. L.R. 887 CA. Quotation from transcript, p.14, per Evans LJ. The advice and examples of appropriate directions in the Judicial College's *Crown Court Compendium: Part 1* (June 2023), Ch.15-1, follow the guidance in *Turnbull*.

(c) Photographs and video films

Replace the first paragraph with:

15-05 A photograph or film of a crime actually being committed, or of some other relevant event, is admissible.[51] Where the quality of the image is sufficiently good,[51a] a jury may be invited to make an identification by comparing it with the appearance of the accused, and this will not be treated as equivalent to a dock identification.[52] Nonetheless, the jury should be given a careful warning about the risks of error in this procedure,[53] and the accused is free to absent himself or herself from the dock.[54] The jury may be assisted by being shown other pictures of the accused.[55] The mere fact that a photograph or film is available which the jury could be asked to compare with the appearance of the accused does not preclude other witnesses from testifying that they have identified the accused as the person depicted.[56] Moreover, if in the circumstances the jury cannot be expected to identify the accused from the photograph or film, for instance because the photograph or film is unclear,[57] or because the accused has changed his appearance,[58] or because the photograph or film has been lost,[59] such a witness may be the only way of establishing who was involved in the relevant event.

[51] *R. v Tolson* (1864) 4 F. & F. 103 at 104; *R. v Cook* [1987] Q.B. 417 CA at 424; *Att.-Gen.'s Reference (No.2 of 2002)* [2002] EWCA Crim 2373; [2003] 1 Cr. App. R. 21. For detailed consideration of the basis of admissibility, see *R. v Nikolovski* (1996) 141 D.L.R. (4th) 647 (Supreme Court of Canada). The law is discussed by Roberts at (2003) 67 J.C.L. 91. The position is the same in Scotland, see *Shuttleton v Orr* [2019] HCJAC 12; 2019 J.C. 98.

[51a] The question whether CCTV footage is "of sufficient nature and quality to be capable of supporting a conclusion on identification" is a threshold matter for the judge in a case where there is a jury: *R. v Parrish* [2021] EWCA Crim 1693 at [27]. This case illustrates the importance of analysing what points the CCTV evidence is being used to support and what processes the jury is being asked to perform; with respect to one defendant in the case (Parrish) the CCTV footage of a gunfight might not have been sufficient to allow him to be identified by simple comparison of the images with his appearance at the trial, however the footage was of sufficient quality to allow the jury to conclude that the person said to be him was the same person (as a result of similarity of clothing, build, and bearing) as someone depicted in other footage, which the defendant admitted showed him, and the CCTV footage was also sufficient for supporting propositions about how events had unfolded, how the participants were located in relation to each other, and when telephones had been used, which were all matters tending to support the prosecution's circumstantial case.

[52] *Att.-Gen.'s Reference (No.2 of 2002)* [2002] EWCA Crim 2373; [2003] 1 Cr. App. R. 21 at [19](i). For objections to dock identifications, see para.15-14. In *Evans v R.* [2007] HCA 59, the High Court of Australia considered a case where the accused had been asked by the prosecution to put on a balaclava, wrap-around sunglasses and overalls so that the jury could compare his appearance with descriptions provided by witnesses and unclear images from a security video. Gummow J and Hayne J concluded that the trial judge should not have permitted this because it was irrelevant, in that the exercise could tell the jury nothing about the physical appearance of the accused that was not readily apparent from observing him in the dock (at [26]). By contrast, Heydon J, with whom Crennan J agreed, thought that the exercise was relevant because it had the capacity to demonstrate whether the accused, when dressed in a way similar to the perpetrator, looked similar to the descriptions given by the witnesses (at [177]). Kirby J agreed with Heydon J on the issue of relevance, but held that the exercise gave rise to unfair prejudice (at [108]). With respect, whilst it may have been correct to reject the extreme position that the evidence was wholly irrelevant, it is strongly arguable that the sort of comparison undertaken by the jury ought not to be encouraged because of the risk that its reliability might be overestimated. In *R. v Savory* [2019] EWCA Crim 1746, the Court of Appeal held that it had not been appropriate for the prosecution (apparently following a suggestion from the trial judge) during cross-examination of the accused to ask him to put on a coat, gloves and balaclava; the Court accepted that the process was undertaken to establish that the clothes were the right size to fit him, but noted that the jury were not instructed to use the demonstration only for this limited purpose, and there was a clear risk that they would inappropriately compare the appearance of the accused with CCTV footage of the disguised robbers.

[53] See further para.15-21. In *R. v Shanmugarajah* [2015] EWCA Crim 783; [2015] 2 Cr. App. R. 14, the Court of Appeal rejected the submission that a warning similar to that recommended in *R. v Turnbull* [1977] Q.B. 224; (1976) 63 Cr. App. R. 132 CA should always be given when a jury is asked to compare a CCTV image with the appearance of the accused in the dock: the court held that there "is no invariable or inflexible rule that a jury have to be expressly warned in every case of the risk that they might make a mistaken identification" (at [29]), and opined that "[m]odern practice in these courts is not to require trial judges to direct the jury as to the obvious" (at [29]).

[54] *R. v McNamara* [1996] Crim. L.R. 750 CA.

[55] *R. v Dodson* (1984) 70 Cr. App. R. 220; *R. v Clare and Peach* [1995] 2 Cr. App. R. 333 CA. Though clearly it would be important that the photographs used were not of such a type as to suggest that the accused had previous convictions. In *R. v Ozger* [2022] EWCA Crim 1238; [2023] 1 Cr. App. R. 23, the jury compared CCTV footage (which an expert had concluded was of insufficient quality for a facial-mapping exercise) with photographs of the accused taken seven months after the incident, which took place nearly three years before the trial. (In commentary on this case in [2023] Crim. L.R. 365, Andrew Roberts draws attention to the significant error rates associated with such comparisons.)

[56] *Att.-Gen.'s Reference (No.2 of 2002)* [2002] EWCA Crim 2373; [2003] 1 Cr. App. R. 21. See also *R. v Ulas* [2023] EWCA Crim 82; [2023] Crim. L.R. 658.

[57] *R. v Clare and Peach* [1995] 2 Cr. App. R. 333 CA.

[58] *R. v Stockwell* (1993) 97 Cr. App. R. 260 CA.

[59] *Taylor v Chief Constable of Cheshire* (1987) 84 Cr. App. R. 191 DC.

(d)   Protection against weak and unfair identification evidence

(iii)   *Important elements of fair identification procedure*

Dock identifications

Replace footnote 147 with:

15-14   147 *Holland v HM Advocate* [2005] UKPC D1; 2005 1 S.C. 3 PC (Scotland). It seems that in Scotland dock identifications are more common than in most common law jurisdictions. See in particular, Lord Hope at [3]: "There is no doubt that Scotland is unique among the jurisdictions in the United Kingdom in the significance that it attaches to dock identification." The criticism of dock identifications in this paragraph was followed in *R. v Long* [2022] EWCA Crim 444 at [23].

3.   DIRECTIONS ON VISUAL IDENTIFICATION EVIDENCE

Replace footnote 156 with:

15-16   156 *R. v Forbes* [2001] 1 A.C. 473 at [27]. A similar warning will frequently be necessary where a witness has identified a suspect informally using social media before participating in a formal identification procedure, particularly where another person drew their attention to specific images: Judicial College, *Crown Court Compendium: Part 1* (June 2023), 15-1 para.6; *R. v Phillips (Conner)* [2020] EWCA Crim 126; [2020] Crim. L.R. 940 at [41].

(a)   Turnbull warnings

Replace footnote 157 with:

15-17   157 *R. v Turnbull* [1977] Q.B. 224 CA. The importance of such warnings has been emphasised many times, for example in *R. v Clifton* [1986] Crim. L.R. 399 CA. The Criminal Procedure Rules 2020 r.25.14(2), provides that "[t]he court must give the jury directions about the relevant law at any time at which to do so will assist jurors to evaluate the evidence". See also *Criminal Practice Directions 2023*, 8.5.1. *R. v Smith (Jordan)* [2019] EWCA Crim 1151, raised the question whether a *Turnbull* direction is appropriate where the defence relies on an eyewitness's identification: in the case, the defence had relied on the fact that two prosecution witnesses had recognised people other than the accused as the perpetrators. The Court of Appeal held that it was "clearly appropriate" for the judge to have directed the jury about the need for caution in approaching this evidence: Leggatt LJ said, at [39]: "The potential dangers of identification evidence and consequent need for care are matters which may not be known to jurors in the way that they are well known to those with experience of criminal justice. Nor do they depend on which party at the trial is relying on such evidence." With respect, we are doubtful whether it would always be appropriate to give such a warning where the defence introduces identification evidence, for example from an eyewitness who testifies to having seen the accused at a place and time inconsistent with him having been elsewhere in order to commit the crime. In *R. v Allen* [2022] EWCA Crim 750 at [19], the Court of Appeal accepted that it would have been inappropriate to give a *Turnbull* warning with respect to defence evidence (witnesses who testified that they had seen a person alive after the date when the prosecution was alleging that she had been murdered by the accused), but held that a brief reference to the risk of honest mistakes was neither inappropriate nor unfair.

(b)   The form of the Turnbull direction

Replace footnote 197 with:

15-23   197 *R. v Graham* [1994] Crim. L.R. 212 CA. The Judicial College's *Crown Court Compendium: Part 1* (June 2023), 15-1 para.12, provides the following helpful list of circumstances that the jury should be directed to consider when putting "caution into practice": "(1) the time during which the witness had the person he/she says was D under observation; in particular the time during which the witness could see the person's face; (2) the distance between the witness and the person observed; (3) the state of the light; (4) whether there was any interference with the observation (such as either a physical obstruction or other things going on at the same time); (5) whether the witness had ever seen D before and if so how many times and in what circumstances (i.e. whether the witness had any reason to be able to recognise D); (6) the length of time between the original observation of the person said to be D (usually at the time of the incident) and the identification by the witness of D [to] the police (often at an identification procedure); (7) whether there is any significant difference between the description the witness gave to the police and the appearance of D."

(f) Other warnings

Replace footnote 234 with:

234 Judicial College, *Crown Court Compendium: Part 1* (June 2023), 15-1 para.6; *R. v Phillips (Conner)* [2020] EWCA Crim 126; [2020] Crim. L.R. 940 at [41]. **15-31**

4. OTHER MEANS OF IDENTIFICATION

(a) DNA evidence

Replace the second paragraph with:

The Court of Appeal had to return to the issue in *R. v Tsekiri*,[249] and on this occasion it held that the approach set out in *R. v Bryon* was not correct. In *R. v Tsekiri* the only evidence identifying the accused as the perpetrator of a robbery was a match between his DNA and the major contributor to a sample containing more than one DNA profile that was taken from the handle on a car door that was opened by the perpetrator; the Court held that this was sufficient to give rise to a case to answer. The Court identified a series of factors that must be assessed in order to decide whether the DNA evidence is, in the particular circumstances of the case, sufficient to establish a case to answer: the magnitude of the random match probability (in this case, it was said to be 1 in a billion); whether the evidence disclosed any innocent explanation for the presence of DNA matching the accused's; the degree of association between the article where the DNA was found and the offence; the moveability of this article; whether there was a geographical association between the accused and the offence; where the sample involved a mix of profiles, whether the match was with the major contributor or a minor contributor to the mix; and, whether the DNA in the sample was likely to be there as a result of primary rather than secondary transfer.[250] In *R. v Belhaj-Farhat*,[250a] the Court of Appeal emphasised that this list was not intended to be exhaustive list and that "each case will depend on its own facts". The appeal turned on the significance of a finding of the accused's DNA on a roll-up cigarette that had been propped up against a frame on the front door inside a flat that had been burgled; the fact that the butt was immediately found in such a place by a resident after she returned to the flat, and that the burglary had taken place in the previous 45 minutes, increased the strength of the evidence.[250b]

15-33

249 *R. v Tsekiri* [2017] EWCA Crim 40; [2017] 1 W.L.R. 2879; [2017] 1 Cr. App. R. 32; see also *R. v Murphy* [2021] NICA 16 (applying the *Tsekiri* approach in Northern Ireland).

250 *R. v Tsekiri* [2017] EWCA Crim 40; [2017] 1 W.L.R. 2879; [2017] 1 Cr. App. R. 32 at [12]–[21]. In *R. v Killick* [2020] EWCA Crim 785, the Court of Appeal rejected a prosecution appeal and held that a trial judge had correctly withdrawn a case from the jury; the case was based entirely on a DNA match between the accused and a screwdriver dropped during a burglary, but the possibility of an innocent deposit of the DNA could not be safely excluded.

250a *R. v Belhaj-Farhat* [2022] EWCA Crim 115 at [28] (see also [32]). This point echoed *R. v Tsekiri* [2017] EWCA Crim 40; [2017] 1 W.L.R. 2879 at [21].

250b The case can be usefully compared with *R. v Metzger* 2023 SCC 5 (Supreme Court of Canada), where the court divided, but a majority allowed an appeal against a conviction for home invasion robbery that depended on the finding, 11 hours after the robbery, of a cigarette butt (with the accused's DNA on it) in a vehicle that had been stolen from the victim and then abandoned: the majority emphasised that the butt provided no proof as to when or why the accused had been in the vehicle. (The other significant evidence potentially implicating the accused was that the victim, who had been hit with a baseball bat, believed that he might have heard one of the intruders say the accused's surname during the robbery.)

(b)   Fingerprints, footmarks and similar body impressions

Replace footnote 262 with:

15-34   [262] Consequently, the provisions in Criminal Procedure Rules 2020 Pt 19 are relevant. See also the *Criminal Practice Directions* 2023 Pt 7.

(c)   Voice recognition

(ii)   Lay listener evidence

Replace footnote 292 with:

15-36   [292] *R. v Deenik* [1992] Crim. L.R. 578 CA. See also, *R. v Crow* [2021] EWCA Crim 617, where the court refused an application for leave to appeal by an accused convicted on the basis of a victim's claimed recognition of his voice from the uttering of the words "Where are you, you cunt?" by a masked attacker.

CHAPTER 16

PHYSICAL CONDITIONS, STATES OF MIND AND EMOTIONS

3. PROOF OF STATES OF MIND AND BODY

(d) Motive and relationship

Replace footnote 90 with:

90 See, for example, *R. v Sule* [2012] EWCA Crim 1130; [2013] 1 Cr. App. R. 3; *R. v Lunkulu* [2015] EWCA Crim 1350; *Myers v The Queen* [2015] UKPC 40; [2016] A.C. 314; [2016] 1 Cr. App. R. 11 (Bermuda); *R. v Stewart* [2016] EWCA Crim 447; *R. v Awoyemi* [2016] EWCA Crim 668; [2016] 2 Cr. App. R. 22; [2017] Crim. L.R. 131; *R. v Simpson* [2019] EWCA Crim 1144 at [13]; *R. v Rashid* [2019] EWCA Crim 2018; *R. v Heslop* [2022] EWCA Crim 897; [2022] 2 Cr. App. R. 20. **16-12**

(f) Fraud and dishonesty

(i) Dishonesty

Replace footnote 124 with:

124 *R. v Jackson-Mason* [2014] EWCA Crim 1993; [2015] 1 Cr. App. R. 6. See also *R. v BRM* [2022] EWCA Crim 385 where a conviction for murder was upheld despite the accused being prevented from leading evidence of his diagnosis with Asperger's Syndrome (now referred to as Autism Spectrum Disorder); the court reasoned that the evidence might have been relevant if the issue had been whether the accused had honestly believed that a particular response to a threat was necessary, or if there was evidence that the condition could lead to delusional beliefs or create hyper-sensitivity to risk, but was not relevant to the issue whether the accused could form an intention to cause really serious injury, nor to whether the accused had (as he claimed) aimed to stab the victim's arm and then accidentally stabbed him a second time. **16-17**

(g) Malice

Replace footnote 149 with:

149 *Brown v Hawkes* [1891] 2 Q.B. 718; *Stuart v Attorney General of Trinidad and Tobago* [2022] UKPC 53; [2023] 4 W.L.R. 21 (PC (Trinidad and Tobago)) at [16] per Lord Burrows JSC; *Roopnarine v Attorney General of Trinidad and Tobago* [2023] UKPC 30 (PC (Trinidad and Tobago)) at [21] per Lord Hamblen JSC. **16-20**

4. Permissible Inferences from States of Mind and Body

(b) Inferences from fear

After the second paragraph, add new paragraph:

16-26   In *Commonwealth of Pennsylvania v Fitzpatrick*,[175a] the Supreme Court of Pennsylvania discussed the admissibility of a note that a wife had written in her day planner the day before she died—"If something happens to me – JOE"—as evidence tending to show that she had been murdered by her husband. The court reasoned that such a note might be admitted as evidence of the deceased's state of mind (under a state of mind exception to the hearsay rule) where *that* state of mind was relevant, but should not be admissible as evidence tending to show the truth of a particular reason for that state of mind, such as that her husband intended to harm her. The court helpfully drew attention to two situations where a deceased person's fear might be relevant in a murder case: where an accused submitted that he had acted in self defence after being attacked by the deceased, and the deceased's fear of the accused made it unlikely that she had attacked him; and where the accused submitted that the deceased had died as a result of an accident, for example, whilst playing with a firearm, and the deceased's fear made it unlikely that she had acted in the way said to have resulted in the accident, for example, because she was afraid of touching firearms.[175b] Applying the law to the facts of the case, the court allowed the appeal, since the deceased's fear that her husband might intend to harm her was only relevant if he did intend to harm her.[175c]

[175a] *Commonwealth of Pennsylvania v Fitzpatrick* (2021) 255 A. 3d 452 (Supreme Court of Pennsylvania).

[175b] *Commonwealth of Pennsylvania v Fitzpatrick* (2021) 255 A. 3d 452 (Supreme Court of Pennsylvania) at 474–475, citing *U.S. v Brown* (1973) 490 F. 2d. 758 (DC Circ.) at 767. The court also identified situations where an accused submitted that a deceased had committed suicide, rather than being unlawfully killed, as situations where the deceased's state of mind might be admissible: if, for example, the deceased's state of mind represented enthusiasm for continuing to be alive.

[175c] There was other evidence in the case, such as a substantial life insurance policy and the accused's desire to proceed with an extra-marital relationship, tending to demonstrate that the accused had a motive to kill the deceased.

(c) Inferences from intention

Replace footnote 187 with:

16-27   [187] C. Tapper, "Hillmon Rediscovered and Lord St. Leonards Resurrected" (1990) 106 L.Q.R. 441. The title refers to *Mutual Life Insurance Co v Hillmon*, 145 U.S. 284 (1892); and *Sugden v Lord St Leonards* (1876) 1 P.D. 154. The *Hillmon* case is discussed in S. Saltzburg, "Solving the State of Mind Mystery" (2023) 59 Criminal Law Bulletin Art.2.

CHAPTER 18

GOOD CHARACTER

1. GOOD CHARACTER OF THE ACCUSED

(d) The judicial direction on good character

(i) Generally

Replace footnote 44 with:

⁴⁴ See now the Judicial College's *Crown Court Compendium Part 1: Jury and Trial Management and Summing Up*, Ch.11, first issued in May 2016, and last updated in June 2023.

18-09

(vi) "Good character" for the purposes of the direction

Replace footnote 80 with:

⁸⁰ See *R. v Sellers* [2018] EWCA Crim 2469 at [29]. See also, *R. v Olive* [2022] EWCA Crim 1141 at [82].

18-16

(vii) The convicted accused

Replace paragraph with:

Under the Rehabilitation of Offenders Act 1974,¹⁰¹ a "spent" conviction is to be treated, in civil cases, as not having taken place. In criminal cases, the Criminal Practice Directions tell criminal courts always to have regard to the general principles of the 1974 Act.¹⁰² Before the decision in *R. v Hunter*,¹⁰³ it was established that, if the defence wished to put forward an accused with a spent conviction as of good character and to invoke the appropriate direction, leave must be sought, it then being a matter for the judge's discretion whether or not to grant it.¹⁰⁴ That position requires reconsideration in the light of *Hunter*. Though, there, Hallett LJ referred to a number of cases involving spent convictions, she made no mention of the significance of them being spent anywhere in her "Conclusions".¹⁰⁵ The consequence would seem to be that "spentness" should be factored into questions about the age of a conviction, as part of a judicial decision as to whether or not the accused counts as being of effective good character.¹⁰⁶ If the answer is in the negative, that spentness will merely be a factor as regards the judge's broad discretion.

18-18

¹⁰¹ See para.20-42.

102 See *Criminal Practice Directions* 2015 (as amended), para.21A.2. It must be added that the 2015 *Directions* have, since publication of the last edition, been revoked by para.1.1.1 of the *Criminal Practice Directions* 2023, except that some of the earlier ones are thereby retained. However, para.21A.2 is not included in those retained. At the time of writing, it was unclear what was the effect of these changes upon the law with regard to spent convictions.

103 *R. v Hunter* [2015] 1 W.L.R. 5367.

104 See *R. v Nye* (1982) 75 Cr. App. R. 247 CA; *R. v Bailey* [1989] Crim. L.R. 723 CA; *R. v Mentor* [2004] EWCA Crim 3104.

105 See *R. v Hunter* [2015] 1 W.L.R. 5367 at [61]–[102]. She did (at [64]) quote a passage from the *Bench Book* that *mentions* them.

106 *R. v Hunter* [2015] 1 W.L.R. 5367 at [79].

(viii)   The unconvicted accused

After the fifth paragraph, add new paragraph:

18-19   A further issue arises if the accused was charged with an offence but later acquitted of it. Here, as will be explained in Ch.19,[118a] for the purposes of the admissibility rules as regards *bad* character, the truth of the evidence must be assumed unless no reasonable jury would believe it to be true. In *R. v BQC*,[118b] one issue for the court was as to the proper effect upon a potential *good* character direction of such evidence having been adduced. It held that the trial judge had been right to give such a direction, but should also have, as she had not, gone on to tell the jury that the accused was entitled to the full benefit thereof unless they were sure that the allegations in question were true.[118c]

118a See at para.19-51.

118b *R. v BQC* [2021] EWCA Crim 1944.

118c See *R. v BQC* [2021] EWCA Crim 1944 at [61].

2.   GOOD CHARACTER OF OTHERS

(a)   **Relevance to a fact in issue**

(i)   Criminal cases

Replace footnote 128 with:

18-21   128 The preceding statement in the text was endorsed by Keene LJ in *R. v Amado-Taylor* [2001] EWCA Crim 1898. See also *R. v Ali* [2006] EWCA Crim 1976 at [36]; *R. v Lodge* [2013] EWCA Crim 987; and, especially, *R. v Mader* [2018] EWCA Crim 2454 at [18] and [22], considered in detail at para.18-22. It was again endorsed in *R. v Braim* [2022] EWCA Crim 352 (see at [27]), in which case *Mader* itself was applied.

CHAPTER 19

BAD CHARACTER OF THE ACCUSED (PROSECUTION ASPECTS)

1. INTRODUCTION TO ACCUSED'S BAD CHARACTER

Replace footnote 16 with:

[16] The leading cases are *R. v Hanson* [2005] 1 W.L.R. 3169 at [15]; *R. v Renda* [2006] 1 W.L.R. 2948 at [3]; *R. v McKenzie* [2008] EWCA Crim 758 at [28]; but see also, *R. v Tangang* [2007] EWCA Crim 469; *DPP v Chand* [2007] EWHC 90 (Admin); [2007] 171 J.P. 285 (an appeal against the decision of a magistrates' court to *exclude* evidence); *R. v Jones, Devall and Gordon* [2007] EWCA Crim 2741; *R. v Tye* [2009] EWCA Crim 1738; *R. v Harris* [2011] EWCA Crim 912; *R. v Brown* [2012] EWCA Crim 773; *R. v Bowman* [2014] EWCA Crim 716; *R. v Loftus* [2015] EWCA Crim 139; *R. v Charles-Wilson* [2015] EWCA Crim 440; *R. v Cushing* [2006] EWCA Crim 1221; *R. v Thompson* [2016] All E.R. (D) 56 (Dec); *R. v Bailey* [2017] EWCA Crim 35; *R. v Bostock* [2020] EWCA Crim 365; *R. v Clifford* [2020] EWCA Crim 724; *R. v Mohammed* [2020] EWCA Crim 761; *R. v Bosa* [2020] EWCA Crim 1219; *R. v Richards* [2022] EWCA Crim 1470.

19-02

Replace the sixth paragraph with:

Two factors stretch trial court autonomy. First, appeal courts are inclined to find there to be discretion, even where there is a very good case for the matter being rule-governed.[18] It is strange to take Parliament's statement that evidence is admissible if, but only if, certain conditions are met as granting the trial judge strong discretion, in the *Wednesbury* sense. Hughes LJ may have had that point in mind when he said, in *R. v McMinn*, that the question whether or not bad character evidence should be admitted under s.101(1)(d) was "correctly described as an exercise of judgment, rather than simply discretion".[19] The second factor seems better to fit judicial orthodoxy, as well as fitting in with the remark in *R. v McMinn*. It is that appeal courts are to display a tolerant attitude to "fact-specific judgements",[20] since the trial judge will be much better placed than an appeal court to make purely factual findings. However, in these respects too, there are limits to appeal court tolerance, those limits perhaps also being set by *Wednesbury* unreasonableness.[21]

[18] Good examples are *R. v Johnson* [2009] EWCA Crim 649 at [34] and [42]; *R. v Khan* [2022] EWCA Crim 1592 at [62].

[19] *R. v McMinn* [2007] EWCA Crim 3024 at [5]. See also, *R. v Reed and Williams* [2007] EWCA Crim. 3083 at [37], where Rix LJ seems to have picked up the same point, as regards s.101(1)(e). The word

"judgment" was also used in another s.101(1)(e) case, *R. v Perkins* [2021] EWCA Crim 1462 at [18]–[20].

[20] See *R. v Renda* [2006] 1 W.L.R. 2948 at [3]. See also, *R. v Murray* [2016] EWCA Crim 278 at [30].

[21] See, e.g. *R. v Murphy* [2006] EWCA Crim 3408 (applied in *R. v McGarvie* [2011] EWCA Crim 1414). See also, *R. v McAllister* [2008] EWCA Crim 1544; [2009] 1 Cr. App. R. 129; *R. v Islam* [2012] EWCA Crim 217.

4. CRIMINAL JUSTICE ACT 2003

(b) The scope of the Act

(ii) "Bad character"

Replace footnote 38 with:

19-12 [38] As explained in *R. v Rowton* (1865) Le. & Ca. 520; 34 L.J.M.C. 57, discussed at paras 18-04 to 18-07.

(c) The gateways to admissibility

Replace footnote 54 with:

19-15 [54] See now, the Criminal Procedure Rules 2020 (as amended), Pt 21.

(d) Res gestae and connected cases

(iii) Res gestae and connected cases under s.98 of the 2003 Act

Replace the first paragraph with:

19-25 As to the exact division between s.98(a) and s.101(1)(c),[88] the authorities are in considerable disarray. There are certainly a large number of cases in which the appeal court, often impressed by the ordinary English meaning of the phrase "has to do with",[89] has taken a wide view of s.98(a), one embracing all of the common law res gestae categories,[90] though it must be added that, in very many of them, it was held that the evidence in question was, in any event, also admissible through some s.101(1) gateway.[91] It even sometimes seems to have been suggested that nothing more is required of the evidence at issue than that it be of simple legal relevance.[92] This widest of views seems clearly to be completely at odds with the structure of s.101 itself; indeed, as Davis LJ said in *R. v H (PD)*[93]:

> "[t]he relevance of ... the ... conviction is not of itself something that can bring a matter within section 98. Relevance alone is not the test".

[88] For a helpful discussion, see Munday [2008] J. Crim. Law 214.

[89] A good example is *R. v Machado* [2006] 170 J.P. 400 at [13], though the court went on, in that case, to take the narrower view.

[90] See, e.g. *R. v Malone* [2006] EWCA Crim 1860; *R. v Tirnaveanu* [2007] EWCA Crim 1239; [2007] 1 W.L.R. 3049; *R. v Saleem* [2007] EWCA Crim 1923; *R. v McNeill* [2007] EWCA Crim 2927 at [14] (where Rix LJ described the (whole) common law as a "sufficient working model"); *R. v Sule* [2012] EWCA Crim 1130; *R. v Hussain* [2013] EWCA Crim 2053; *R. v Hastings-Coker and Smith* [2014] EWCA Crim 555; *R. v Okokono* [2014] EWCA Crim 2521; *R. v Marray* [2014] EWCA Crim 2910; *R. v Ali Ditta* [2016] EWCA Crim 8 at [7]; *R. v Hanson* [2016] EWCA Crim 1228; *R. v Campbell* [2017] EWCA Crim 213; *R. v Lovell* [2018] EWCA Crim 19; [2018] 1 Cr. App. R. (S.) 48; *R. v KM* [2018] EWCA Crim 605; *R. v H* [2018] EWCA Crim 2868; [2019] 1 W.L.R. 3744; *R. v Lucas and Floan* [2019] EWCA Crim 213; *R. v Soloman* [2019] EWCA Crim 1356; *R. v Kumar-Sethi* [2019] EWCA Crim 1486;

R. v Murray [2019] EWCA Crim 1535; *R. v Dixon-Kenton* [2021] EWCA Crim 673; *R. v Stanton* [2021] EWCA Crim 1075; *R. v Chand* [2021] EWCA Crim 1587.

[91] Two recent examples, both concerned with evidence said to be relevant to the accused's motive for committing the crime charged, are *R. v Manjra* [2021] EWCA Crim 853; and *R. v Stanton* [2021] EWCA Crim 1075. In the former, the court clearly thought it admissible via s.101(1)(c). In the latter, rather surprisingly, the court ruled it inadmissible under s.101(1)(c), but admissible under s.101(1)(d) (see at [30] and [34]). Of course, the appeal court may decide that the trial judge was wrong to find that s.98(a) applied, yet rule that the evidence in question properly satisfied one of the s.101 gateways—see, e.g. *R. v McGowan, Dawuda-Wodu, Baker and Backhouse* [2023] EWCA Crim 247 at [33].

[92] See, e.g. *R. v McNeill* [2007] EWCA Crim 2927 at [14]; *R. v Penney* [2022] EWCA Crim 191 at [18]. Though *R. v O, C and D* [2010] EWCA Crim 1336 might appear to be similar effect, the case may properly be regarded as affirming that the evidence at hand was admissible under s.101(1)(d).

[93] *R. v H (PD)* [2016] EWCA Crim 1659 at [22].

Replace footnote 94 with:

[94] *R. v Hussain* [2013] EWCA Crim 2053. See also, *R. v Oloyowang* [2021] EWCA Crim 1412, though there the s.98(a) argument was, perhaps, more persuasive.

Replace the fourth paragraph with:

The very important case, *R. v Mullings*,[98] sounds a similar note. There, the prosecution had been permitted to call evidence of the accused's possession of documents indicative of support of one Manchester gang,[99] and antipathy towards another, in order to advance its case that, when part of a group containing members of the former gang confronting those of the latter, he must have known that others were carrying firearms with intent to endanger life, and must have shared that intent. The court held that, because of the absence of any close temporal connection, that evidence did not "have to do with" the alleged facts. An example that it gave of evidence that would satisfy s.98(a) is instructive. It envisaged evidence that the accused might, at the very time of the confrontation, have been shouting out similar sentiments of support and antipathy. The temporal connection would undoubtedly then be shown, but it is clear enough that the factual one would too, such that the shouting would properly have been accounted, at common law, part of the transaction under review.[100] Furthermore, the court added the very important point, already adverted to in the text, that:

> "[t]he wider s.98(a) is construed, and the wider the embrace of evidence which 'has to do' with the facts of the alleged offence, the less effective the statutory purpose becomes"

with the consequence that "the narrower view of s.98(a) is to be preferred".[101] This reasoning seems wholly convincing.[102]

[98] *R. v Mullings* [2010] EWCA Crim 2820; [2011] 2 Cr. App. R. 2. See also, *R. v Hewgill* [2011] EWCA Crim 1778; *R. v Rostami* [2013] EWCA Crim 1363; *R. v IA and others* [2013] EWCA Crim 1308; *R. v Sullivan* [2015] EWCA Crim 1565; (2015) 179 J.P. 552; *R. v King* [2019] EWCA Crim 2434; *R. v Heron* [2020] EWCA Crim 966; *R. v Byrne* [2021] EWCA Crim 107; *R. v Porritt* [2021] EWCA Crim 1115; *R. v Singh* [2022] EWCA Crim 1108.

[99] There is a series of cases decided during the last decade that all relate to gang activity, starting with *R. v Sule* [2012] EWCA Crim 1130. Though, in some, s.98(a) has been relied upon by the appeal court— see *Sule* itself; *R. v Lunkulu* [2015] EWCA Crim 1350; *R. v Stewart* [2016] EWCA Crim 447; (2016) 180 J.P. 205; *R. v Dixon-Kenton* [2021] EWCA Crim 673; *R. v Abdi* [2022] EWCA Crim 315; *R. v Heslop, Hassan and Constable* [2022] EWCA Crim 897; [2022] 2 Cr. App. R. 20—in others, s.101(1)(c) was the route to admissibility—see *R. v Hoare* [2016] EWCA Crim 886, whilst, in three cases, that route was provided by s.101(1)(d)—see *R. v Lewis* [2014] EWCA Crim 48; *R. v Awoyemi* [2016] EWCA Crim 668; *R. v Rashid and Tshoma* [2019] EWCA Crim 2018.

[100] To similar effect are *R. v Brand* [2009] EWCA Crim 2878; *R. v Loftus and Comben* [2009] EWCA Crim 2688; *R. v McPherson* [2010] EWCA Crim 2906; *R. v Hart* [2014] EWCA Crim 2686 at [10], per Laws LJ; and *R. v Sullivan* [2015] EWCA Crim 1565; (2015) 179 J.P. 552 at [50], where *R. v Mullings* [2011] 2 Cr. App. R. 2 was referred to.

[101] See *R. v Mullings* [2011] 2 Cr. App. R. 2 at [32], per Pitchford LJ.

[102] The case also scotches a suggestion in *R. v Fox* [2009] EWCA Crim 653 that the phrase "has to do with the alleged facts" contemplates only the factual elements of the alleged offence, so not any element of mens rea—see [2011] 2 Cr. App. R. 2 at [29]. See also, Ormerod [2009] Crim. L.R. 881. To the same effect is *R. v IA and others* [2013] EWCA Crim 1308.

Replace the second paragraph with:

19-26   The Commission envisaged only misconduct of police[107] or accused being embraced, and, in *R. v Scott*,[108] the judge's decision to reject an argument that s.98(b) applied to defence evidence that the complainant had sought to intimidate a witness into believing that the accused really had raped her was upheld on appeal, because, "[t]he misconduct has to have some closer link with the actual investigation of the offences or with their actual prosecution".[109] However, this does not entail that third party misconduct will never be caught, and *Scott* was distinguished in *R. v Apabhai*.[110] There, Apabhai alleged that his co-accused Amani had given him seven days to pay Amani £125,000, in return for Amani not changing his statement to the investigating customs officers such as to place all of the blame for the offences at hand upon Apabhai. The appeal court upheld the judge's decision that that evidence was caught by s.98(b). Here, the alleged misconduct was that of an accused, but the issue to which it related was not one between that accused and the prosecution, which is what the Law Commission appears to have had in mind. In *R. v Singh*,[110a] by contrast, the misconduct at issue was that of a potential witness that the defence sought to have tendered by the prosecution for cross-examination. However, it is to be noted that that person had given evidence against Singh at a first trial for the murder for which he was now being retried. Though it upheld the trial judge's ruling that s.98(b) could not be relied upon, the Court of Appeal cast no doubt on the holding in *Apabhai* that the ambit of that subsection is not restricted to prosecution misconduct. Rather, the problem was that the present alleged misconduct was not "misconduct in connection with the investigation or prosecution of" the offence of murder now charged, for the purposes of s.98(b). Therefore, it still remains to be decided whether, in some circumstances, the courts will be prepared to extend s.98(b) to cover misconduct by a complainant or other third party.

[107] In *R. v Denton* [2020] EWCA Crim 410, the misconduct of a trading standards officer who had been performing functions usually those of the police was rightly held caught by s.98(b).

[108] *R. v Scott* [2009] EWCA Crim 2457. That case was not cited in *R. v Louanjli* [2021] EWCA Crim 819, where the court seemed inclined to think that rather similar behaviour did not amount to qualifying misconduct, but eventually (at [28]) ruled it irrelevant anyway.

[109] *R. v Scott* [2009] EWCA Crim 2457 at [38], per Aikens LJ.

[110] *R. v Apabhai* [2011] EWCA Crim 917; followed in *R. v Haxihaj* [2016] EWCA Crim 83.

[110a] *R. v Singh* [2022] EWCA Crim 1108, especially at [39].

(iv)   Res gestae and connected cases under s.101(1)(c) of the 2003 Act

In the eighth paragraph, after "… that is more prejudicial than probative.", add new footnote 131a:

[131a] *R. v Shiekh* [2013] EWCA Crim 907, where the court ruled that the trial judge had been wrong to allow evidence to be called of the accused's rape conviction in order to explain why he had been subject to a sexual offences prevention order at the time of the present alleged offence, may well be an example of a case where the trial judge should have excluded that evidence under s.78(1), though the higher court made no mention of that provision—see at [8] and [9].

19-28

(e)   Important matters in issue between prosecution and accused

(i)   The three-stage test in Hanson and its application

Replace the first paragraph with:

Though *R. v Hanson*,[132] the leading case on gateway (d), directly concerned use of convictions as probative via propensity reasoning, and the provisions of s.103 in particular, certain remarks of Rose LJ have much more general significance. His Lordship suggested that a three-stage test needed to be satisfied, and that test has been very often applied since *Hanson*, both at trial and on appeal.[133] In his words[134]:

19-30

> "Where propensity to commit the offence is relied upon there are thus essentially three questions to be considered.
>
> 1.   Does the history of conviction(s) establish a propensity to commit offences of the kind alleged?
> 2.   Does that propensity make it more likely that the defendant committed the offence charged?
> 3.   Is it unjust to rely on the conviction(s) of the same description of category; and, in any event, will the prosecution be unfair if they are admitted?"

His Lordship went on to emphasise the importance of several factors in evaluating the case for admission.[135] A relevant propensity was more likely to be shown where it had been exercised more than once, though similarity in modus operandi, or the behaviour's unusualness, would tend towards its establishment. Account should be taken of the age of the conviction(s), with admission of old convictions more likely seriously to affect adversely the fairness of the proceedings, unless they could properly be said to show a "continuing propensity".[135a] Likewise, trial fairness would tell against admission of bad character evidence where the rest of the prosecution case was weak. Finally, the sentence passed would not normally be probative or admissible at the prosecution's behest. How these factors have been applied in the later cases will be dealt below,[136] but consideration must first be given to the application of law to the conjoined appeals in that case itself.

[132] *R. v Hanson* [2005] 1 W.L.R. 3169.

[133] There are too many examples for them to be listed here.

[134] *R. v Hanson* [2005] 1 W.L.R. 3169 at [7].

[135] *R. v Hanson* [2005] 1 W.L.R. 3169 at [9]–[12].

[135a] This is how the point was put by Rose LJ in *R. v Hanson* [2005] 1 W.L.R. 3169 at [11]. Yet, in *R. v A'Hearne* [2022] EWCA Crim 1784, the court affirmed the trial judge's decision to allow admission in evidence of the accused's previous convictions for violence over a period of about 15 years, justifying its ruling (at [18]) on the basis that those convictions were indicative of "a lifetime of violence".

However, the last of them had occurred fully 20 years before the offence presently charged, which makes it hard to see how the old propensity was really a "continuing" one.

[136] See para.19-31.

Replace footnote 138 with:

[138] There are many cases supporting the view that paedophilic activities and attitudes are both persistent and exceptionally unusual—see, e.g. *R. v Cox* [2007] EWCA Crim 3365; *R. v Alec Edward A* [2009] EWCA Crim 513; *R. v Haystead* [2010] EWCA Crim 3221; *R. v D, P and U* [2011] EWCA Crim 1474 (distinguished in *R. v W* [2011] EWCA Crim 2463); *R. v Balcombe-Jestico* [2011] EWCA Crim 1630; *R. v Malaty* [2012] EWCA Crim 24; *R. v Malik* [2014] EWCA Crim 142; *R. v Wells* [2015] EWCA Crim 2; *R. v Thompson* [2016] All E.R. (D) 56 (Dec); *R. v P* [2022] EWCA Crim 1582.

Replace footnote 140 with:

19-31   [140] *R. v Murphy* [2006] EWCA Crim 3408 at [16]. No reference was made to Murphy in either *R. v Cloud* [2022] EWCA Crim 1668 or *R. v Palmer* [2022] EWCA Crim 1709, in both of which cases it is rather hard to see that the one crime in question really carried any "very special and distinctive feature".

Replace footnote 148 with:

[148] There are a host of examples of it failing—see *R. v Robinson* [2007] EWCA Crim 2479; *R. v Shrimpton* [2007] EWCA Crim 3346; *R. v Burton* [2008] EWCA Crim 376; *R. v James* [2009] EWCA Crim 2347; *R. v Kingdom* [2009] EWCA Crim 2935; *R. v Louis* [2010] EWCA Crim 735; *R. v Evans* [2010] EWCA Crim 2253; *R. v Hedge* [2010] EWCA Crim 2252; *R. v Harding* [2010] EWCA Crim 2145; *R. v KW* [2010] EWCA Crim 2734; *R. v Brown* [2011] EWCA Crim 80; *R. v P* [2011] EWCA Crim 2216; *R. v Visvaniathan* [2017] EWCA Crim 517; *R. v Rose* [2017] EWCA Crim 1458; *R. v Douglas* [2019] EWCA Crim 686; *R. v Pedley* [2019] EWCA Crim 1308; *R. v Smith* [2020] EWCA Crim 38; [2020] 1 W.L.R. 4921; *R. v Kydd* [2020] EWCA Crim 1226; *R. v Belhaj-Farhat* [2022] EWCA Crim 115.

Replace footnote 158 with:

19-32   [158] *R. v Edwards* [2006] 1 Cr. App. R. 31 (Chohan); *R. v Smith* [2006] All E.R. (D) 280 (Feb); *R. v Shrimpton* [2007] EWCA Crim 3346; *R. v Woodhouse* [2009] EWCA Crim 498; *R. v Gumus* [2009] EWCA Crim 1355; *R. v Bellfield* [2012] EWCA Crim 279; *R. v Fearon* [2012] EWCA Crim 577; (perhaps) *R. v Contostavlos* [2013] EWCA Crim 779; *R. v Spencer* [2013] EWCA Crim 1180; *R. v J(KMS)* [2016] EWCA Crim 1079; *R. v Visvaniathan* [2017] EWCA Crim 517; *R. v Smith* [2022] EWCA Crim 176; *R. v Jackson and Hartley* [2023] EWCA Crim 145. It is less clear that the similarities in *R. v Gillespie* [2011] EWCA Crim 3152, or some of those in *R. v Singh* [2012] EWCA Crim 1305, would have satisfied that test.

(ii)   Propensity and coincidence

Replace footnote 161 with:

19-33   [161] See *R. v Wallace* [2008] 1 W.L.R. 572; *R. v Freeman and Crawford* [2008] EWCA Crim 1863; [2009] 1 Cr. App. R. 137; *R. v Jordan* [2009] EWCA Crim 953; *R. v McAllister* [2009] 1 Cr. App. R. 129; *R. v Norris* [2009] EWCA Crim 2697; *R. v Ali* [2010] EWCA Crim 1619; *R. v Kamara* [2011] EWCA Crim 1146; *R. v Cambridge* [2011] EWCA Crim 2009; *R. v Suleman* [2012] EWCA Crim 1569; *R. v O'Leary* [2013] EWCA Crim 1371; *R. v Soloman* [2019] EWCA Crim 1356; *R. v Adams* [2019] EWCA Crim 1363. In both *R. v BQC* [2021] EWCA Crim 1944 at [58]; and *R. v Khan* [2022] EWCA Crim 1592 at [60], it was accepted that it may sometimes be appropriate for the judge to direct the jury that it might properly use the evidence in question on both a coincidence basis and a propensity one.

Replace footnote 165 with:

[165] In this respect, the author disagrees with Spencer, *Evidence of Bad Character*, 3rd edn (2016), paras 4.88–4.93 and Fortson and Ormerod [2009] Crim. L.R. 313 at 325–328, though he has the support of Redmayne [2011] Crim. L.R. 177 at 188–192. See also, *R. v Kawa and Davies* [2023] EWCA Crim 845, which is considered at para.19-35.

(iii)   Proof issues

Replace the second paragraph with:

In short, the issue in question is whether or not the jury should be directed that   **19-35**
it is only if they find the propensity in question proved to them beyond reasonable
doubt that they may use it in deciding if the accused committed the offence charged.
But, within that issue, there is a sub-issue, namely whether or not, if more than one
example of exercise of that propensity is relied upon by the prosecution, they should
be directed that no such example may be used by them, in that way, unless found
by them *itself* to have been proved beyond reasonable doubt. The answer given to
the first question, in *R. v Mitchell*, was that they *should be* given the direction in
question; the answer to the second that such a direction *should not be* given.[177] In
other words, they were not to be directed to conduct a *segregated* examination of
the various examples of exercise of the propensity put before them, but to be
directed simply to decide, having considered all of them, if the propensity at issue
had been proved.

[177] The answers are stated most clearly in *R. v Mitchell* [2017] A.C. 571 at [54], per Lord Kerr, with
whom all the other members of the court agreed. In both *R. v Gabbana* [2020] EWCA Crim 1473; [2020]
4 W.L.R. 160; and *R. v Peace* [2022] EWCA Crim 879, the appeal court seemed to be content that the
Mitchell requirement of a direction was satisfied even though it had not been explicitly put to the jury
in that way. As was stated in *Peace* (at [53]), it was sufficient for the need for the jury to be satisfied
beyond reasonable doubt of the existence of the propensity in question to have been conveyed to them
"by the summing up as a whole and it [being] part of the implicit framework in which the jury were
operating vis-à-vis the evidence."

After the second paragraph, add new paragraphs:

In *R. v Kawa and Davies*,[177a] an issue in the case was whether it had been Kawa
himself or the victim, who had been stabbed to death, that had brought the knife in
question to the scene. The appeal court upheld the trial judge's decision that
evidence of other occasions on which Kawa or Davies had been found in possession of knives was admissible as relevant to that issue. In doing so, it ruled that,
because the prosecution was not relying on any propensity of the two accused to
carry knives, there had been no need for the judge to give the *Mitchell* direction that
the jury could properly rely on the extraneous evidence thereof only if they were
satisfied that that evidence established such a propensity.[177b] This does seem to be
another case involving a rather surprising view of what does and does not amount
to propensity reasoning.[177c]

[177a] *R. v Kawa and Davies* [2023] EWCA Crim 845.

[177b] See *R. v Kawa and Davies* [2023] EWCA Crim 845 at [43].

[177c] For other such cases, see para.19-33.

It is noteworthy that Lord Kerr, in *Mitchell*, went on to add the following statement about the overall significance of a propensity issue[178]:

> "It is necessary to emphasise, however, that propensity is, at most, an incidental issue. It
> should be made clear to the jury that the most important evidence is that which bears
> directly on the guilt or innocence of the accused person. Propensity cannot alone establish
> guilt and it must not be regarded as a satisfactory substitute for direct evidence of the ac-
> cused's involvement in the crime charged."

[178] See *R. v Mitchell* [2017] A.C. 571 at [55].

(vii) Relevant to an important matter in issue

Replace footnote 225 with:

19-39   [225] Instructive examples are *R. v Wood* [2008] EWCA Crim 587; *R. v McCarry and Waters* [2009] EWCA Crim 1718; *R. v Slack and Johnson* [2010] EWCA Crim 1149; *R. v Mockble* [2010] EWCA Crim 2540; *R. v Olu* [2010] EWCA Crim 2975; [2011] 1 Cr. App. R. 404; *R. v Maina* [2010] EWCA Crim 3228; *R. v Okenarhe* [2011] EWCA Crim 616; *R. v Harris* [2011] EWCA Crim 912; *R. v Nicholas and Dennie* [2011] EWCA Crim 1175; *R. v McGrory* [2013] EWCA Crim 2336; *R. v Powell (Kevin)* [2014] EWCA Crim 596; *R. v Cox* [2014] EWCA Crim 804; *R. v C and T* [2014] EWCA Crim 1807; *R. v Miles* [2015] EWCA Crim 353; *R. v Khan and Rahman* [2015] EWCA Crim 1755; *R. v Cerqua* [2015] EWCA Crim 2385; *R. v Grant-Murray and Henry* [2017] EWCA Crim 1228; *R. v Brough* [2018] EWCA Crim 1903; *R. v Kiyago* [2019] EWCA Crim 1905; *R. v McNally* [2020] EWCA Crim 333; *R. v Barton and Booth* [2020] EWCA Crim 575; *R. v Hepburn* [2020] EWCA Crim 820; *R. v Williams-Reid* [2021] EWCA Crim 429; *R. v Afzal* [2021] EWCA Crim 533; *R. v Mahamud* [2022] EWCA Crim 381; *R. v Dogan* [2022] EWCA Crim 1752.

(f)   Proof and prejudice

(i)   Probative value

Cogency

Replace footnote 273 with:

19-50   [273] See also, Criminal Procedure Rules 2020 (as amended), r.21.5(b).

Replace footnote 275 with:

[275] See *R. v N(H)* [2011] EWCA Crim 730 at [41]. That case was followed in *R. v AT* [2013] EWCA Crim 1850 at [95]. See also, *R. v BQC* [2021] EWCA Crim 1944 at [55]–[58].

Replace the fourth paragraph with:

As regards the power to direct an acquittal or discharge the jury, it may arise, once the case for the prosecution has closed, in respect of evidence admitted under any of gateways (c)–(g). Section 107(1) makes no mention of this power arising only on a defence application, but two cases intimate that that is so,[278] whilst another is to the opposite effect.[279] If the court is satisfied, both that the evidence in question is contaminated, and that the contamination is such that, given its importance to the case, a conviction for the offence charged (or a lesser included one) would be unsafe, it must direct an acquittal, or, if it considers that there should be a retrial, discharge the jury. In *R. v Card*,[280] the case for discharge was strong, for the facts involved parental influence and pressure on a 13-year-old who complained of sexual assault, yet the judge had ruled against it. That ruling was overturned on appeal; though the judge was the exclusive finder of fact, the s.107(1) powers were not discretionary. However, it is important to note that, in *R. v DZ and JZ*, Lord Judge CJ intimated that those powers are to be exercised sparingly.[281]

[278] See *R. v Channell* [2011] EWCA Crim 2067 at [25]; *R. v Marke* [2023] EWCA Crim 505 at [14].

[279] See *R. v Woolf* [2011] EWCA Crim 2764 at [31].

[280] *R. v Card* [2006] EWCA Crim 1079; [2006] 1 W.L.R. 2994. cf. *R. v Woolf* [2011] EWCA Crim 2764, where *Card* was distinguished.

[281] *R. v DZ and JZ* [2012] EWCA Crim 1845 at [15].

Replace the second paragraph with:

19-51   The 2003 Act left *R. v Z* untouched,[285] so the difficult consequential issues raised by it remain significant. Two of them have been resolved, but not the third. First, it is clear that the ruling in *R. v H*,[286] that, for purposes of the rule of exclusion, evidence of uncharged criminal conduct must be deemed 100 per cent credible, applies no less to evidence of a crime of which the accused was acquitted.[287] Secondly, *R. v Z* itself was concerned with acquittals by juries that had considered the case as a whole. But a judge may order a verdict of not guilty without ever putting the accused in charge of the jury and has power to direct an acquittal even though the accused is already in its charge. It is now clear that these cases are to be treated no differently.[288] The third question remains unresolved. What if a conviction is overturned on appeal, given that an appeal may be allowed for a variety of reasons, some consistent with guilt, others not?[288a]

[285] See e.g., *R. v O'Dowd* [2009] EWCA Crim 905 at [37]; *R. v Hamidi* [2010] EWCA Crim 66 at [34]; *R. v Wiltshire* [2010] EWCA Crim 1874; *R. v Denton* [2018] EWCA Crim 456; *R. v Halliday* [2019] EWCA Crim 1457; *R. v Golam-Rassoude* [2020] EWCA Crim 704; *R. v Hajdarmataj* [2019] EWCA Crim 303; *R. v Timmis* [2021] EWCA Crim 159; *R. v Chowdhury and Chowdhury* [2021] EWCA Crim 694; *R. v Shinn* [2023] EWCA Crim 493 at [46].

[286] *R. v H* [1995] 2 A.C. 596 HL, considered at para.19-49.

[287] See *R. v Morgans* [2010] EWCA Crim 3089 at [23]; *R. v MP* [2012] EWCA Crim 401 at [23]. There remains grave difficulty in reconciling this with the presumption of innocence under art.6(2) of the ECHR: see Tapper (2001) 117 L.Q.R. 1 at 3.

[288] See *R. v Morgans* [2010] EWCA Crim 3089; *R. v Small* [2010] EWCA Crim 3241. It is particularly hard to understand how evidence so weak that it failed to "pass the judge" is properly made available to a later jury. That said, there are situations where the accused has been formally acquitted, but without the evidence in question having been considered by either the jury or the judge, as when acquittal has been ordered after the prosecution has decided not to present any evidence, a point relied upon in *R. v Halliday* [2019] EWCA Crim 1457 at [22]. Though *Halliday* was not referred to in *R. v Mahmood* [2022] EWCA Crim 1573, that case is to the same effect.

[288a] In *R. v Portman* [2022] EWCA Crim 1200 (considered in detail at para.22-39), an issue did arise as to evidence given in another case by the present complainant, where that other accused had had his conviction overturned on appeal but, as will be apparent, that case did not concern an overturned conviction of the *present accused*.

Replace the first paragraph with:

R. v Z was applied to a rather different situation in *R. v Edwards and Rowlands*.[289] **19-52** There, the police had, some years before, officially informed the accused that he would not be prosecuted for certain offences. He was later charged with them, after similar complaints had emerged. Those charges themselves were *stayed* by the judge. His decision that the alleged underlying facts could be relied on, as regards the newer charges, was upheld. In *R. v Nguyen*,[290] *Edwards and Rowlands* was applied to a case in which the Crown had decided not to prosecute, rather than being prevented, by judicial order, from doing so. Of course, in neither of these cases had there been an acquittal.

[289] *R. v Edwards and Rowlands* [2006] 1 W.L.R. 1524 (Smith).

[290] *R. v Nguyen* [2008] EWCA Crim 585. See also, *R. v RK* [2022] EWCA Crim 1523 at [16].

After the second paragraph, add new paragraph:

An issue somewhat akin to the one about acquittals and connected outcomes has arisen in several cases, most recently in *R. v AYS*.[293a] It concerns situations where the prosecution seeks to rely upon some extraneous misconduct of the accused that does not count as criminal unless the rebuttable presumption of *doli incapax* for children aged at least 10 but under 14 has been rebutted. Though that rebuttable presumption has been abolished,[293b] its abolition has been held not to have retrospective effect.[293c] In consequence, cases may still arise where, at the time of the misconduct in question, the presumption was applicable. For such cases, it has been held that, as long as the misconduct satisfies the relevant 2003 Act admissibility test, it is not rendered inadmissible on the present criminal charge by virtue of the fact that the accused has not, in relation to *that* misconduct, been proved to have known that what they were doing was seriously wrong.[293d]

[293a] *R. v AYS* [2023] EWCA Crim 730. See also, *R. v H* [2010] EWCA Crim 312; and *R. v DM* [2016] EWCA Crim 674; [2016] 4 W.L.R. 146.

[293b] By the Crime and Disorder Act 1998 s.34. See also, para.6-31 hereof.

[293c] See *R. v H* [2010] EWCA Crim 312.

[293d] See, in particular, *R. v AYS* [2023] EWCA Crim 730 at [25]–[26].

(ii)   Prejudicial effect

Moral prejudice

Replace footnote 316 with:

19-60   [316] See, in particular, *R. v McKenzie* [2008] EWCA Crim 758 at [22]–[24]. See also, *R. v McAllister* [2009] 1 Cr. App. R. 129; *R. v Gumbrell* [2009] EWCA Crim 550; *R. v O'Dowd* [2009] EWCA Crim 905; *R. v McCarry and Waters* [2009] EWCA Crim 1718; *R. v DS* [2010] EWCA Crim 1016; *R. v Rhodes* [2010] EWCA Crim 2771; *R. v Walker* [2019] EWCA Crim 1825; *R. v Shinn* [2023] EWCA Crim 493.

(h)   Directions to the jury

Replace footnote 360 with:

19-66   [360] Issued by the Judicial College (successor to the Judicial Studies Board) in May 2016, and now replaced by a Compendium issued in June 2023. The part relating to evidence of bad character is to be found in Chs 12 and 13.

Replace the third paragraph with:

There is no reason at all to suppose that the Compendium, the approach of which is broadly similar to that of its predecessor, is intended to strike a different note. In any event, emphasis has been placed, in three decisions[363] concerned with various s.101(1) gateways, upon the need for the trial judge to pay full attention to the Compendium before deciding how to tailor directions to the case at hand. In the most important of the three, *R. v PHH*, the court took the opportunity of setting out[364] what it regarded as the principal features of Ch.12 of the Compendium. They were:

(i)   where the bad character evidence is disputed, the jury must be reminded of the arguments on both sides and warned to rely only on matters proved to the criminal standard;

(ii)   where evidence is admitted through more than one gateway, directions must be given in respect of all relevant matters in relation to each of them; and

(iii)   the issues to which the evidence is potentially relevant must be identified in detail, with the jury directed as to the limited purposes for which it may be used, as well as to any purpose for which it may not be used.[365]

[363] *R. v PHH* [2017] EWCA Crim 2046; *R. v Baynes and Mahoney* [2017] EWCA Crim 2109; *R. v Hackett* [2019] EWCA Crim 983. Three other decisions deal with the particular problems that arise when both s.98(a) and a s.101 gateway are relied upon by the prosecution—see *R. v RJ* [2017] EWCA Crim 1943; [2018] Crim. L.R. 478; *R. v MA* [2019] EWCA Crim 178; *R. v AAM* [2021] EWCA Crim 1720.

[364] See *R. v PHH* [2017] EWCA Crim 2046 at [33].

[365] It noteworthy that, in *R. v Everson* [2021] EWCA Crim 1178 at [24], without referring either to Ch.12 or to *R. v PHH*, Holroyde LJ stated that, where no suggestion had been made, during the course of the proceedings, that any other use might be made be made of the evidence in question, there was no need for a direction not so to use it.

(i)   Duty to give reasons

Replace footnote 372 with:

[372] See s.110(2). See also, Criminal Procedure Rules 2020 (as amended), r.21.5. There is no duty to give reasons for any ruling that falls outside those that are specifically covered—see *R. v Channell* [2011] EWCA Crim 2067.   **19-68**

(j)   Joinder and severance of counts

Replace the first paragraph with:

Though the 2003 Act itself made no change to the law concerning joinder and severance of counts, one was later effected by a 2018 amendment to the Criminal Procedure Rules. Before then, originally under r.9 of the Indictment Rules 1971, different counts could be joined on the same indictment only if either "founded on the same facts" or "form[ing] or [being] a part of a series of offences of the same or a similar character".[374] However, the 2020 Rules now state at r.3.29(4)[375]:   **19-69**

"Where the same indictment charges more than one offence, the court may exercise its power to order separate trials of those offences if of the opinion that—

(a)   the defendant otherwise may be prejudiced or embarrassed in his or her defence (for example, where the offences to be tried together are neither founded on the same facts nor form or are part of a series of offences of the same or a similar character); or

(b)   for any other reason it is desirable that the defendant should be tried separately for any one or more of those offences."

Therefore, what necessarily *denied joinder* under r.9 is now merely *a reason for severance* under r.3.29(4).[376]

[374] And later under the Criminal Procedure Rules 2015, r.3.21(4).

[375] See Criminal Procedure Rules 2020 (as amended), r.3.29(4).

[376] As was, in effect, recognised in both *R. v Ali* [2018] EWCA Crim 1011 at [21]; and *R. v Toner* [2019] EWCA Crim 447; [2019] 1 W.L.R. 3826 at [11] and [13]. See also, *R. v Ivor* [2021] EWCA Crim 923.

Replace the second paragraph with:

Though one later case seemed to make it clear that the separate treatment direction is mandatory,[387] other, later authorities appear to conflict as to whether the direction that evidence on the one is not properly evidence on the other entails a case-dependent discretion or a duty. The former view was taken in *R. v H*,[388] but the latter one in *R. v Adams*,[389] where, though the prosecution had not relied at all on cross-admissibility, the trial judge had failed as Leggatt LJ put it to direct the jury that[390]:   **19-70**

"in considering each count, they should have regard only to the evidence which was directly relevant to that count and should ignore evidence relating to other counts".

In his Lordship's view, they "ought to have been [so] directed",[391] and the error in that respect was the reason why the court allowed the appeal. The language used by Leggatt LJ seems clearly to smack of duty, rather than discretion, and, indeed, he went on to describe himself as having difficulty understanding the actual ruling in *R. v H* itself, where the court had treated a direction similar to the one given by the judge in *Adams* as sufficient.[392] That said, it may be possible to reconcile the actual decision in *Adams* with the discretion view on the basis that the judge there had abused that discretion. In that regard, the following words of Rix LJ in *H*[393] were endorsed by the *Adams* court[394]:

> "Everything depends on the directions and facts of a particular case, and the danger that the jury might seek to use the evidence of one complainant as evidence of his guilt on counts concerned only with another complainant."

[387] See *R. v C(D)* [2012] EWCA Crim 1852 at [14].

[388] *R. v H* [2011] EWCA Crim 2344; following the pre-Act case of *R. v F* [2005] EWCA Crim 3217; and the post-Act case of *R. v Mackay* [2010] EWCA Crim 167. See also, *R. v Khan* [2012] EWCA Crim 2361.

[389] *R. v Adams* [2019] EWCA Crim 1363.

[390] *R. v Adams* [2019] EWCA Crim 1363 at [18].

[391] *R. v Adams* [2019] EWCA Crim 1363 at [18].

[392] *R. v Adams* [2019] EWCA Crim 1363 at [20].

[393] *R. v H* [2011] EWCA Crim 2344 at [31].

[394] *R. v Adams* [2019] EWCA Crim 1363 at [20]. Those words were also referred to in *R. v AHC* [2022] EWCA Crim 925 at [25], where the at least apparent clash between the two earlier cases was considered. The actual decision in *AHC* seems consistent with the reconciliation point made in the present text. In *R. v Cloud* [2022] EWCA Crim 1668; [2023] 1 Cr. App. R. 19 at [28], the court alluded to the clash, but found that, on the particular facts, it did not need to address the issue.

(k)   Rules of court

Replace footnote 396 with:

19-71   [396] See now, the Criminal Procedure Rules 2020 (as amended), Pt 21.

CHAPTER 20

BAD CHARACTER OF THE ACCUSED (DEFENCE ASPECTS)

2. CRIMINAL JUSTICE ACT 2003

(b) Important matters in issue

Replace footnote 16 with:

[16] See paras 19-15 and 19-71, and, in particular, the Criminal Procedure Rules 2020 (as amended), Pt 21.

20-05

(d) Correcting a false impression

(ii) Loss of "shield"—assertion elements

Replace footnote 46 with:

[46] *R. v Weir (Somanathan)* [2006] 1 W.L.R. 1885. See also, *R. v Ullah* [2006] EWCA Crim 2003; *R. v Chable* [2009] EWCA Crim 496; *R. v Gillespie* [2011] EWCA Crim 3152; and, more recently, *R. v Molliere* [2023] EWCA Crim 228; *R. v Hussain, Malik and Ditta* [2023] EWCA Crim 311; [2023] 2 Cr. App. R. (S.) 27.

20-12

(e) Attacks on another person's character

(iii) The meaning of "attack"

Fairness to the accused

Replace footnote 133 with:

[133] *R. v O* [2009] EWCA Crim 2235; (2009) 173 J.P. 616. See also, *R. v Headech* [2016] EWCA Crim 1032; *R. v McDonagh* [2022] EWCA Crim 1384; *R. v Molliere* [2023] EWCA Crim 228.

20-31

(vi) Judicial directions

Replace footnote 194 with:

[194] See *R. v Highton* [2005] 1 W.L.R. 3472 at [10] (emphasis in original). To similar effect are *R. v Singh* [2007] EWCA Crim 2140 at [9]; *R. v Letts and Chung* [2007] EWCA Crim 3282 at [23] and [25]; *R. v Lamaletie and Royce* [2008] EWCA Crim 314 at [13]; *R. v Collier* [2022] EWCA Crim 1651.

20-38

(vii) Leave and judicial warnings?

Replace footnote 209 with:

20-39   [209] For discussion of all of these points, see para.19-15, and, in particular, the Criminal Procedure Rules 2020 (as amended), Pt 21.

(g)   Spent convictions

Replace footnote 217 with:

20-42   [217] As amended to October 2020. It must be added that the 2015 *Directions* have, since publication of the last edition, been revoked by para.1.1.1 of the *Criminal Practice Directions* 2023, except that some of the earlier ones are thereby retained. However, para.21A.2 is not included in those retained. At the time of writing, it was unclear what was the effect of these changes upon the law with regard to spent convictions.

CHAPTER 21

BAD CHARACTER OF THE CO-ACCUSED

2. CRIMINAL JUSTICE ACT 2003

(c) Evidence of substantial probative value on an important matter

(i) The general test

Replace footnote 15 with:

[15] This appears to have been the governmental understanding of the word—see Explanatory Notes to the Criminal Justice Act 2003, para.375, referring to evidence of "only marginal or trivial value". Of course, if the evidence in question has no *real* relevance at all, it will be inadmissible anyway—see, e.g. *R. v Mohammedzai* [2022] EWCA Crim 162; *R. v Khan* [2022] EWCA Crim 1478.

21-07

Replace footnote 25 with:

[25] In *R. v Byrne* [2021] EWCA Crim 107 at [139], the court described the approach in *Platt* as being the same as that in *Phillips*, adding that "substantial" was an ordinary word that should not be glossed. By contrast, in *R. v Perkins* [2021] EWCA Crim 1462 at [18]–[20], the *Phillips* gloss seems to have been straightforwardly applied.

(v) Absence of leave requirement

Replace footnote 75 with:

[75] See now the Criminal Procedure Rules 2020 (as amended), Pt 21.

21-19

(f) Spent convictions

Replace paragraph with:

The absolute right of the accused to cross-examine about the convictions, or other bad character, of a co-accused who had given evidence against them applied, under the old law, no less to spent convictions than to any other ones.[86] There is no reason to suppose that the position is different under gateway (e).[87]

21-22

[86] *R. v Corelli* [2001] Crim. L.R. 913; *R. v Lee* [2004] All E.R. (D) 287, both CA. Of course, under the 2003 Act, the accused will not be limited to cross-examination, but may call direct evidence.

[87] Though the reader is referred to the point made in the text about the law relating to spent convictions after the *Criminal Practice Directions* 2015 were replaced by the Criminal Practice Directions 2023 (see para.18-18, fn.102, para.20-42, fn.217 and para.22-38, fn.158), any change to the law in that respect

could not affect the accused's absolute right to cross-examine about and/or call evidence of the spent convictions of a co-accused.

CHAPTER 22

BAD CHARACTER OF PERSONS OTHER THAN THE ACCUSED

3. CRIMINAL JUSTICE ACT 2003

(a) The basic provision and its scope

Replace the fifth paragraph with:

Finally, not only witnesses are protected. Most obviously, a person in some way **22-19** involved in the events will be covered, even though they do not testify. Two examples are an untraced observer and a deceased "victim". Subject to the point that it is hard to see how a deceased properly counts as a "person",[71] there is no reason for restricting the scope of s.100 to witnesses, especially when one purpose of its enactment seems to have been that no citizen should be needlessly exposed to character attacks by those accused of crime.[72] And indeed, in *R. v Jukes*,[73] it was held that it extended to a co-accused who had pleaded guilty (and had thereby ceased to be a "defendant").

[71] There seems to be no case explicitly dealing with this point but, in both *R. v Martin* [2017] EWCA Crim 488 and *R. v O'Casey* [2021] EWCA Crim 1581, it was clearly assumed to be the position, whilst it is certainly the position under s.101(1)(g)—see para.20-25.

[72] In both *R. v Ibrahim* [2021] EWCA Crim 1935 and *R. v Odupitan* [2021] EWCA Crim 2040, it was assumed that s.100 *did* apply to a non-witness who had not been involved in the events at hand, though in neither case was argument to the contrary put to the court and, in *Odupitan*, the evidence was found to fail the substantial probative value test anyway (see at [17] and [18]).

[73] *R. v Jukes* [2018] EWCA Crim 176 at [32] and [33]. See also, *R. v Doyle* [2017] EWCA Crim 340.

Replace footnote 81 with:

[81] Criminal Procedure Rules 2020 (as amended), Pt 21, especially rr.21.2 and 21.3. For further discus- **22-20** sion, see para.19-71.

(b) All parties in agreement

Replace footnote 83 with:

[83] *R. v Sixto* [2012] EWCA Crim 2615. A contrasting case, where the argument was full and detailed, **22-21** is *R. v Roe* [2023] EWCA Crim 316—see at [44].

(d) Substantially probative evidence

(i) Issue relevance

Replace footnote 104 with:

22-27 104 See *R. v Walsh* [2012] EWCA Crim 2728 at [21] and [24]. See also, *R. v WD* [2012] EWCA Crim 152; *R. v Hussain* [2015] EWCA Crim 383; *R. v Hodkinson* [2015] EWCA Crim 1509. Of course, sometimes the evidence in question will be excluded as having "little or no probative value" anyway: see, e.g. *R. v Turner* [2021] EWCA Crim 303 at [15]; *R. v Simpson* [2021] EWCA Crim 302 at [25]; *R. v Al-Safee* [2022] EWCA Crim 396 at [34].

Replace footnote 114 with:

114 Examples are *R. v Sixto* [2012] EWCA Crim 2615 at [49]–[50]; *R. v Walsh* [2012] EWCA Crim 2728 at [17]; *R. v Dizaei* [2013] EWCA Crim 88 at [37]–[38]; *R. v M* [2014] EWCA Crim 1457 at [63]; *R. v Jackson* [2014] EWCA Crim 2477 at [10]; *R. v King* [2015] EWCA Crim 1631; *R. v Burchell* [2016] EWCA Crim 1559 at [20]; *R. v Hawkins* [2018] EWCA Crim 406; *R. v Stanley* [2018] EWCA Crim 974; *R. v Carroll* [2019] EWCA Crim 1396; *R. v Umo and Benjamin* [2020] EWCA Crim 284; [2020] 4 W.L.R. 163 at [37]; *R. v TG* [2020] EWCA Crim 939 at [31] and [32]; *R. v Bogdanovic* [2020] EWCA Crim 1229 at [46].

Replace paragraph with:

22-29 Section 100(1)(b) also requires the matter in issue to be one of substantial importance in the case as a whole. In *R. v Brewster and Cromwell*, Pitchford LJ described this as a "significant hurdle",118 and there are three recent cases119 in which the appeal court held that that hurdle had not been cleared.

118 *R. v Brewster and Cromwell* [2011] 1 W.L.R. 601 at [23]. See also, *R. v Mara* [2013] EWCA Crim 807 at [23].

119 *R. v Jukes* [2018] EWCA Crim 176; [2018] 2 Cr. App. R. 9; *R. v Duesbury* [2021] EWCA Crim 1481; *R. v Wilson* [2022] EWCA Crim 1438.

(ii) Credibility relevance

Replace footnote 147 with:

22-33 147 *R. v Nyemba* [2008] EWCA Crim 939. See also, *R. v W* [2022] EWCA Crim 1438.

(iv) Spent convictions

Replace the first paragraph with:

22-38 A non-accused's convictions may be spent, under the terms of the Rehabilitation of Offenders Act 1974. So, the provisions dealing with spent convictions in criminal proceedings clearly apply no less to witnesses than to the accused, and, perhaps, even to non-witnesses.158 When an application is made for leave to refer to a spent conviction, the judge enjoys wide discretion to decide whether or not such a reference may be made, but, in so deciding, the judge is required always to have regard to the general principles of the 1974 Act.159 However, it should be borne in mind that the interests of an unconvicted accused are at stake. In this respect, it is to be noted that the pre-2003 Act cases emphasised that, where, on a matter of importance, there was a "head-on collision" between the testimony of the accused and of a prosecution witness, which the jury would inevitably have to resolve, an appeal court would be very likely to find wrong in principle a decision to refuse leave to cross-examine the latter about spent convictions.160 With a defence witness, the accused's interests clearly tell in favour of cross-examination being disallowed, though the dangers of prejudice to that accused are clearly not as great as where their own spent convictions are at issue.

[158] See the wording of *Criminal Practice Directions* 2015, Division V paras 21A.1 and 21A.2. For a general discussion, see para.20-42. It must be added that the 2015 *Directions* have, since publication of the last edition, been revoked by para.1.1.1 of the *Criminal Practice Directions* 2023, except that some of the earlier ones are thereby retained. However, para.21A.2 is not included in those retained. At the time of writing, it was unclear what was the effect of these changes upon the law with regard to spent convictions.

[159] See *Criminal Practice Directions 2015*, Division V para.21A.2, but note the point made in fn.158.

[160] See *R. v Evans* (1992) 156 J.P.R. 539 CA at 542. The phrase "head-on collision" is taken from *R. v Paraskeva* (1982) 76 Cr. App. R. 162 CA at 164. See also *R. v Whelan* [1996] Crim. L.R. 423 CA; *R. v Lawrence* [1995] Crim. L.R. 815.

(v)   Unconvicted criminality (s.109) and acquittals

After the fourth paragraph, add new paragraph:

Finally, it is worth referring to *R. v Portman*,[173a] where, again, no reference was made to *R. v Z*. There, the complainant (Falter) of racially aggravated harassment, alarm or distress contrary to s.31(1)(b) of the Crime and Disorder Act 1998 had testified that the accused had made racist comments to him. On appeal against his conviction for that offence, Portman had challenged the trial judge's decision not to allow him to adduce evidence of the quashing of an earlier conviction of a third party for that same offence, that quashing having allegedly been based on a decision that Falter, the complainant in that case too, had lied when testifying that the third party had made racist comments to him. Portman's appeal was dismissed, essentially because there was no proper basis for inferring that the appeal court in the earlier case had positively concluded that Falter had given false evidence. That would seem to leave open for argument, in some later case, that, if the earlier appeal clearly had been allowed on that kind of basis, then the evidence in question should, other things being equal, be admissible at the present trial.   **22-39**

[173a] *R. v Portman* [2022] EWCA Crim 1200.

4.   SPECIAL PROTECTION FROM BAD CHARACTER EVIDENCE (RAPE AND ALLIED OFFENCES)

(b)   The position under statute

(i)   Scope of the Act

Replace the third paragraph with:

Equally, it applies only if the evidence is, or questions are, "about sexual behaviour" of the complainant. That term means, by s.42(1)(c), "any sexual behaviour or other sexual experience". Unsurprisingly, this has been taken to include questions about the complainant's sexual orientation, at least where they were "suggestive of sexual activity".[201a] And, in general, those two terms have been interpreted widely. So, questions asked about a photograph of a complainant scantily dressed, described as "quite graphic", have been held to be about sexual behaviour.[202] More surprisingly, it was held in one case that evidence of a complainant of being pregnant was comprehended, though one might argue that it was really about a result of the behaviour itself,[203] and, indeed, there is a later case going   **22-46** the other way.[204] It also seems clear that the phrase embraces *absence* of sexual behaviour, for example a claim to be a virgin.[205]

[201a] See *R. v T* [2021] EWCA Crim 318 at [44].

[202] *R. v T* [2012] EWCA Crim 2358.

[203] *R. v Uddin* [2010] EWCA Crim 1818. In *R. v Moody* [2019] EWCA Crim 1222, evidence of the complainant's "pregnancy fear" was, rather less surprisingly, held to be about sexual behaviour.

[204] *R. v P(RP)* [2013] EWCA Crim 2331, though no reference was made to *Uddin*.

[205] The position, as to this, is considered at para.22-57.

Replace the third paragraph with:

22-47   As to what has the capability of showing the complaint to be false, there is clear authority that the mere fact that the complainant herself did not pursue the other complaint, or delayed in making it, does not tend to show it to be false.[215] The position is the same where the prosecution has decided not to put the complaints in question before a court.[216] Moreover, an acquittal at trial of the person accused does not at all show that the complainant must have lied.[217]

[215] See *R. v All-Hilly* [2014] 2 Cr. App. R. 530 and *R. v TE* [2016] EWCA Crim 314 (both not pursued); *R. v Tomkins* [2022] EWCA Crim 156 (delayed).

[216] See *R. v Ali* [2017] EWCA Crim 1211; *R. v DR* [2018] EWCA Crim 1315.

[217] See *R. v Gorania* [2017] EWCA Crim 1538.

(iii)   The grounds for leave

Under s.41(4)

Replace footnote 252 with:

22-56   [252] *R. v Archer* [2003] EWCA Crim 2072 at [14]. However, some important words of caution about the danger of over-extending limitations on the applicability of s.41(4) were expressed in *R. v T* [2021] EWCA Crim 318 at [48].

Under s.41(5)

Replace footnote 269 with:

22-57   [269] *R. v Soroya* [2006] EWCA Crim 1884. Though no reference to *Soroya* was made in *R. v Battle* [2022] EWCA Crim 705, it was there affirmed (at [19] and [21]) that s.41 has no application to evidence sought to be adduced by the prosecution.

CHAPTER 23

LEGAL PROFESSIONAL PRIVILEGE

1. THE NATURE OF LEGAL PROFESSIONAL PRIVILEGE

(a) Introduction

After the first paragraph, add new paragraph:

In *Candey Ltd v Bosheh*[3a] Arnold LJ declined to treat Lord Millett's words as a   **23-01**
complete statement of the nature of the right:

> "The effect of privilege is to confer an enhanced degree of protection for a particular genus
> of confidential information. Thus privilege enables the party (or one of the parties) entitled
> to the privilege to obtain an injunction to restrain use of the information, including use
> of the information by a person who has knowledge of it (in particular, where that person
> either already has copies of privileged documents or has come into possession of them)
> in legal proceedings (at least provided that the injunction is obtained before the informa-
> tion has been adduced in evidence at trial)."

[3a] *Candey Ltd v Bosheh* [2022] EWCA Civ 1103; [2022] 4 W.L.R. 84 at [116].

5. CLAIMING PRIVILEGE

(a) The duty of the lawyer in claiming privilege

Replace footnote 201 with:

[201] CPR r.31.19(5) does not apply where PD 57AD is applicable.   **23-36**

(b) Manner of claim for privilege under the CPR

Replace footnote 207 with:

[207] CPR r.31.19 (1) (2) and (8) have survived PD 57A but not the rest of CPR r.31.19.   **23-37**

(c)   The Disclosure Pilot rule

The title of this sub-section should be changed to: "PD 57AD".

Replace the first paragraph with:

23-39   Practice Direction 57 AD, previously known as the Disclosure Pilot applies in England and Wales in the Commercial Court, Chancery Division, Technology and Construction Court, Circuit Commercial Court and the Admiralty Court. It over-rides CPR Pt 31 save where expressly stated to the contrary. It has only a limited effect of privilege because privilege is a substantive fundamental right and PD 57AD is essentially procedural. Nevertheless, it affects the manner of claiming of privilege in a variety of respects which are set out where applicable. As in other courts in England & Wales PD 57AD does not apply, it is also necessary to set out the CPR Pt 31 position.

Replace the first line of the second paragraph with:
Where PD 57AD applies, it provides[209]:

[209] CPR PD 51U para.14.

(d)   Individual listing of privileged documents?

In the fifth paragraph, after "Where", replace "the Disclosure Pilot" with:
23-40   PD 57AD

Replace the sixth paragraph with:

The pragmatic view is that, whether PD 57AD or CPR Pt 31 apply, there is no real difficulty in listing privileged documents by class rather than individually and the potentially difficult wording of CPR Pt 31, not followed in PD 57AD, should not require listing of privileged documents in any way different from what has always been done. That said, in appropriate cases the courts are beginning to make orders for listing of privileged documents individually, whether because of the terms of CPR Pt 31, or simply as part of the court's powers, and it is that line of cases which needs to be considered.[214]

[214] In *Stockman Interhold SA v Arricano Real Estate Plc* [2017] EWHC 1337 (Comm) Sir Richard Field said at [19] the case before him was not "the sort of exceptional circumstances in which the court might order the listing of privileged communications."

At the end of the final quote, after ", or can, be challenged.", add new footnote 217a:

[217a] See also *Tonstate Group Ltd v Wojakovski* unreported 11 February 2022 Ch D.

(f)   The Court's power to inspect

Replace the first paragraph with:

23-43   The court has a power to inspect under CPR r.31.19 (6) or under PD 57AD under para.14.3. It was once said by the Court of Appeal that the court would rarely inspect when a properly formulated claim to privilege was contained in the list.[221] In a case not involving privilege, *Wallace Smith Trust v Deloitte Haskins & Sells*[222] the Court of Appeal set out a much greater enthusiasm for inspection by the court:

"The judge has a discretion whether or not to inspect the documents. But if the party seeking discovery shows that the production of the documents may be necessary for the fair disposal of the action an order should normally only be refused after the court has examined the documents and considered them in the light of the material already in the applicant's possession. Indeed, as is apparent from the speech of Lord Wilberforce in *Science Research Council v Nasse*,[223] the court will need to inspect the documents where relevance is admitted but it is asserted that the documents are confidential. Similarly, inspection is likely to be the only safe course where it seems probable that the documents contain a version of events given soon after their occurrence and at a time when the recollection of the witness would have been fresh."

Particularly where the matter arises at trial, inspection by the court dispels any suggestion that there are sinister undisclosed documents lurking under some dubious claim for privilege or irrelevance. Skilful advocacy can sometimes give rise to a suspicion that there is more beneath the surface than is actually the case. So there are times when inspection by the court resolves all the difficulties.

[221] *Westminster Airways Ltd v Kuwait Oil Co Ltd* [1951] 1 K.B. 134 at 136.

[222] *Wallace Smith Trust Co (In Liquidation) v Deloitte Haskins & Sells* [1996] 4 All E.R. 403 at 413.

[223] *Science Research Council v Nasse* [1979] 3 W.L.R. 762 at 769–770.

6. PRIVILEGE: PROBLEM AREAS

(c) Copies

Replace footnote 248 with:
[248] Under PD 57AD para.13.4.

23-49

After "Under", replace "the Disclosure Pilot" with:
PD 57AD

(e) Giving a clue to the legal advice

At the end of the final paragraph, after "… as to what the legal advice might have been.", add new footnote 277a:
[277a] See *University of Dundee v Chakraborty* [2022] EAT 150; [2022] I.R.L.R. 1003.

23-53

7. LEGAL ADVICE PRIVILEGE: THREE RIVERS

(f) Challenge to Three Rivers

In the second paragraph, after "… rejected this analysis as inconsistent with Three Rivers (No.5).", add new footnote 339a:
[339a] See *Glaxo Wellcome UK Ltd v Sandoz Ltd* [2018] EWHC 2747 (Ch) at [20] per Chief Master Marsh: "Preparatory work of compiling information by persons with no authority to seek or receive legal advice will never be subject to legal advice privilege".

8. THE BREADTH OF LEGAL ADVICE PRIVILEGE

(c) Documents sent to multiple addressees

At the end of the third paragraph, replace "commujnication." with:
communication.

23-71

(d) Knowledge derived from the retainer

In the third paragraph, after "References to 'spring-cleaning' documents have a", replace "perjorative" with:

23-72 pejorative

(f) Client's name, address and details

23-76 *From the start of the second paragraph, delete "There are two relevant recent authorities."*

After the third paragraph, add new paragraph:
The Court of Appeal did review the issue in *Loreley Financing (Jersey) No 30 Ltd v Credit Suisse Securities (Europe) Ltd*[408a] where it was argued that the identity of the persons communicating with a solicitor in relation to litigation were covered by litigation privilege. Males LJ said that in order to determine the question[408b]:

> "it is necessary to consider whether disclosure of that identity would inhibit candid discussion between the lawyer and the client (or the person communicating on behalf of the client). If so, the identity of such persons should be privileged. But if not, to extend privilege to the identity of such persons is unnecessary and may deprive the court of relevant evidence needed in order to arrive at a just determination of litigation."

[408a] *Loreley Financing (Jersey) No 30 Ltd v Credit Suisse Securities (Europe) Ltd* [2022] EWCA Civ 1484; [2023] 1 W.L.R. 1425.

[408b] *Loreley Financing (Jersey) No 30 Ltd v Credit Suisse Securities (Europe) Ltd* [2022] EWCA Civ 1484; [2023] 1 W.L.R. 1425 at [37].

9. LITIGATION PRIVILEGE

(a) The requirements for litigation privilege

After the final paragraph, add new paragraph:
23-79 In *Al-Sadeq v Dechert LLP*[427a] Murray J held[427b] that the right to claim litigation privilege extended to those who had sufficient interest in the litigation in contemplation, such as the victim of a crime, rather than limited to those who were actual or prospective parties to the litigation in question. The judge reached the conclusion after citing all the privilege textbooks (none of which supported it) and an authority that held the contrary.[427c] This decision is unlikely to be correct and rides a coach and horses over existing principles.

[427a] *Al-Sadeq v Dechert LLP* [2023] EWHC 795 (KB).

[427b] *Al-Sadeq v Dechert LLP* [2023] EWHC 795 (KB) at [212].

[427c] *Minera Las Bambas v Glencore Queensland Ltd* [2018] EWHC 286 (Comm) per Moulder J.

(f) What is "litigation" for this purpose?

At the end of the third paragraph, after "… a fair hearing contrary to art.6.", add new footnote 480a:
23-87 [480a] See the discussion of Re L in *Al Maktoum v Al Hussein* [2021] EWCA Civ 1216; [2022] 2 F.L.R. 206.

At the end of the fourth paragraph, after "… which would have been obtained in civil proceedings.", add new footnote 491a:

491a See *Qatar v Banque Havilland SA* [2021] EWHC 2172 (Comm) at [104] per Deputy Judge David Edwards KC discussing *Tesco* and *R. v Jukes* [2018] EWCA Crim 176; [2018] 2 Cr. App. R. 9.

23-88

(g) When is litigation in reasonable prospect

At the end of the fourth paragraph, after "… where there are regulatory investigations.", add new footnote 512a:

512a See also *Qatar v Banque Havilland SA* [2021] EWHC 2172 (Comm) per Deputy Judge David Edwards KC.

23-92

CHAPTER 24

OTHER FORMS OF PRIVILEGE

4. WITHOUT PREJUDICE PRIVILEGE

(r) Unambiguous impropriety

At the end of the second paragraph, after "… on a without prejudice basis.", add new footnote 289a:

24-50 [289a] See in relation to family mediations *LS v PS* [2021] EWFC 108; [2022] 4 W.L.R. 19 per Roberts J.

5. PRIVILEGE AGAINST SELF-INCRIMINATION

(m) Statutory abrogation: construing the statute

In the second list, replace list item "(a)" with:

24-73 (a) Section 13 of the Fraud Act 2006 removes the privilege where the proceedings in which disclosure is sought are proceedings in relation to property (which includes money) and the risk must be of incrimination for an offence involving fraudulent conduct or a fraudulent purpose. The section was considered in detail by the Court of Appeal in *Kensington International v Congo*.[442] and by the Deputy Judge in *Trafalgar Multi Asset Trading Co Ltd v Hadley*.[442a]

[442] *Kensington International v Congo* [2007] EWCA Civ 1128; see also *JSC Bank v Ablyazov* [2009] EWCA Civ 1124; and *McKay v All England Tennis Club (Championships) Ltd* [2020] EWCA Civ 695.

[442a] *Trafalgar Multi Asset Trading Co Ltd v Hadley* [2023] EWHC 1184 (Ch) per Deputy Judge Nicholas Thompsell at [153].

CHAPTER 25

FACTS EXCLUDED BY PUBLIC POLICY

2. PUBLIC INTEREST IMMUNITY TODAY

(c) Government procedure in claiming public interest immunity

Replace footnote 39 with:

[39] *Al Rawi v Security Service* [2011] UKSC 34; [2012] 1 A.C. 531, 544. See also *R. (Hoareau) v Secretary of State for Foreign and Commonwealth Affairs* [2018] EWHC 3825 (Admin); and more recently in *R. (Public and Commercial Services Union) v Secretary of State for the Home Department* [2022] EWHC 823 (Admin); [2022] A.C.D. 53; *R. (on the application of AAA) v Secretary of State for the Home Department* [2022] EWHC 2191 (Admin); [2022] A.C.D. 117.   **25-06**

3. PUBLIC INTEREST IMMUNITY IN PRACTICE: CIVIL CASES

(a) The claim to immunity under the Civil Procedure Rules

Replace the first paragraph with:
CPR r.31.19 provides[42]:   **25-08**

"**31.19**—(1)   A person may apply without notice for an order permitting him to withhold disclosure of a document on the ground that disclosure would damage the public interest.
(2)   Unless the Court orders otherwise, an order of the Court under paragraph (1):
(a)   must not be served on any other person;
(b)   must not be open to inspection by any person.
(3)   The person who wishes to claim that he has a right or a duty to withhold inspection of a document, or part of a document, must state in writing:
(a)   that he has such a right or duty; and
(b)   the grounds on which he claims that right or duty.
(4)   The statement referred to in paragraph (3) must be made:
(a)   in the list in which the document is disclosed; or
(b)   if there is no list, to the person wishing to inspect the document.

(5)   The party may apply to the Court to decide whether a claim made under paragraph (3) should be upheld.

(6)   For the purpose of deciding an application under paragraph (1) (application to withhold disclosure) or paragraph (3) (claim to withhold inspection) the Court may:

(a)   require the person seeking to withhold disclosure or inspection of a document to produce that document to the Court;

(b)   invite any person, whether or not a party, to make representations.

(7)   An application under paragraphs (1) or (5) must be supported by evidence.

(8)   This Part does not affect any rule of law which permits or requires a document to be withheld from disclosure or inspection on the ground that its disclosure or inspection would damage the public interest."

[42] CPR r.31.19 (1) (2) and (8) survive PD 57AD (formerly the Disclosure Pilot) although the rest of CPR r.31.19 does not. The purpose seems to be to make clear the principle is maintained but otherwise align the procedure to the PD 57AD.

(b)   Closed material procedure

In the first paragraph, after "Parliament duly did provide such procedures.", add new footnote 54a:

25-09   [54a] See *Ramoon v Cayman Islands* [2023] UKPC 9.

Replace footnote 57 with:

[57] *Competition and Markets Authority v Concordia International RX* [2018] EWCA Civ 1881; [2019] 1 All E.R. 699; following *AHK v Secretary of State for the Home Department* [2013] EWHC 1426 (Admin) Ouseley J. For a case where disclosure to a tight confidentiality ring was considered workable and proportionate see *R. v (Public and Commercial Services Union) v Secretary of State for the Home Department* [2022] EWHC 823 (Admin); [2022] A.C.D. 53, DC.

(d)   Public interest immunity in civil cases today

Replace the fifth paragraph with:

25-12   The Court of Appeal held in *Competition and Markets Authority v Concordia International*[84] that it is not appropriate to disclose public interest immunity material into a confidentiality ring, particularly in relation to the obtaining and challenging of warrants. Use of confidentiality rings was limited to the protection of commercially sensitive information.

[84] *Competition and Markets Authority v Concordia International* [2019] 1 All E.R. 699; distinguished in *R. (Public and Commercial Services Union) v Secretary of State for the Home Department* [2022] EWHC 823 (Admin); [2022] A.C.D. 53, DC where disclosure of relevant but sensitive material relating to the Government's pushback policy regarding migrant vessels in the English Channel to a tight confidentiality club was considered to be a workable and proportionate solution.

(e)   Waiver of public interest immunity

Replace footnote 86 with:

25-13   [86] *Wiley* [1995] A.C. 274, applied in *R. (Jordan) v Chief Constable of Merseyside Police* [2020] EWHC 2274 (Admin); [2020] A.C.D. 125.

6.   TELEPHONE INTERCEPTS

Replace footnote 151 with:

25-31   [151] In *R. (on the application of Schofield) v Secretary of State for the Home Department* [2021] EWHC 902 (Admin) the Divisional Court held that the bar on the use of intercept evidence in court under s.56(1) and Sch.3 para.21(4) was not incompatible with ECHR art.2 in relation to a killing for which the state was allegedly responsible. So too in *R. (on the application of National Council for Civil Liberties) v Secretary of State for the Home Department* [2019] EWHC 2057 (Admin); [2020] 1 W.L.R. 243 the bulk surveillance powers under IPA were not incompatible with arts 8 and 10. However in earlier litigation *R. (on the application of National Council for Civil Liberties) v Secretary of State for the Home Department* [2018] EWHC 975 (Admin); [2019] Q.B. 481 the Divisional Court had held that IPA Pt 4 was incompatible with fundamental rights in EU law, in that in the area of criminal justice, access to retained data was not limited to the purpose of combating "serious crime", and access to retained data was not subject to prior review by a court or an independent administrative body. The court decided against making an order of disapplication but required the Act to be amended by 1 November 2018. On 31 October 2018 the Data Retention and Acquisition Regulations 2018 came into force to address this ruling. These regulations increased the threshold for accessing communications data only for the purposes of serious crime and requires that authorities consult an independent Investigatory Powers Commissioner before requesting data. A further challenge, *R. (on the application of the National Council for Civil Liberties) v Secretary of State for the Home Department* [2022] EWHC 1630 (Admin); [2022] 1 W.L.R. 4929, held that ability of the security and intelligence services to obtain access to retained data for crime purposes was incompatible with retained EU law but otherwise dismissed the challenge.

At the end of the final paragraph, after "… contains miscellaneous and general provisions.", add new footnote 151a:

[151a] See *Liberty v Security Service* [2023] H.R.L.R. 5.

CHAPTER 26

LOSS AND WAIVER OF PRIVILEGE

1. WAIVER OF PRIVILEGE: THE PRINCIPLES

(a) Confidentiality

After the sixth paragraph, add new paragraph:

26-01   In another case concerning documents on a company's server, *Jinxin Inc v Aser Media Pte Ltd*[4a] Deputy Judge Simon Salzedo KC cavilled at the import of the "reasonable expectation of privacy" test from the law of privacy and considered confidentiality was a more appropriate test in the law of privilege: it better reflected the relation between information, persons and uses and the fact that documents could be privileged against one person but not another.

[4a] *Jinxin Inc v Aser Media Pte Ltd* [2022] EWHC 2856 (Comm); [2023] 1 W.L.R. 1084.

Replace the second paragraph with:

26-02   In *Paragon Finance v Freshfields*[8] the Court of Appeal held that, when a client sues his solicitor in relation to the confidential relationship between them, there is an implied waiver of privilege between them in relation to the materials necessary for the determination of that suit. It may be noted that there was never any confidentiality between client and solicitor in relation to those documents.[9] However, the issue in such circumstances is better focused on the uses to which those documents may be put rather than whether they are confidential between the parties.[10]

[8] *Paragon Finance v Freshfields* [1999] 1 W.L.R. 1183 (see Ch.24).

[9] Thus, in *Singla* [2012] EWHC 1176 (Ch) at [14], discussed in Ch.24, Briggs J said that, in cases where a common interest is prayed in aid to obtain disclosure of privileged documents, the issue is confidentiality not privilege: the documents are treated as not confidential between the particular parties.

[10] See *Candey Ltd v Bosheh* [2022] EWCA Civ 1103; [2022] 4 W.L.R. 84 at [79]–[81] where Coulson LJ doubted a passage in the previous edition of this work which suggested that the court in TSB might have decided the case on the basis that there was no confidentiality between solicitor and client. See also

Arnold LJ at [118]. The focus is on permitted uses rather than confidentiality; see similarly *ENRC v Dechert LLP* [2016] EWCA Civ 375; [2016] 1 W.L.R. 5027.

(g)   What sort of reference constitutes a waiver?

After "But it is not easy to see where the dividing line is.", add new footnote 64a:

64a For recent attempts to rationalise the principles see *PCP Capital Partners LLP v Barclays Bank Plc* [2020] EWHC 1393 (Comm); [2020] Lloyd's Rep. F.C. 460 per Waksman J; *Kyla Shipping Co Ltd v Freight Trading Ltd* [2022] EWHC 376 (Comm) per DJ Charles Hollander KC; *Clements v Frisby* [2022] EWHC 3124 (Ch) per Judge Cawson KC.

26-11

2.   COLLATERAL WAIVER

(b)   Deployment in interlocutory proceedings and at trial

After the third paragraph, add new paragraph:

The authorities were reviewed by Judge Paul Matthews in *Pickett v Balkind*.[88a] The court held that a waiver of privilege was indivisible and that if there is a deliberate disclosure of information by a party to its opponent, even for an interlocutory purpose, it ceases to be confidential as against that party, and hence loses its privilege.[88b]

26-15

88a *Pickett v Balkind* [2022] EWHC 2226 (TCC); [2022] 4 W.L.R. 88.

88b Not following the decision of Birss J in *Property Alliance Group Ltd v Royal Bank of Scotland Plc* [2015] EWHC 3272 (Ch).

(c)   "The issue in question"

At the end of the secon paragraph, after "… what fairness requires to be disclosed.", add new footnote 97a:

97a See also *E20 Stadium LLP v Allen & Overy LLP* [2022] EWHC 1808 (Comm) per Moulder J.

26-16

3.   WAIVER OF PRIVILEGE: PARTICULAR CASES

(c)   Documents referred to in pleadings

Replace footnote 146 with:

146 The wording is similar under PD 57AD at 21.

26-23

(i)   Documents referred to in expert reports and instructions to the expert

Replace footnote 158 with:

158 Under PD 57AD to similar effect.

26-29

4.   LIMITED AND IMPLIED WAIVER

(f)   Limited waiver: discussion

After the second paragraph, add new paragraph:

In *Mond v Insolvency Practitioners Association*[109a] Deputy Judge Jonathan Hilliard KC declined to decide what he regarded as a difficult issue on the ambit of a waiver expressed as a limited waiver on a summary basis, recognising that there

26-39

are a number of strands of case-law on the limited waiver doctrine, that how they should be brought together is open to serious argument, and that the case-law is continuing to develop. He regarded as the most difficult issue, where the law is developing, to be how far the limited waiver principle extends as between the same parties when privileged documents are disclosed.

[109a] *Mond v Insolvency Practitioners Association* [2023] EWHC 477 (Ch).

5. Implied Waiver of Privilege

(d) ENRC: problems of analysis

After the first paragraph, add new paragraph:

26-43   ENRC puts the emphasis on the use which it is intended to make of the documents and recognises that it may be impermissible for documents disclosed for one purpose to be used for a different purpose. The Court of Appeal emphasised this in *Candey Ltd v Bosheh*.[227a]

[227a] *Candey Ltd v Bosheh* [2022] EWCA Civ 1103; [2022] 4 W.L.R. 84 per Arnold LJ at [118].

Replace the fourth paragraph with:

26-45   There is one authority which goes significantly further. In *Hakendorf v Countess of Rosenborg*[234] the solicitor obtained a freezing injunction against the client in a claim for unpaid fees, relying on privileged documents of the client. The client objected to the use of the privileged documents. Tugendhat J said,[235] rejecting the client's objection, that there was an analogy to be drawn with *Paragon*: the former client cannot put the former solicitor in that position, and at the same time deny the solicitor the use of materials relevant to the action. This decision is potentially out of step with other implied waiver cases because the client has taken no positive (whether by claim or defence) step to bring into play the doctrine of implied waiver. The decision was considered by the Court of Appeal in *Candey Ltd v Bosheh*,[235a] albeit in somewhat inconclusive terms. Both Coulson and Arnold LJJ had sympathy for the suggestion that a solicitor was entitled in suing for fees to put before the court privileged invoices which established the entitlement to those fees but thought that the *Hakendorf* decision was on any view expressed too widely.

[234] *Hakendorf v Countess of Rosenborg* [2004] EWHC 2821 (QB).

[235] *Hakendorf* [2004] EWHC 2821 (QB) at [82].

[235a] *Candey Ltd v Bosheh* [2022] EWCA Civ 1103; [2022] 4 W.L.R. 84.

6. Loss of Privilege through Inadvertence and Fraud

(b) Inadvertent disclosure in the course of proceedings

Replace the second paragraph with:

26-48   Save where the PD 57AD (formerly the Disclosure Pilot) applies, CPR r.31.20 now regulates the position where there has been inadvertent inspection of a privileged document. This was a new rule introduced under the CPR. It was initially assumed that it had been intended to change the law, but subsequent authorities made clear this was not so.

Replace the first paragraph with:

26-50   In courts where PD 57AD applies, CPR r.31.20 is no longer applicable. But the replacement rule, PD 51U para.19, is not much different:

"19.1 Where a party inadvertently produces a privileged document, the party who has received the document may use it or its contents only with the permission of the court.

19.2 Where a party is told, or has reason to suspect, that a document has been produced to it inadvertently, that party shall not read the document and shall promptly notify the party who produced it to him. If that party confirms that the document was produced inadvertently, the receiving party shall, unless on application the court otherwise orders, either return it or destroy it, as directed by the providing party, without reading it."

Whilst this looks at first blush like a change in the law, it does not seem to affect the position. If a party is told that a document has been disclosed inadvertently before reading it, then if he reads it he will be subject to all the remedies available against someone who knowingly reads confidential and privileged material. This chapter is concerned with the more difficult issues which arise when a person reads a document *before* realising that it is privileged or disclosed by mistake. PD 57AD does not deal with this. It can thus be assumed that the principles will be much the same as before.

Replace the third paragraph with:

There is no definition of the word "use" in CPR r.31.20 or in PD 57AD. Does the obligation to seek leave from the court arise if the party wishes to make merely internal use (such as considering strategy) of the document? And, as can be seen from the citation from *Atlantisrealm* below, the word has significance in other contexts too. In *Single Buoy Moorings v Aspen Insurance UK Ltd*[250] Teare J rejected the submission that "use" meant "tendered in evidence." He said that that it was:

26-50

> "too narrow a meaning of 'use' to say that it requires that the documents must be tendered in evidence in court or even that the documents must be deployed in a letter, pleading or statement. All will depend upon the circumstances of the particular case. In the present case the March documents had not merely been provided to the Defendant by the Claimant but the Claimant had deployed them in support of an argument which it wished to persuade the Defendant was correct. The documents were therefore read and evaluated by the Defendant, or rather by its solicitor. I consider that that amounts to making use of the documents for the purpose of the *Al Fayed* principles. The solicitor was invited to read them and consider whether they supported the Claimant's case. He did so as a part of his professional duty as a solicitor."[251]

[250] *Single Buoy Moorings v Aspen Insurance UK Ltd* [2018] EWHC 1763 (Comm) Teare J.

[251] *Single Buoy Moorings v Aspen Insurance UK Ltd* [2018] EWHC 1763 (Comm) at [16].

After the first paragraph, add new paragraph:

In *Pickett v Balkind*[259a] Judge Paul Matthews said:

26-52

> "I cannot see a proper basis for granting an injunction to restrain a party from using otherwise confidential information in the document mistakenly disclosed, unless either that party has done (or not done) something, and that act (or omission) affects its conscience, or (perhaps) has not yet suffered any prejudice by acting in reliance on it."

[259a] *Pickett v Balkind* [2022] EWHC 2226 (TCC); [2022] 4 W.L.R. 88 at [43].

After "… disclosure to the hypothetical reasonable solicitor.[269]*", add:*

It has been suggested that in cases of doubt a solicitor should examine metadata which may give an indication as to whether there has been a mistake,[269a] although this seems fact-specific.

269a *Glaxo Wellcome UK Ltd v Sandoz Ltd* [2018] EWHC 2747 (Ch) at [50] per Chief Master Marsh. See also *Flowcrete UK v Vebro Polymers* [2023] EWHC 22 (Comm) per Deputy Judge Nigel Cooper KC.

(f) The inadvertent disclosure rules—are they fit for purpose?

In the final paragraph, after "… US and Australian examples.", replace "The Disclosure Pilot" with:

26-55   PD 57AD

7. Loss of Privilege through Fraud

(a) No privilege in iniquity

At the end of the final paragraph, after "… iniquity which negates the privilege.", add new footnote 314a:

26-59   314a See *Lakatamia Shipping Co Ltd v Su* [2022] EWHC 3115 (Comm) per Jacobs J where the judge held that the lawyers were being used as an instrument to perpetuate the deception of Lakatamia and of the court in relation to the existence and whereabouts of Mr Su's assets and that fell within the iniquity exception.

CHAPTER 27

THE COLLATERAL UNDERTAKING

1. DEVELOPMENT OF THE UNDERTAKING

(c) The collateral undertaking under the CPR

Replace the second paragraph with:
PD 57AD, formerly the Disclosure Pilot repeats CPR 31.22.   **27-05**

(e) Demise of the "compulsion" principle

Replace the eighth paragraph with:
It is for consideration whether the court could use PD 57AD as a basis for restor-   **27-12**
ing the compulsion principle. The *SmithKline Beecham* decision is founded on the
definition of "disclosure" in CPR r.31.2 "a party discloses a document by stating
that the document exists or has existed". Under PD 57AD para.1.4 "disclose" is said
to "comprise a party stating that a document that is or was in its control has been
identified or forms part of an identified class of documents and either producing a
copy, or stating that a copy will not be produced". If the court was so minded, it
would be open to it to use the change in wording as a basis for distinguishing
SmithKline Beecham and holding that the compulsion principle again determines
whether the collateral undertaking exists. No one has yet argued this. But given that
the Court of Appeal in *SmithKline Beecham* relied upon the "fresh start" in the CPR
and the definition of "disclose" in CPR Pt 31 there must be a decent argument that
the court can use the change as a basis for getting rid of this wretched decision.

2. PARTICULAR CASES

Replace footnote 76 with:

[76] This section assumes that the court does not, under PD 57AD, use the change in wording to revert   **27-14**
to the compulsion principle as canvassed above.

CHAPTER 28

THE RULE AGAINST HEARSAY

3. JUSTIFYING THE RULE

Replace footnote 63 with:

28-11 [63] O. Wellborn, "Demeanour" (1991) 76 Cornell L. Rev. 1075; V. Munro, "Handle with care: Jury deliberation and demeanour-based assessments of witness credibility" (2022) 26 I.J.E.P. 381. Observation of facial expression may be actually harmful in evaluating credibility, O. Wellborn, "Demeanour" (1991) 76 Cornell L. Rev. 1075, 1087.

CHAPTER 30

HEARSAY IN CRIMINAL PROCEEDINGS

1. GENERAL

(a) Scope of this Chapter

Replace the first paragraph with:

This chapter concentrates on Ch.2 of Pt II of the Criminal Justice Act 2003. This Act codifies the law on hearsay for "criminal proceedings in relation to which the strict rules of evidence apply".[1] These are trials on indictment, sentencing hearings,[2] preparatory hearings[3] and hearings pursuant to s.4A of the Criminal Procedure (Insanity) Act 1964.[4] The strict rules of evidence do not apply to committal,[5] bail,[6] and summary[7] proceedings, or those proceedings leading to the imposition of a Criminal Behaviour Order,[8] a Closure of Premises Order,[9] a Knife Crime Prevention Order,[10] a Serious Disruption Prevention Order,[10a] a Domestic Abuse Protection Order[11] or a Psychoactive Substance Prevention Order.[12] Although a confiscation proceeding is an extension of a sentencing hearing, and therefore in essence criminal in character, it lies outside the scope of the 2003 Act's hearsay regime because of the "formidable difficulties that would arise were that regime to be applied to proceedings in which the prosecution relies on 'information', as opposed

30-01

to 'evidence', and in which proof is less strict". In practice, a judge hearing a confiscation application is more likely to be concerned with the weight than the admissibility of information, but should its admissibility be a live issue:

> "the Criminal Justice Act 2003 regime, applied by analogy, will furnish the most appropriate framework for adjudicating such issues. When considering questions of weight, the 'checklist' contained in s.114(2) (and the matters set out in s.116) of the CJA, suitably adapted to address weight rather than admissibility, will provide a valuable (if not exhaustive) framework of reference."[13]

[1] Criminal Justice Act 2003 s.134. This does not include extradition proceedings (*Friesel v Government of USA* [2009] EWHC 1659 (Admin) at [33]) or bail proceedings (which are not criminal proceedings, see *R. (Thomas) v Greenwich Mag. Ct.* [2009] EWHC 1180 (Admin) at [16]; cp. *PP v Sollihin bin Anhar* [2014] SGHC 228 at [19] or an application for a criminal behaviour orders (Anti-social Behaviour, Crime and Policing Act 2014 s.23(2)) or when on conviction a court makes a psychoactive substance prohibition order (as the proceedings are civil, see Psychoactive Substances Act 2016 s.32).

[2] cp. *R. v Clark* [2015] EWCA Crim 2192; [2016] 1 Cr. App. R. (S.) 52 at [12].

[3] *R. v H* [2005] EWCA Crim 2083; [2006] 1 Cr. App. R. 4.

[4] *R. v Chal* [2007] EWCA Crim 2647.

[5] *R. (Firth) v Epping Magistrates' Court* [2011] EWHC 388 (Admin) where the advice was given to admit evidence and leave the final decision as to its admissibility to a higher court.

[6] *R. (Thomas) v Greenwich Magistrates' Court* [2009] EWHC 1180 (Admin) at [16]. cp. *PP v Sollihin bin Anhar* [2014] SGHC 228 at [19].

[7] The hearsay provisions in the Criminal Justice Act 2003 supersede Magistrates Court Act 1980 s.5D, see *R. (CPS) v City of London Magistrates' Court* [2006] All E.R.(D) 37.

[8] *R. v W* [2006] EWCA Crim 686; [2007] 1 W.L.R. 339 (CA); [2006] 2 Cr. App.R. (S.) 110; *R. v Uddin* [2015] EWCA Crim 1918; [2016] 4 W.L.R. 24 (CA) at [37]. The Civil Evidence Act 1995 applies.

[9] *Taylor v Solihull MBC* [2020] EWHC 412 (Admin). The Civil Evidence Act 1995 applies.

[10] Offensive Weapons Act 2019 s.19(8) and (9); Magistrates' Courts (Knife Crime Prevention Orders) Rules 2020 r.5. Rules 3, 4, 5 of the Magistrates' Courts (Hearsay Evidence in Civil Proceedings) Rules 1999, as adapted by r.5, apply. Guidance advises that hearsay only be used to prove what are key issues "where oral evidence cannot be called (for example, where the only witness has made a statement but cannot be found)": Home Office, *Knife Crime Prevention Orders Practitioners' Guidance* July 2021, available at *https://assets.publishing.service.gov.uk/government/uploads/system/uploads/attachment_data/file/998039/KCPO_Practitioners__Guidance_-July_2021.pdf*, p.15.

[10a] Public Order Act 2023 s.119(8) and (9). This is not yet in force.

[11] Domestic Abuse Act 2021 s. 48(2). This is not yet in force.

[12] Psychoactive Substance Act 2016 s.32. The proceedings are civil.

[13] *R. v Zuman* [2021] EWCA Crim 399 at [64] (emphasis added). This case follows *R. v Clipston* [2011] EWCA Crim 446; [2011] 2 Cr. App. R. (S) 101 at [64] (where the witness was in court but declined to answer questions). See also *R. v Hameed* [2020] EWCA Crim 1768 at [20], [39] (where the witness who made the statement was not in court).

3. HEARSAY DEFINED

To the end of the third paragraph, add:

30-04   As a matter of logic this should apply also to an AI device such as the virtual home device Amazon Echo that does not require a human being to press a record button in order for a conversation to be picked up and stored as an audio file.

4. HEARSAY BY AGREEMENT

Replace the first paragraph with:

By virtue of s.114(1)(c), if all[86] parties agree, any statement not made in oral evidence (including multiple hearsay)[87] is admissible as evidence of a matter stated in it.[88] Agreement may be express or implied.[89] When hearsay is relied upon during the trial by the prosecution without objection from a legally represented defendant, the trial court is entitled to infer implied consent and an application made retrospectively at the close of the prosecution case does not alter this.[89a] The Criminal Procedure Rules Pt 20 impose a pre-trial notice requirement that a party intends to adduce hearsay evidence pursuant to ss.114(1)(d), 116, 117(1)(c) and 121.[90] Whether this notice procedure has to be followed in respect of hearsay evidence whose use is agreed has not been judicially decided.[91] If, where notice is required by Pt 20, and it is given, no other party objects to the admissibility of the statement concerned, the court must treat the hearsay as admissible by agreement.[92]

30-11

[86] If only some agree and no fixed hearsay gateway applies, it may be possible to admit the hearsay statement via s.114(1)(d), if this is in the interests of justice, see *R. v Flisher* [2012] EWCA Crim 794 at [33].

[87] Criminal Justice Act 2003 s.121(1)(b).

[88] *R. (Meredith) v Harwich Justices* [2006] EWHC 336 Admin at [10].

[89] *R. v Shah* [2012] EWCA Crim 212 at [13]; *Arowolo v DPP* [2013] EWHC 1671 (Admin) at [23]; *Small v Crown Court* [2014] EWCA Crim 1616 at [41].

[89a] *R. v Phair* [2022] NICA 66 at [111].

[90] SI 2020/759 20.2. The statement or other document containing the evidence must be served with the notice, unless it has already been served.

[91] *R. v Turner* [2020] EWCA Crim 1241 at [59]. There is no notice requirement if hearsay is adduced under a common law hearsay exception preserved in the 2003 Act. There is also no requirement to give notice when offering documents pursuant to s.117 that were not specifically prepared from criminal proceedings. By analogy, the notice provisions ought not to apply to the admission of hearsay by agreement. Also, in the case of the hearsay gateways to which the notice procedure expressly applies, the party entitled to notice may waive this entitlement: CrimPR 20.5. Arguably, agreement to admissibility is no different from waiver of the notice requirement.

[92] CrimPR 20.4.

6. UNAVAILABLE WITNESS

(c) Statutory requirements for admissibility

(i) Oral evidence is admissible

Replace the first paragraph with:

Section 116(2)(a) requires the judge to be satisfied that were the maker of the statement available as a witness at the trial, he or she could have given direct evidence of the matter stated. This condition is not satisfied, for example, if the evidence is irrelevant or the content of the statement is protected by legal professional privilege or the statement was made under compulsion and was preceded by a claim of privilege against self-incrimination in circumstances where the maker of the statement would have been entitled to refuse to disclose it to the court.[156] It was not met in *R. v Kadir*[156a] because it was unclear how much of the tendered statement itself had a hearsay basis. The section also requires the maker of the statement to have been a competent witness *at the time when the statement was made*, a precondition that is made explicit in s.123(1). In *R. v Marshall*[157] the Court of Ap-

30-28

peal ruled that a diagnosis of dementia does not automatically render an out-of-court statement inadmissible and that the maker's capacity may be proved without reliance on expert evidence. In this case evidence from relatives was held to be acceptable. Once the statement maker's capacity is proved, Sharp LJ said, the issue becomes one of reliability for the jury:

> "The meaning of 'capability' for the purposes of section 123 is set out in subsection (3). It provides that a witness has capability if he is capable of (a) understanding questions put to him about the matter stated and, (b) giving answers to such questions which can be understood. Section 123(4) then deals with how the issue, if raised, is to be decided. It says at (b) that in determining the issue the court may receive expert evidence and evidence from any person to whom the statement in question was made and, at (c) the burden of proof lies on the parties seeking to adduce the statement and the standard of proof is the balance of probabilities."[158]

[156] *R. v Hayes* [2015] EWCA Crim 1944 at [53]–[59].

[156a] *R. v Kadir* [2022] EWCA Crim 1244; [2023] 1 W.L.R. 532.

[157] *R. v Marshall* [2004] EWCA Crim 2957.

[158] *R. v Marshall* [2014] EWCA Crim 2957 at [8].

(iv) Admissibility with leave: witness unavailable through fear

Replace footnote 221 with: *R. v Pinnock* [2006] EWCA Crim 3119; *R. (Robinson) v Sutton Coldfield Magistrates' Court* [2006] EWHC 307 (Admin) at [24]; [2006] 4 All E.R. 1029; [2006] 2 Cr. App. R. 208; *R. v Davies* [2006] EWCA Crim 2643; cp. *R. v Manning* [2004] EWCA Crim 2847; *R. v Boulton* [2007] EWCA Crim 942; *R. v Kelly* [2007] EWCA Crim 1715. cp. *R. (Cleary) v Highbury Corner Magistrates' Court* [2006] EWHC (Admin) at 1869 [30]; [2007] 1 All E.R. 270 (civil case concerning hearsay evidence and closure orders); *R. v Houlder* [2019] EWCA Crim 1064 at [7], [15]; *R. v A'Hearne* [2022] EWCA Crim 1784.

Replace list with:

30-34   (1) "Through fear the relevant person does not give (or does not continue to give) oral evidence in the proceedings, either at all or in connection with the subject matter of the statement."

A causal link between the refusal or failure to give evidence and the fear must be established—in the case of the prosecution, to the criminal standard.[236] Fear that is relevant is fear at the time the witness is expected to testify.[237] The word "fear" is interpreted broadly and includes fear of reliving the incident through the giving of evidence[238] and "fear of the death or injury of another person or fear of financial loss".[239] The fear does not have to be attributable to the defendant or those acting on the defendant's behalf[240] and does not require a hostile approach to have been made to the witness.[241] Fear may be induced by a climate of fear in the area where the witness lives or the reputation of the defendant.[242] What matters is that the witness, through a genuine fear, does not testify. Fear of the ordeal of giving evidence in a court *of law will not do*.[243] To admit the statement of a prosecution witness who finds giving evidence too intimidating to contemplate would "tilt the balance too far against the accused ... who is thereby deprived of the ability to cross-examine."[244] If the witness is intimated by the prospect of giving evidence in the presence of the defendant, that kind of fear may be capable of being addressed by the special measures provisions found in the Youth Justice and Criminal Evidence Act 1999.[245] The fear of re-living an incident, is not necessarily something that special measures can alleviate.[246] In *R. v Doherty*[247] the Court of Appeal drew attention to the need to assess unavailability through fear subjectively. Objective justification for fear is to be considered as part of the question of unfairness under s.116(4). A chamber of the ECtHR indicated in *Horncastle* that "subjective fear of the witness" is not an adequate reason to deny the defendant an opportunity to examine the witness.

> "The trial court must conduct appropriate enquiries to determine, first, whether or not there are objective grounds for that fear, and, second, whether those objective grounds are supported by evidence."[248]

The "through fear" requirement may be satisfied even though the witness is present in the courthouse[249] or has already given substantial evidence, provided the evidence in relation to the subject-matter of the hearsay statement is withheld through fear.[250] No specific provision is made within s.116 for the witness who through fear gives false evidence or who answers some questions and refuses to answer others,[251] but in either situation the court can declare the witness to be hostile and give leave to prove a prior inconsistent statement,[252] which by virtue of s.119 of the 2003 Act becomes evidence of what it states.[253]

(2) Admitting the statement is "in the interests of justice".[254]

In deciding where the interests of justice lie, the 2003 Act states in s.116(4) that the judge is to have regard to the statement's contents, the risk that admission or exclusion will result in unfairness to any party (especially ability to challenge the statement), the possibility of a special measures direction, and any other relevant circumstance.[255] Where it is highly probable[256] that the witness's fear is attributable to the accused or his associates, this is a factor that supports the admissibility of the statement "since otherwise a premium is put by the criminal justice system on the intimidation of witnesses",[257] and because witnesses and victims have rights too.[258] In *R. v Wilson*[259] Hughes LJ was critical of the weight the trial judge had attached to the opinion of the defence ("This is not a matter for the defendant, although his submissions must be considered")[260] and to the fact that if compelled to testify, the witness would have to be treated as hostile.

If leave is granted, the jury is not informed of the reason for this.[261] When leave is refused, the reason must be supplied to the parties.[262]

---

[236] *R. v Shabir* [2012] EWCA Crim 2564 at [64].

[237] *R. v H* [2001] All E.R. (D.) 150.

[238] *Morgan v DPP* [2016] EWHC 3414 (Admin) at [33].

[239] Criminal Justice Act 2003 s.116(3). Query: does it extend to the fear of a co-accused who has pleaded guilty of being prejudiced in sentencing if called as a defence witness? See C. Tapper, "Use of third party confessions: R. v Finch" (2007) 11 E & P 318, 321.

[240] *R. v Horncastle* [2009] EWCA Crim 964 at [86]; *Horncastle v R.* [2009] UKSC 14 at [68].

[241] *R. v B* [2006] EWCA Crim 1978.

[242] *R. v Horncastle* [2009] EWCA Crim 964 at [84].

243 In *R. v Parkinson* [2004] EWCA Crim 3195, which was decided under the Criminal Justice Act 1988 s.23(3), it was held that nervousness about being questioned and having one's business activities investigated by the police does not suffice.

244 Per Tipping J, *R. v Manase* [2001] 2 N.Z.L.R. 197 CA at [30].

245 The special measures include use of screens, live links and video call evidence and the removal of wigs and gowns (to make the experience of giving evidence less intimidating). Use of live-link evidence is governed by Criminal Justice Act 2003 s.51. Under the temporary Covid-epidemic version of s.51 then in force, the trial judge in *R. v Kadir* [2022] EWCA Crim 1244; [2023] 1 W.L.R. 532 at [39], upheld the decision of the trial judge not to allow a witness in Bangladesh to give evidence for the defence via a WhatsApp video call link. The Court of Appeal agreed that the power to direct that evidence be given via WhatsApp existed under the temporary and normally in force legislation. Each case turns on all the circumstance and, the Court of Appeal emphasised, the onus is on the party seeking to introduce the evidence to supply the trial judge with all the information necessary to decide where the interests of justice lie. In *Kadir* the appellant's counsel failed to do this. No effort was made to sound out the facilities and required permissions in Bangladesh for the giving of testimony from Bangladesh to a court in a foreign jurisdiction which meant that the judge was in no position to decide whether it was in the interests of justice to make a live video link direction. The acceptability, in principle, of WhatsApp as "other arrangement" for in the definition of a live video link in s.56(2D) does not mean that all video call software will be equally acceptable. WhatsApp uses end to end encryption, other software may not.

246 *Morgan v DPP* [2016] EWHC 3414 (Admin) at [31].

247 *R. v Doherty* [2007] EWCA Crim 2716; 171 J.P. 79 at [28].

248 *Horncastle v United Kingdom* [2014] ECJR 4184/10; (2015) 60 E.R.R.R. 31 at [133].

249 *R. v Greer* [1998] Crim. L.R. 572 CA. See also *R. v Gray* [2004] EWCA Crim 1000; *R. v Arnold* [2004] EWCA Crim 1293 at [26]. But see *R. v Saunders* [2012] EWCA Crim 1185 at [34] where it was assumed that if a witness was willing to testify, but would not tell the whole truth out of fear s.116(2)(e) did not apply. The evidence was admitted under s.114(1)(d) instead.

250 cp. *R. v Ashford JJ, Ex p. Hilden* [1993] Q.B. 555.

251 That, it is submitted, is not appropriately described as a situation in which the witness "does not continue" to give evidence. The word "continue" more naturally implies a situation in which the witness disappears or refuses to give any further evidence.

252 Criminal Procedure Act 1865 s.3.

253 LRC, Report 245, para.8.53 and fn.83.

254 Criminal Justice Act 2003 s.116(4); *R. v Doherty* [2007] EWCA Crim 2716; *R. v Millar* [2017] EWCA Crim 639.

255 Criminal Justice Act 2003 s.116(4)(a)–(d).

256 *R. v Sellick* [2005] EWCA Crim 651 at [52], [57]; *The Times,* 22 March 2005, CA; which was approved on this point by Lord Mance in *R. v Davis* [2008] UKHL 36; [2008] 3 W.L.R. 125.

257 *R. v Horncastle* [2009] EWCA Crim 964 at [83], per Thomas LJ.

258 *Horncastle v United Kingdom* [2014] ECJR 4184/10; (2015) 60 E.R.R.R. 31 at [133].

259 *R. v Wilson* [2012] EWCA Crim 1509.

260 *R. v Wilson* [2012] EWCA Crim 1509 at [54(vi)].

261 *R. v Shabir* [2012] EWCA Crim 2564 at [37].

262 *R. v Denton (Clive)* [2001] 1 Crim. App. R. 6.

Replace paragraph with:

30-35   To comply with art.6 of the ECHR (see discussion later in this chapter), where the evidence of a witness who is unavailable for any of the reasons specified in s.116 is important to the prosecution's case, the judge must consider whether the out-of-court statement is potentially reliable and the practicability of the jury testing and assessing its reliability.[263] The factors mentioned in s.116(4) have been mentioned in numerous cases in which a witness is unavailable for a reason other than fear.[264] Yet the admissibility of a statement by a witness who is dead, unfit to testify, abroad or cannot be found is not, according to the terms of the 2003 Act, contingent on satisfying the court of the factors mentioned in s.116(4)[265] (or s.114(2))[266]; admissibility is automatic. In practice, to avoid infringing art.6(3)(c), the courts routinely consider whether a statement produced by the prosecution should, as a matter of discretion, be excluded under s.78 of the Police and Criminal Evidence Act 1984 and in deciding this, judges find it helpful to consider the factors mentioned in s.116(4) and/or s.114(2).[267]

[263] *R. v Millar* [2017] EWCA Crim 639 at [34]–[43].

[264] e.g. *R. v Z* [2009] EWCA Crim 20; [2009] Cr. App. R. 34 at [27]; *Brett v DPP* [2009] EWHC 440 (Admin) at [13].

[265] This is tacitly acknowledged in *R. v Horncastle* [2009] EWCA Crim 964 at [75].

[266] *R. v Jagnieszko* [2008] EWCA Crim 3065.

[267] See e.g. *R. v Ibrahim* [2012] EWCA Crim 837 at [106]; *R. v BC* [2019] EWCA Crim 623 at [31].

7.   BUSINESS AND SIMILAR DOCUMENTS

(a)   Introduction

Replace list with:

"Business and other documents   **30-37**

Section 117—(1)   In criminal proceedings a statement contained in a document is admissible as evidence of any matter stated if—
  (a)   oral evidence given in the proceedings would be admissible as evidence of that matter,
  (b)   the requirements of subsection (2) are satisfied, and
  (c)   the requirements of subsection (5) are satisfied, in a case where subsection (4) requires them to be.
  (2)   The requirements of this subsection are satisfied if—
  (a)   the document or the part containing the statement was created or received by a person in the course of a trade, business, profession or other occupation, or as the holder of a paid or unpaid office,
  (b)   the person who supplied the information contained in the statement (the relevant person) had or may reasonably be supposed to have had personal knowledge of the matters dealt with, and
  (c)   each person (if any) through whom the information was supplied from the relevant person to the person mentioned in paragraph (a) received the information in the course of a trade, business, profession or other occupation, or as the holder of a paid or unpaid office.
  (3)   The persons mentioned in paragraphs (a) and (b) of subsection (2) may be the same person.
  (4)   The additional requirements of subsection (5) must be satisfied if the statement—
  (a)   was prepared for the purposes of pending or contemplated criminal proceedings, or for a criminal investigation, but
  (b)   was not obtained pursuant to
    (i)   a request under section 7 of the Crime (International Co-operation) Act 2003
    (ii)   an order under paragraph 6 of Schedule 13 to the Criminal Justice Act 1988,
    (iii)   an overseas production order under the Crime (Overseas Production Orders) Act 2019,

[109]

(all of which relate to overseas evidence).

(5)   The requirements of this subsection are satisfied if—

(a)   any of the five conditions mentioned in section 116(2) is satisfied (absence of relevant person etc), or

(b)   the relevant person cannot reasonably be expected to have any recollection of the matters dealt with in the statement (having regard to the length of time since he supplied the information and all other circumstances).

(6)   A statement is not admissible under this section if the court makes a direction to that effect under subsection (7).

(7)   The court may make a direction under this subsection if satisfied that the statement's reliability as evidence for the purpose for which it is tendered is doubtful in view of—

(a)   its contents,

(b)   the source of the information contained in it,

(c)   the way in which or the circumstances in which the information was supplied or received, or

(d)   the way in which or the circumstances in which the document concerned was created or received."

(b)   Requirements for admissibility

Replace paragraph with:

30-39   Section 117 (unlike s.116) applies exclusively to statements that, when tendered to the court, are contained in documents.[291] A "document" is "anything in which information of any description is recorded".[292] Section 117 does not require, as did certain earlier legislation, that the document take the form of a "record".[293] The requirements for admissibility are:

(1)   The relevant part of the document is produced. The appeal succeeded in *Motor Depot Ltd, Philip Wilkinson v Kingston Upon Hull City Council*[294] because the prosecution had used s.117 to put an employee of a car manufacturer who lacked personal knowledge of the facts into the witness box without also producing the relevant parts of the record. It was not good enough that the witness had looked up where the car had been registered and whether it was still under warranty before coming to court.

(2)   The information in the record could have been given orally in the proceedings.[295] This means that besides the hearsay rule there is no bar to its admissibility, such as, for example, a lack of relevance[296] or that the matter is protected by legal professional privilege.

(3)   The statement in the document contains information that originated with a person who either had personal knowledge of the matters dealt with or may reasonably be supposed to have had such knowledge.[297] This person does not have to be the person who made the statement in the document.[298] In *Wellington v DPP* the Divisional Court permitted s.117 to be relied upon to prove a police record which stated an alias by which the defendant was known. This was information which it was reasonable to suppose had been supplied by police officers who had personal knowledge of the fact.[299]

(4)   The document itself, or the part containing the statement, was created or received by a person in the course of a specified activity—broadly, in the course of a trade or occupation or as the holder of a paid or unpaid office.[300] In *R. v Carrington*[301] (which was decided under Criminal Justice Act 1988 s.24) a note recording a car registration number made by a shop employee

in the course of her job, at the dictation of a customer, was held admissible. The same note made by a bystander would not be. When an image is uploaded onto a social media website provider such as Facebook, the provider of that website receives it at the point at which it was added to the provider's database.[302]

(5) The information from the person with personal knowledge may be supplied directly to the maker or recipient of the statement in the document,[303] or that information may have been supplied via one or more intermediaries, provided that each intermediary in the chain received it in the course of one of the specified activities.[304]

(6) Everyone who created, transmitted or received the document had, at that time, the necessary competence to give evidence in a court of law.[305]

In some cases, a document is simultaneously admissible under ss.116(1) and 117.[305a] Although in English law the admission of anonymous hearsay is, in principle, prohibited,[306] the conditions set out above have the effect of allowing anonymous hearsay in the form of business documents to be admitted as evidence.[307] Furthermore, the section allows the admission of compound hearsay that could not be provided orally by the final recipient of the information,[308] and does so without the additional requirements for multiple hearsay laid down in s.120 applying.[309]

[291] It is no objection that the statement was originally an oral one, provided that it is tendered to the court in documentary form. cf. *Perinchief v R.* [2018] Bda LR 65 at [26].

[292] Criminal Justice Act 2003 s.134(1). It can, for example, be a label on a bottle containing a specimen of blood taken from the accused: *Khatibi v DPP* [2004] EWHC 83 at [44] (Admin). See also *R. v Usayi* [2017] EWCA Crim 1394 at [35].

[293] cf. Criminal Evidence Act 1965 s.1, and Police and Criminal Evidence Act 1984 s.68(1). The courts adopted an unduly narrow interpretation of this word: see, e.g. *R. v Tirado* (1974) 59 Cr. App. R. 80.

[294] *Motor Depot Ltd, Philip Wilkinson v Kingston Upon Hull City Council* [2012] EWHC 3257 (Admin); (2013) 177 J.P. 41 at [24].

[295] Criminal Justice Act 2003 s.117(1)(a). See also *Perinchief v R.* [2018] Bda LR 65 at [20].

[296] e.g. *R. v Hayes* [2015] EWCA Crim 1944.

[297] Criminal Justice Act 2003 s.117(2)(a). See *Grazette v DPP* [2012] EWHC 3863 (Admin); (2013) 177 J.P. 259 at [11]–[14]. cf. *Perinchief v R.* [2018] Bda LR 65 at [26].

[298] Criminal Justice Act 2003 s.117(3). e.g. *R. v Usayi* [2007] EWCA Crim 1394 at [35].

[299] *Wellington v DPP* [2007] EWHC 1061 (Admin); (2007) 171 J.P. 497 at [31]. Contrast *R. v Humphris* [2005] EWCA Crim 2030; (2005) 169 J.P. 441 where only the victim of the offence could have had personal knowledge of the details in the record.

[300] Criminal Justice Act 2003 s.117(2)(a). *R. v Lockley and Corah* [1995] 2 Cr. App. R. 554 (on Criminal Justice Act 2003 s.24) holds that transcripts of evidence in a previous trial are admissible under the predecessor to s.117 (viz. s.24). In *R. v Clowes* [1992] 3 All E.R. 440 (Central Criminal Court) where a witness summons received by liquidators in the course of their profession was held admissible under Criminal Justice Act 1988 s.24.

[301] *R. v Carrington* (1994) 99 Cr. App. R. 376; [1994] Crim. L.R. 438.

[302] This is discussed by M. O'Florinn and D. Ormerod, "Social networking material as criminal evidence" [2012] Crim L.R. 486, 494-496. They argue that the person who posts a message on a website makes a statement, but that the social media provider is the one who creates the document in which it is contained.

[303] Criminal Justice Act 2003 s.24(2)(c). It is the receipt of the document rather than the information in it that matters: *Perinchief v R.* [2018] Bda LR 65 at [20].

[304] Criminal Justice Act 2003 s.24(2)(c). For a case in which this requirement was not satisfied see *Maher v DPP* [2006] EWHC 1271 at [14]–[15].

[305] Criminal Justice Act 2003 s.123.

305a E.g. *R. v W* [2022] EWCA Crim 1438 (statement by a deceased gynaecologist who had performed a termination on a girl under the age of 16).

306 *R. v Ford* [2010] EWCA Crim 2250.

307 *White v Nursing and Midwifery Council* [2014] EWHC 520 (Admin) at [12].

308 See, e.g. *R. v Hinds* [1993] Crim. L.R. 528 CA and commentary by D. Birch at 530.

309 Criminal Justice Act 2003 s.121(1)(a).

13. INCLUSIONARY DISCRETION

General observations

Replace the third paragraph with:

30-50 English courts have approved the use of s.114(1)(d) by the prosecution many times.[406] For example, in *R. v Hengari-Ajufo*[407] that the Court of Appeal upheld a decision to use s.114(1)(d) to admit an out-of-court statement by a prosecution witness who failed to identify the defendants as the persons responsible for a fatal stabbing as he had previously done to friends of the deceased. Apart from the fact that the Crown had ensured that their hostile witness was at court, the Court of Appeal considered it significant that: the statement had been made to reliable persons who were available for cross-examination; included a number of details that the statement-maker could not possibly have known could be proved by objective means; and there were ways such as CCTV evidence to explore the danger of misidentification.

406 e.g. *R. v Taylor* [2006] EWCA Crim 260; [2006] 2 Cr. App. R. 14; *R. v Isichei* [2006] EWCA Crim 1815; (2006) 170 J.P. 753; *R. v Singh* [2006] EWCA Crim 660; [2006] 1 W.L.R. 1564; *R. v Kavallieratos* [2006] EWCA Crim 2819; *R. v Nguyen* [2020] EWCA Crim 140; *Salem v Camden LBC* [2021] EWHC 2530 (Admin); [2022] L.L.R. 187.

407 *R. v Hengari-Ajufo* [2016] EWCA Crim 1913. See also *R. v Saunders* [2012] EWCA Crim 1185. In both cases s.116(2) did not apply because the witness was willing to give evidence.

Replace the fourth paragraph with:

30-51 More recently, in *R. v Warnick*[423] the Court of Appeal said that the inclusionary discretion should not have been used to admit the out-of-court statement of a frightened witness given a finding that the witness might have given evidence had better efforts been made to explain the available safeguards to the witness. Not only had the judge nullified the purpose of the conditions specified in s.116, but it was also difficult to see how factor (g)[424] of the "interests of justice" test (discussed in para.30-53) was satisfied. Likewise in *R. v Inglis*[424a] the Court of Appeal concluded that a text message was wrongly admitted pursuant to s.114(1)(d) in circumstances were the proper steps to secure evidence in person from the statement-maker, an important witness, had not been attempted. The prosecution took a "short-cut"— the effect of which was "to secure contents of [a text] message as part of the prosecution case whilst denying the appellant any opportunity to challenge its reliability by cross-examination" and this was unacceptable. Had the prosecution taken appropriate steps and failed to secure the attendance of the witness, the position might have been different because the ability of the defendant to give evidence about the statement might have been a weightier factor in favour of admitting the evidence.[424b] By way of contrast, in *Salem v Camden LBC*[424c] the decision to utilise s.114(1)(d) to admit a business document that was inadmissible via s.117 was upheld. In this instance, the evidence was created by professional employees of a local authority for the authority. This evidence was presumed to be reliable; securing oral evidence would have caused delay; and admitting the document was incapable of causing prejudice to the defendant.

423 *R. v Warnick* [2013] EWCA Crim 2320.

424 Criminal Justice Act 2003 s.114(2)(g): "whether oral evidence of the matter stated can be given".

424a *R. v Inglis* [2021] EWCA Crim 1545.

424b *R. v Inglis* [2021] EWCA Crim 1545 at [34].

424c *Salem v Camden LBC* [2021] EWHC 2530 (Admin); [2022] L.L.R. 187.

Replace list with:

(a) the probative value of the statement (assuming it to be true) in relation to a matter in issue[435] or its value for understanding other evidence in the case; **30-53**
(b) the availability of alternative evidence;
(c) the importance of the evidence to a party's case[436];
(d) the circumstances in which the statement was made[437];
(e) the apparent reliability of the maker of the statement[438];
(f) the apparent reliability of the evidence of the making of the statement[439];
(g) whether oral evidence of the matter stated can be given[440] and, if not, why not[441];
(h) difficulty of controverting the statement[442];
(i) risk of prejudicing the party against whom the statement is adduced[443];
(j) any other factor the court considers relevant such as, for example, the tender age of the witness,[444] or the fact that the jury would gain little from seeing the witness testify in person because the witness could only communicate by pointing to letters on an alphabet board and in a previous trial the witness has previously been cross-examined on oath.[445]

435 *R. v Seton* [2010] EWCA Crim 450.

436 The more important and reliable the statement, the stronger the case for admission, *R. v Cole and Keet* [2006] EWCA Crim 197 at [38], per Hughes LJ.

437 cp. *Rees v Commissioner for Police for the Metropolis* [2017] EWHC 273 (QB) at [171].

438 *R. v Musone* [2007] EWCA Crim 1237 at [25]–[26]; *R. v Walker* [2007] EWCA Crim 1698; *R. v Awar* [2021] EWCA Crim 1811 at [38], [51]. cp. *R. v Khelawon* 2006 SCC 57. This fact that the witness is unreliable is not decisive: *R. v J* [2011] EWCA Crim 3021.

439 *R. v Marsh* [2008] EWCA Crim 1816; *R. v M* [2011] EWCA Crim 2341; *R. v Awar* [2021] EWCA Crim 1811 at [51]–[53].

440 In *R. v ED* [2010] EWCA Crim 1213 the trial judge failed to take into account the fact that the prosecution was at fault in not giving the witness enough notice that she would be required to give oral evidence. In *R. v CW* [2010] EWCA Crim 72 at [41]–[44] the Court of Appeal criticised the trial judge for not scrutinizing with sufficient care why it was suggested that the maker of the statement should not be called as a witness.

441 *R. v Khan* [2009] EWCA Crim 86; *R. v Z* [2009] EWCA Crim 20; *R. v L* [2008] EWCA Crim 973; [2008] 2 Cr. App. R. 18; *R. v Nuygen* [2020] EWCA Crim 140 at [60].

442 *R. v S* [2007] EWCA Crim 335; [2008] 2 Cr. App. R. 26; *R. v CW* [2010] EWCA Crim 72. This factor does not include putting the defendant at the tactical disadvantage of having to testify: *R. v Horsnell* [2012] EWCA Crim 227 at [58].

443 See *R. v Williams* [2014] EWCA Crim 1862 at [76] for an example of what does not constitute prejudice. See also *R. v Nguyen* [2020] EWCA Crim 140 where the lateness of the prosecution's application (during the closing argument) was found not to have significantly prejudice the appellant in the circumstances of the case.

444 *R. v Burton* [2011] EWCA Crim 1990; *R. v J* [2011] EWCA Crim 3021.

445 *R. v Sadiq* [2009] EWCA Crim 712.

15.   Statutory Counter-measures to Prevent Unfairness

(d)   Discretionary exclusion

Replace the second paragraph with:

30-75   The fact that hearsay tendered by the prosecution contains evidence of identification whose accuracy cannot be explored with the identifying witness does not mean that it cannot safely be left to the jury to be considered in the context of all the evidence against the defendant.[587] What is unfair always depends on the particular facts of the case. Exclusion under s.78 was said not to be justified on the grounds of fairness where the defendant alleged that the identification was malicious and untruthful.[588] *R. v Sohal*[589] went the other way. The Court of Appeal ruled that the s.78 discretion should have been used to exclude witness statements regarding the defendant's identity by two unavailable witnesses.[590] This was because (i) it was unlikely that both statements were verbatim records of what the witnesses had reported; (ii) the evidence was of limited relevance to the prosecution's case; and (iii) letting the witness statements about what had been said in the witnesses' presence go to the jury left the jury in the invidious position of having to "grapple[…] with the difficult concept that the [co-defendant's] statement …was indicative of his dishonesty when he said it, but was not indicative of dishonesty on the part of the [defendant] when the [defendant] repeated it." The fact that hearsay evidence, once admitted pursuant to s.116 and/or s.117, requires further explanation does not warrant its exclusion, if its admission does not otherwise prejudice the defendant.[590a]

[587] *R. v Akhtar* [2018] EWCA Crim 2872 at [65]–[66].

[588] *R. v Thomasson* [2021] EWCA Crim 114 at [31].

[589] *R. v Sohal* [2019] EWCA Crim 1237 at [48].

[590] See also *R. v Kiziltan* [2018] 4 W.L.R. 43 CA where the trial judge was held to have erred in admitting the out-of-court statement of the victim of a kidnap attempt who had disappeared before giving evidence and was alleged by the defendant to have colluded with the defendant's ex-lover to implicate him falsely in a crime he had not committed. When the judge had investigated the kidnap victim's disappearance before admitting her statement, it had emerged that the defendant's ex-lover had ignored a judicial instruction not to discuss the evidence she had given against the defendant and had in fact done so with the kidnap victim, the very person with whom the defendant alleged she had conspired against him. This, plus the fact that the victim was reported as having said that he "did not feel right" about giving evidence, raised concerns about the reliability of the identification in the tendered statement which should, therefore, have been excluded under s.78.

[590a] *R. v W* [2022] EWCA Crim 1438 at [32], [39].

Replace the third paragraph with:

The Court of Appeal will only find against the trial judge's exercise of s.78 (or s.126) "if it concludes that a decision was reached which was outside the band of legitimate decisions available to the judge."[591] In *R. v BC*[592] the Court of Appeal decided that although some judges might have excluded the deceased victim's emotional suicide note and admitted as evidence against the defendant only her ABE evidence, this was not of itself a reason to interfere with the trial judge's careful and measured ruling which he followed up with a warning to the jury to keep "cool heads." Should a judge be satisfied that unreliability in conjunction with the importance to the prosecution of a hearsay statement threatens the defendant's right to a fair trial, there is only one way to exercise the PACE s.78 discretion: for exclusion.[593]

[591] *R. v BC* [2019] EWCA Crim 623 at [37]. See also *R. v Lindsay* [2020] EWCA Crim 420 at [8] which is concerned with PACE s.78 and *R. v W* [2022] EWCA Crim 1438 at [42]. There is no need for a trial

judge to refer in terms to s.78 when deciding whether to exercise the discretion: *R. v Rochester* [2020] EWCA Crim 1224 at [13].

[592] *R. v BC* [2019] EWCA Crim 623.

[593] *R. v Ibrahim* [2012] EWCA Crim 837 at [38], [106]. Distinguished on its facts in *R. v RB* [2023] NICA at [62]. The question when admitting hearsay evidence violates art.6 is discussed in detail later in the chapter.

(e) Stopping case because of unconvincing hearsay

Replace footnote 599 with:

[599] *R. v Riat* [2012] EWCA Crim 1509 at [29], and see e.g. *R. v RB* [2023] NICA 24 a sex case in which the deceased complainant had a significant learning disability and communication difficulties.

30-77

Replace the fourth paragraph with:

It is to be noted that in this passage Hughes LJ does not envisage an actual finding by the trial judge that the hearsay evidence *has been shown to be* reliable, because this is a jury matter.[605] Hughes LJ envisages that the same test is to be applied whether the question the trial judge has to decide is the admissibility of the hearsay statement or the application of s.125 after its admission: can the hearsay "*safely* be held to be reliable" by a jury?[606] Where the contested hearsay evidence of an unavailable complainant is of central importance to the prosecution's case, the trial judge may lawfully decide to admit that evidence despite its shortcomings and later decide, after having again reviewed the strength and weaknesses of the hearsay evidence, its importance to the case as a whole and the tools available to the jury to assess its reliability, that it is unfair to the defendant for it to be left to the jury to assess its reliability (i.e. a conviction on the basis of that evidence would be unsafe) and on that basis to terminate the proceedings pursuant to s.125.[607] Evidence that is demonstrably reliable cannot result in a s.125 direction.[608]

[605] *R. v RT* [2020] EWCA Crim 1343; [2021] 1 Cr. App. R. 14 at [20].

[606] The outcome in *R. v Bennett* [2008] EWCA Crim 248 is consistent with this approach. In *Bennett* the question before the Court of Appeal was whether prior inconsistent interviews that had been admitted by virtue of s.119 as evidence of the matters stated should have been excluded under s.125. Latham LJ said at [21]: "There was other material … which was at least consistent with the basic thrust of the content of the interviews. In those circumstances, provided the jury was given proper warning as to how to approach this material … the judge was perfectly entitled to ask the jury to consider it". Whether the *Riat* approach or that taken in *Ibrahim* is preferable is considered later in the chapter.

[607] *R. v RB* [2023] NICA 24 at [60] and [64]: "[A] judge cannot be straight jacketed by an earlier ruling otherwise [s.15] …would have no purpose." The appellate court will not intervene at the behest of the prosecution if the terminating ruling is reasonable (a high bar) because it is not the business of the higher court simply to substitute its own view: *R. v RB* at [66]. *R. v RB* also shows that the trial judge's failure to spell out explicitly the reason for the change of mind is not necessarily a fatal flaw in the trial judge's ruling.

[608] *R. v Rodgers* [2013] NICA 71 at [22]. In this case the defence found it difficult to challenge expert evidence purely because of its inherent reliability.

16. OTHER COUNTER-MEASURES TO PREVENT UNFAIRNESS

(a) Directing the jury

Replace the first paragraph with:

If hearsay evidence is admitted, including by agreement of the parties,[614a] it must be the subject of a direction to the jury.[615] This is probably a requirement of both art.6 and English domestic law.[616] The direction should be tailored to the circumstances of the case and the judge should discuss the content with counsel

30-79

before delivering it[617]:

> "We take the view that what is said by the judge should not be drafted in words written in stone but should be words appropriate to the case which in the opinion of the judge meet the fairness of the course that has been taken with the evidence of the witness who does not appear and generally appropriate to the circumstances of the case."[618]

[614a] *R. v Da Costa* [2022] EWCA Crim 1262.

[615] *Grant v The State* [2006] 2 W.L.R. 835; *R. v Cole and Keet* [2007] 1 W.L.R. 2716 at [38]; *R. v Carter* [2009] EWCA Crim 964; *R. v Claridge* [2013] EWCA Crim 203; *R. v Nguyen* [2020] EWCA Crim 140 at [77].

[616] *R. v Sellick* [2005] EWCA Crim 651; *The Times,* 22 March 2005, CA.

[617] *R. v Hardwick* [2003] EWCA Crim 369 at [20]; *R. v S* [2016] EWCA Crim 1908.

[618] *R. v Sellick* [2005] EWCA Crim 65 at [19], per Curtis J. See also *R. v Denton* [2001] 1 Cr. App. R. 16; *R. v Lobban* [2004] EWCA Crim 1099 at [44].

Replace the second paragraph with:
Where the maker of the statement is not in court, the judge should warn about the inability to test the maker of the statement about its contents by cross-examination,[619] that the statement has not been verified on oath[620] (although omission to do so is not necessarily a legitimate ground of appeal,[620a] if the jurors must have been aware of this fact)[621] and that the jurors did not see it made[622] (unless a video-recording is provided). It is desirable that the jury be told to consider the statement in the context of all the evidence,[623] and that the judge draw attention to its strengths and weaknesses.[624] Potential weaknesses include:

- inconsistencies between the contents of the statement and other evidence[625];
- contradictory accounts by the witness of material issues[626];
- uncertainty about whether the statement was made[627];
- the emotionally charged nature of the statement[628];
- that in an historic case, a confession that had been admitted only to explain the reason for the long delay in complaining about the offence to the police, was not evidence of that which was confessed[629]; and
- anything that casts doubt on the credibility of the maker of the statement, such as a criminal record or mental health issues.[630]

Potential strengths include:

- a video-recording of the making of the statement[631];
- no reason for the maker of the statement to misrepresent the matter stated[632]; and
- independent evidence supporting the statement's reliability.[633]

[619] *N v HM Advocate* [2003] S.L.T. 761 at [37]; *Grant v The State* [2006] UKPC 2; [2007] 1 A.C. 1 at [21].

[620] *Grant v The State* [2006] UKPC 2; [2007] 1 A.C. 1 at [21].

[620a] *R. v Da Costa* [2022] EWCA Crim 1262 at [20].

[621] *R. v Kitziltan* [2018] 4 W.L.R. 43 at [20]. However, in *Kitziltan* at [22], where collusion between an unavailable and an available witness was alleged, and an illicit communication took place during the trial between the two, jurors should have been directed "to consider whether there may be a link between the reason for" the witness's unavailability and the assertion of collusion, "and, if so, whether that affected their view of the credibility" of the unavailable witness's identification of the defendant in his hearsay statement.

[622] This applies also to a prior consistent or inconsistent statement by a trial witness that in consequence of s.119 or s.120 of the Criminal Justice Act 2003 is admissible as evidence of the matter stated.

[623] *Grant v The State* [2006] UKPC 2; [2007] 1 A.C. 1 at [21].

[624] *R. v Shabir* [2012] EWCA Crim 2564 at [44]–[46], [72].

[625] *R. v Gavin*, unreported, 3 May 2000 CA at [31]; *R. v Allawi* [2015] EWCA Crim 1964 at [23].

[626] *R. v S* [2016] EWCA Crim 1908.

[627] *R. v Smith* [2019] EWCA Crim 1151 at [47]–[48]. The Court of Appeal said that the judge had given a direction unduly favourable to the defence, in so far as he had said that the statement should be disregarded unless the jurors were "sure" it had been made. All the jurors were required to be sure about was that the defendants had committed the crime.

[628] *R. v BC* [2019] EWCA Crim 623 at [37] where the statement was a suicide note.

[629] *R. v Smith* [2020] EWCA Crim 777 at [58].

[630] e.g. *R. v Shabir* [2012] EWCA Crim 2564 at [44]. cf. *R. v Shaid* [2019] EWCA Crim 412 where the deceased had a bad character and was addicted to spice.

[631] e.g. *R. v Friel* [2012] EWCA Crim 2871 at [23].

[632] *R. v Friel* [2012] EWCA Crim 2871 at [23].

[633] *R. v Friel* [2012] EWCA Crim 2871 at [23] at [24].

17.   HEARSAY AND EUROPEAN CONVENTION ON HUMAN RIGHTS

Replace paragraph with:

30-83   The right of confrontation embodied in art.6(3)(d) and the English hearsay rule are not co-extensive and reliance on what both legal regimes classify as hearsay does not automatically violate art.6.[652a] Article 6(3)(d) protects a criminal defendant against accusations by anonymous witnesses[653] and reinforces the principle of equality of arms by conferring on the defence the same right to call and cross-examine witnesses as the prosecution.[654] The expression "witness" in art.6(3)(d) extends beyond those persons who testify at the trial.[655] It refers to anyone (including an accomplice)[656] who has supplied the authorities with information for the prosecution on which the prosecution relies.[657] Since art.6(3)(d) is not about hearsay evidence per se, it probably does not come into play when an out-of-court statement by an actual testifying witness is admitted pursuant to s.119 or s.120 of the Criminal Justice Act 2003.[658] It is also doubtful whether it is relevant when a business record is admitted under s.117[659] or a court receives the transcript of the oral testimony of a witness in an earlier contested trial.[660] How art.6(3)(d) affects spontaneous utterances admissible under the preserved res gestae doctrine has not been conclusively determined.[661] It may be that a distinction will be drawn between spontaneous utterances in which the defendant is accused of the crime and those that do not make such an accusation. Article 6(3)(d) seems to be otiose when the parties agree that all the evidence is to take the form of hearsay.[662]

[652a] *SA-Capital OY v Finland* App. No. 5556/10 10 Feb. 14, 2019 at [66]–[92].

[653] *Kostovski v Netherlands* (1990) 12 E.H.R.R. 434.

[654] *R. v Horncastle* [2009] EWCA Crim 984 at [76].

[655] *Asch v Austria* (1993) 15 E.H.R.R. 597.

[656] *Kaste and Mathisen v Norway* (2006) 48 E.H.R.R. 45 (In a joint trial, the prosecution read out D1's deposition to the police. Because D1 had declined to testify by invoking his right to silence, the court did not permit D2 to cross-examine D1 about the contents of the deposition. The ECtHR said that D1 was a "witness" against D2, that D2 should have been given the opportunity to put questions directly to D1 (who could refuse to answer specific questions on the grounds of self-incrimination) and that art.6(3)(d) was therefore infringed).

[657] *Windisch v Austria* (1990) 13 E.H.R.R. 281 at [23]; *Delta v France* (1993) 16 E.H.R.R. 574 at [34]; *Trevedi v United Kingdom* (1997) 89 D & R 136. In *Crawford v Washington* 124 S.Ct.1354, 158 L.Ed.

2d 177 (2004), the US Supreme Court distinguished testimonial evidence (that is, formal accusations) made with a view to a criminal prosecution such as witness statements, responses during police questioning, evidence before a Grand jury or during a previous trial and non-testimonial statements such as business documents and statements made informally to friends and to those providing medical assistance. The latter may be hearsay, but their admission as evidence does not interfere with the right of confrontation guaranteed by the Sixth Amendment. See also para.28-12.

[658] cp. *X v FRG* (1980) 17 D. & R. 231; *Hauschildt v Denmark* (1989) 49 D. & R. 86, 102. cp. *R. v KGB* (1993) 79 C.C.C. (3d) 257, 281–282 SCC.

[659] "[T]here is no case where the European Court found a breach [of Art.6(3)(d)] in situations where the court had not been concerned with what might be called in English terms a 'witness statement' i.e. a statement made by a potential witness to the police or the prosecuting authorities" *R. v Owen* [2001] EWCA Crim 1019 at [18], per Keene LJ. The Court of Appeal did not have to decide whether the admissibility of a business document is affected by art.6(3)(d) in *R. v Carter* [2009] EWCA Crim 964 at [156] because the document was not relied upon by the prosecution for a hearsay purpose.

[660] As in *R. v Sadiq* [2009] EWCA Crim 712. This is because the defence had the opportunity to cross-examine the witness during the previous proceedings.

[661] The Court of Appeal thought it probably did not apply in *R. v Horncastle* [2009] EWCA Crim 964 at [35] but then gave as an example of reliable hearsay just such a statement ibid at [61]. On the admissibility at common law of spontaneous utterances see *Andrews v DPP* [1987] A.C. 281 HL a case discussed in Ch.31.

[662] *Arnarsson v Iceland* Application 44671/98, 15 July 2003. cp. Criminal Justice Act 2003 s.131(1)(a).

Replace the first paragraph with:

30-84   The ECtHR has long recognised that the art.6(3)(d) right is not absolute: "Article 6 does not grant the accused an unlimited right to secure the appearance of witnesses in court."[663] The court is interested in the importance of the hearsay evidence in the proceedings and the overlapping issue of the overall fairness of the proceedings given the admission of contested hearsay evidence. The first consideration has induced the ECtHR to draw a distinction between those trials in which the prosecution would have failed had the prosecutor been unable to rely on hearsay evidence and those in which it would not. In *Al-Khawaja and Tahery v United Kingdom*,[664] the ECtHR, sitting as a Chamber, held that in consequence of art.6(3)(d), the admission of sole or decisive hearsay evidence in a criminal trial infringed the defendant's Convention rights. Previously in *Luca v Italy* that court had said:

> "[W]here a conviction is based solely or to a decisive degree on depositions that have been made by a person whom the accused has had no opportunity to examine or to have examined, during the investigation or at the trial, the rights of the defence are restricted to an extent that is incompatible with the guarantees provided by Article 6."[665]

[663] *A.L. v Finland* Application no. 23220/04 27 January 2009 at [37].

[664] *Al-Khawaja and Tahery v United Kingdom* App. No. 26766/05, 20 January 2009.

[665] *Luca v Italy* (2003) 36 E.H.R.R. 46 at [40].

Replace list with:

30-95   (1) *The circumstances in which the out-of-court statement was made* "The circumstances of the making of the hearsay statement may be such as to reduce the risk of unreliability, for example if it is spontaneous[732] ... The disinterest of the maker of the statement may reduce the risk of deliberate untruth."[733] No motive to lie was a factor in *Doran*,[734] *Friel*[735] and *Adeojo*.[736] In *S*[737] a substantially reduced risk that the witness had not actually said what was contained in the written statement was taken into account. In *B(J) v HM Advocate*, a Scottish case in which the complainant was incompetent to testify because of Alzheimer's disease by the trial, the court mentions as one of several factors that her allegations "had been taken by a police officer in a relatively formal way in the first instance at least, and that police officer was available to be cross-examined".[737a]

(2) *Availability of material about the absent witness's credibility and/or accuracy* "The availability of good admissible testing material concerning the reliability of the witness may show that the evidence can properly be tested and assessment."[738] This includes documentary evidence[739] a prior inconsistent statement[740] and, in certain circumstances, the defendant's own testimony from the witness box.[741] In *Vidgen v Netherland*[742] the ECtHR drew attention to the fact that the witness (an accomplice) had incriminated himself in the out-of-court statement. Significant inconsistencies between accounts of the crime by absent witnesses, however, may also be a reason to exclude hearsay.[743] In *Wilson*, another appeal conjoined to *Riat*, and the only one to be upheld, a key concern was that the statements of the eyewitnesses, all of whom were unavailable for cross-examination, "revealed material differences in important respects. In particular, there was a vast difference between the accounts of how the assault started and further differences in the descriptions of the assailants, both of which matters were of considerable significance".[744] Where the out-of-court statement includes a visual identification of the defendant, another eyewitness, although unable to make a direct identification, may be able to testify and be cross-examined about the conditions under which the absent witness saw the defendant.[745] In *B(J) v HM Advocate* the availability of evidence of the statement-maker's deteriorating faculties at the time that the statements were made was treated as a factor, as was the fact that the defendant entered the witness box and denied the allegations.[745a]

(3) *Independent evidence supporting the reliability of the statement* "Independent dovetailing evidence may reduce the risk both of deliberate untruth and innocent mistaken ..."[746] The supporting evidence may be direct, for example, an admission (*Bennett, Friel/Allawi*[747])[748],[749], or circumstantial, for example, lies (*Riat*,[750] *Doran*,[751] *Bennett*,[752] *Adeojo*,[753] *Strotten*[754]) an implausible explanation (*Clare*),[755] similar fact evidence (*Doran*,[756] *Al-Khawaja, Barney*,[757] *Strotten*[758]), inconsistent statements (*Allawi*[759]) discovery of a weapons on the defendant's premises that could have been used to commit the crime (*Adeojo*),[760] telephone data placing the defendant at or in the vicinity of the crime scene at the relevant time (*Fergus*,[761] *Adeojo*[762]), CCTV evidence (*Adeojo*,[763] *Allawi*,[764] *Houlder*[765]) and injuries to victims that were consistent with the description of the commission of the crime in the statement (*Friel*).[766]

(4) *Prior opportunity to cross-examine the absent witness* The ECtHR does not insist the opportunity for cross-examination occur during the trial. In *R. v Deakin*[767] the Court of Appeal upheld a decision to admit the statement of a witness living in North Cyprus whose attendance at the trial could not be secured because the defence was able to cross-examine the witness during an earlier trial involving the same defendants and allegations. Conversely, in *Schatschaschwili v Germany*[768] the trial was unfair because an investigating judge had held the pre-trial hearing at which the statements of the only eye-witnesses (who were later unavailable) were taken without the defendant present, and thus able to test their evidence.

(5) *Counterbalancing procedural measure* Correct application of statutory

safeguards[769] (as to which see ss.114(2), 116(4), 121(1)(c), 124, 125, 126(1)(b) and PACE s.78) and a full and proper direction to the jury about the weaknesses of any hearsay evidence that is admitted[770] is necessary, but not of itself sufficient, for Convention compliance. An audio-recorded statement is helpful for admissibility because it eliminates the risk of inaccurate transmission from the witness to the courtroom and enables the jury to consider "not just the words recorded but the manner in which the witness responded to questions".[771] In *Riat*[772] and the conjoined *Doran* appeal,[773] where the prosecution adduced a video-recording, the Court of Appeal took into account the fact that the jury was able to see the witness making the statement. In *B(J) v HM Advocate*[773a] the Scottish appellate court dismissed an argument that because the jury was in a remote location it could not adequately assess the demeanour of the witness whose evidence was offered to corroborate that of the incompetent complainant.

[732] A factor in *R. v Riat* [2012] EWCA Crim 1509 at [36](i); and seemingly in *R. v Claridge* [2013] EWCA Crim 203 where the witness had identified the defendant (who was known to her) in a 999 call immediately her boyfriend was attacked.

[733] *R. v Riat* [2012] EWCA Crim 1509 at [6] cp. at [25].

[734] *R. v Doran* [2012] EWCA Crim 1509 at [42](iv).

[735] *R. v Riat* [2012] EWCA Crim 1509 at [22](f), [23].

[736] *R. v Adeojo* [2013] EWCA Crim 41 at [30], [81].

[737] *S v HMA* [2020] HCJAC 42 at [20].

[737a] *B(J) v HM Advocate* [2022] HCJAC 38; 2022 S.C.C.R. 283 at [37].

[738] *R. v Riat* [2012] EWCA Crim 1509 at [6], cp. [25]. There was abundant material to test the complainant's credibility and reliability in *Riat* ibid at [36]–[37]. See also *R. v Adeojo* [2013] EWCA Crim 41 at [46].

[739] *R. v Evans* [2010] EWCA Crim 2516 at [20].

[740] *R. v Evans* [2010] EWCA Crim 2516 at [25]. cp. *R. v Riat* [2012] EWCA Crim 1509 at [36](viii).

[741] e.g. *R. v Jabbar* [2013] EWCA Crim 801 at [36].

[742] *Vidgen v Netherland* (2019) 69 E.H.R.R. SE3 at [42]. In addition there was corroborating evidence.

[743] cp. *Trampevski v Macedonia* App. No. 4570/07, 10 July 2012 at [48]–[49].

[744] *Trampevski v Macedonia* App. No. 4570/07, 10 July 2012 at [61] (conjoined to *Riat*).

[745] *R. v Adeojo* [2013] EWCA Crim 41 at [30], [46], [81].

[745a] *B(J) v HM Advocate* [2022] HCJAC 38 at [37].

[746] *R. v Adeojo* [2013] EWCA Crim 41 at [6].

[747] *R. v Allawi* [2015] EWCA Crim 1964.

[748] *R. v Friel* [2012] EWCA Crim 2871 at [5], [33].

[749] *R. v Friel* [2012] EWCA Crim 2871 at [36]; *R. v Adeojo* [2013] EWCA Crim 41 at [15], [46], [81].

[750] *R. v Friel* [2012] EWCA Crim 2871 at [36](i), (vi),(vii).

[751] *R. v Friel* [2012] EWCA Crim 2871 at [42](v).

[752] *R. v Friel* [2012] EWCA Crim 2871 (conjoined to *Riat*).

[753] *R. v Adeojo* [2013] EWCA Crim 41 at [15](ii), [35].

[754] *R. v Strotten* [2015] EWCA Crim 1101.

[755] *R. v Friel* [2012] EWCA Crim 1509 (conjoined to *Riat*)

[756] *R. v Friel* [2012] EWCA Crim 1509 at [42] (v).

[757] *R. v Barney* [2014] EWCA Crim 589 at [17].

758 *R. v Strotten* [2015] EWCA Crim 1101.

759 *R. v Allawi* [2015] EWCA Crim 1964 at [24].

760 *R. v Adeojo* [2013] EWCA Crim 41 at [11].

761 *R. v Fergus* [2012] EWCA Crim 2248 at [49].

762 *R. v Fergus* [2012] EWCA Crim 2248 at [15](ii). Neither the discovery of the weapons nor the telephone data is mentioned as "supporting evidence" at [82].

763 *R. v Fergus* [2012] EWCA Crim 2248 at [82].

764 *R. v Allawi* [2015] EWCA Crim 1964 at [24].

765 *R. v Houlder* [2019] EWCA Crim 1064 at [16].

766 *R. v Friel* [2012] EWCA Crim 2871 at [5], [8], [35].

767 *R. v Deakin* [2009] EWCA Crim 2541 at [14].

768 *Schatschaschwili v Germany* (2016) 63 E.H.R.R. 14.

769 *R. v Ibrahim* [2012] EWCA Crim 837; *R. v Claridge* [2013] EWCA Crim 203 at [13].

770 *R. v Friel* [2012] EWCA Crim 2871 at [23], [24], [31]; *R. v Claridge* [2013] EWCA Crim 203 at [19].

771 *R. v Adeojo* [2013] EWCA Crim 41 at [81].

772 *R. v Friel* [2012] EWCA Crim 1509 at [36](iv). In *R. v Fergus* [2012] EWCA Crim 2248 at [49] the Court of Appeal took into account that what "went on during the [VIPER] identification procedures was before the jury in totality by virtue of its recording".

773 *R. v Friel* [2012] EWCA Crim 1509 at [40], [42]. See also *R. v Friel* [2012] EWCA Crim 1509 at [4], [22](d), [23], [31].

773a *B(J) v HM Advocate* [2022] HCJAC 38 at [28], [39]: "The use of remote juries was an established feature of the criminal justice system at the time of the trial and built upon the court's experience of witnesses, particularly complainers in sexual cases, giving evidence remotely. The suggestion that this impacted on the jury's ability to assess the evidence of NB is nothing more than an unvouched assertion."

18. MISCELLANEOUS PROCEDURAL MATTERS

(b) Proof of admissibility

Replace paragraph with:

An application to admit an out-of-court statement for a hearsay purpose may be **30-101** made at the Plea and Directions Hearing or pre-trial review.[804] This avoids disrupting the flow of the trial. If there is a disputed issue on admissibility during the trial, the judge should embark on a trial within a trial.[805] No voir dire was conducted in *R. v Wright*.[805a] The trial judge justified this by pointing out that the witness had already expressed her reluctance to come to court; holding a voir dire might require her to give evidence twice. The Court of Appeal said that as part of the proper exercise of his trial management power, the trial judge was entitled to forgo the voir dire and see how the witness's evidence came out, given that he had the power to stop the case if this evidence, which was "plainly of crucial importance to the prosecution",[805b] turned out to be unfairly prejudicial to the defence.

804 See *Practice Direction (Criminal Proceedings Consolidation)*, para.41; [2002] 1 W.L.R. 2870.

805 *R. v Minors and Harper* (1989) 89 Cr. App. R. 102 (a decision on Police and Criminal Evidence Act 1984 ss.68, 69). The other party must be permitted to cross-examine any witness called: *R. v Wood and Fitzsimmons* [1998] Crim. L.R. 213 CA.

805a *R. v Wright* [2022] EWCA Crim 1722 [14]–[16].

805b *R. v Wright* [2022] EWCA Crim 1722 at [8], per Judge Menary KC.

After the first paragraph, add new paragraph:

When a voir dire is held it should not be held in the judge's room in the absence of the defendant (save with his consent or in exceptional circumstances)[806] or the shorthand writer.[807] If cross-examination is warranted, defence counsel should be given the opportunity to cross-examine the witnesses called on the voir dire (including, normally, if he be a witness, the person who is said to be afraid to give evidence at the trial).[808] There may be circumstances in which the judge, having heard submissions from counsel, considers that that this is not the appropriate cause.[809] The court may rely on its own observation of a witness[810] and the witness's inability to explain his refusal to give evidence[811] (in addition to any other evidence) in deciding whether a witness is in fear. When a court is asked to admit a document, a preliminary hearsay issue may arise about its authenticity.[812] In deciding on the admissibility of a document, inferences may be drawn from the face of the document about the personal knowledge of the person who supplied the information, the purpose of the document and its provenance.[813] A further written statement by the same witness will not do,[814] but another statement properly admitted in its own right may be relied upon.[815]

[806] If a witness is afraid of the defendant devices such as screens or television links which preserve the right of the defendant to be present may be used: *R. v Lobban* [2004] EWCA Crim 1099 at [30].

[807] *R. v Lobban* [2004] EWCA Crim 1099 at [27].

[808] *R. v Lobban* [2004] EWCA Crim 1099 at [36]–[37].

[809] *R. v Lobban* [2004] EWCA Crim 1099 at [38].

[810] *R. v Ashford Magistrates' Court, Ex p. Hilden* (1993) 96 Cr. App. R. 92 DC (a Criminal Justice Act 1988 decision).

[811] *R. v Gray* [2004] EWCA Crim 1000 at [29].

[812] For example, if reliance is placed on a signature. See *R. v Jenkins* [2002] EWCA Crim 2475. cp. *R. v Stubbs* [2002] EWCA Crim 2254.

[813] *R. v Foxley* [1995] 2 Cr. App. R. 523 (a Criminal Justice Act 1988 decision); *Vehicle and Operator Services Agency v George Jenkins Transport Ltd* [2003] EWHC 2879 (Admin) (decided under the Criminal Justice Act 1988); *Khatibi v DPP* [2004] EWHC 83, [42] (Admin) (decided under the Criminal Justice Act 1988). But cf. *R. v Feest* [1987] Crim. L.R. 766 CA.

[814] *R. v Belmarsh Magistrates' Court, Ex p. Gilligan* [1998] 1 Cr. App. R. 14, DC (a witness's fear); *R. v Case* [1991] Crim. L.R. 192 CA. Both cases were decided when the Criminal Justice Act 1988 was in force.

[815] *R. v Castillo* [1996] 1 Cr. App. R. 438 (a Criminal Justice Act 1988 decision).

CHAPTER 31

RES GESTAE AND CERTAIN OTHER EXCEPTIONS TO THE
HEARSAY RULE IN CRIMINAL PROCEEDINGS

2. SPONTANEOUS (OR EXCITED) UTTERANCES

Replace footnote 21 with: "T. Lau, "Reliability of Excited Utterance Hearsay Evidence" (2018) 87 Mississippi L.J. 599; E. Keat, "Wither, hither and thither, res gestae? A comparative analysis of its relevance and application" (2021) 25 E. & P. 326; R. Coffey, "Fight, flight, freeze…or lie? Rethinking the principles of res gestae evidence in the light of its revival" (2023) 27 E. & P. 51. Coffey argues that this hearsay exception adds nothing to the hearsay regime under the 2003 Act, blurs the operation of s.114(1)(d), and rests on assumptions about how trauma victims behave that run counter to modern neuroscience."

(a) Status of the rule

After "… under the excited utterance hearsay exception.", add new footnote 22a:

[22a] e.g. *R. v Milne* [2022] EWCA Crim 753 at [12]. On appeal it was found that the evidence was wrongly admitted because it lacked probative value: *R. v Milne* [2022] EWCA Crim 753 at [27].

31-03

(f) Availability of declarant

Replace footnote 92 with:

[92] *R. v Brown* [2019] EWCA Crim 1143. Consider also the facts of *Brown v Sestras* [2023] EWHC 1220 (KB). In these civil proceedings, the trial judge took into account an anonymous telephone tip-off to police, which had been made within four hours of a road accident. The caller had identified the type of

31-16

car responsible (a black 5-door Mercedes with blacked out windows), described how it had been driven, and reported the registration plate number. An attempt to trace the maker of this statement, whom the judge found had been motivated by a genuine desire to help, was unsuccessful.

(g) Alternative grounds of admissibility

Replace footnote 96 with:

31-17   [96] Steph. Dig. Art.3 illustration a; *The Times,* 8 March 1856. Cp. *R. v Gorman* [2019] EWCA Crim 2271 where the statement maker was not aware that a crime had been committed when she identified the defendant as the caller.

11.   EXPERT EVIDENCE

Replace the first paragraph with:

31-49   In *R. v Abadom*[321] the Court of Appeal confirmed that, of necessity, a witness whom the court is satisfied has the necessary professional expertise, when asked for an opinion about an issue, may draw upon secondary material of a general nature such as is commonly relied upon by experts in the field in forming opinions.[322] It is common for police officers to be allowed to give evidence of local drug-dealing patterns and gang activities.[323] Very likely some of their expertise, and hence their opinions, are derived from hearsay as opposed to first-hand experience of the local crime scene. A prerequisite of the admissibility of an expert's opinion evidence is that the trial court is presented with admissible evidence of the primary facts to which the opinion relates.[323a] The *Abadom* common law hearsay exception, which is considered further in Ch.33, has been retained by the Criminal Justice Act 2003 s.118(1):

"The following rules of law are preserved.

Expert evidence

8.   Any rule of law under which in criminal proceedings an expert witness may draw on the body of expertise relevant to his field."

The common law exception is supplemented by a new statutory exception created by s.127(2) of the Criminal Justice Act 2003 which permits a testifying expert to rely on the work of an assistant without the assistant having to be called to give oral evidence, unless the court, on application by a party, decides this to be against the interests of justice.[324] The assistant's evidence is presented to the court as a written statement.[325]

[321] *R. v Abadom* [1983] 1 W.L.R. 126 CA. For a discussion of the case law on which this decision is based see R. Pattenden, "Expert Opinion Evidence Based on Hearsay" [1982] Crim. L.R. 85. See also *Wilson v HM Advocate* [2009] HCJA 58 at [63].

[322] *R. v Zundel* (1987) 31 C.C.C. (3d) 97, 146, Ont. CA. See also *HKSAR v Kissel* [2013] HKCA 622 at [134]–[135] in which the Court of Appeal in Hong Kong relied on what was said in R. Pattenden, "Expert Opinion based on Hearsay" [1982] Crim. L.R. 85.

[323] T. Ward and S. Fouladvand, "Bodies of Knowledge and Robes of Expertise: Expert Evidence about Drugs, Gangs and Human Trafficking" [2021] Crim. L.R. 442. However, "case workers …are [not] experts in human trafficking or modern slavery (whether generally or in respect of specified countries) and for that fundamental reason cannot give opinion evidence in a trial on whether an individual was trafficked or exploited": *R. v Brecani* [2021] EWCA Crim 731 at [54].

[323a] The expert can give evidence of representations made to him that constitute primary facts if the purpose is to explain the basis of his opinion and not to prove those facts. This is because the evidence of the representations is not adduced for a hearsay purpose.

[324] Criminal Justice Act 2003 s.127(4). Matters to be considered are specified in s.127(5). Notice must be given of the intention of the expert to rely on the assistant's statement: s.127(1)(c), (d). See further details in Ch.33.

[325] Criminal Justice Act 2003 s.127(3).

CHAPTER 32

**COMMON LAW EXCEPTIONS TO THE RULE AGAINST HEARSAY:
EVIDENCE OF REPUTATION OR FAMILY TRADITION; PUBLISHED
WORKS; PUBLIC INFORMATION; BANKERS' BOOKS; ANCIENT
DOCUMENTS**

Replace the first paragraph with:

32-01   This chapter examines a number of common law hearsay exceptions that have survived the virtual abolition of the hearsay rule in civil proceedings[1] by the Civil Evidence Act 1995.[2] Five of these relate to reputation, family tradition or both. Reputation as evidence comprises collective gossip about a person of which the person in question is not necessarily aware. Reputation evidence is hearsay when its relevance depends upon the gossipers speaking the truth, which is frequently the case when character is a substantive issue in the trial. If its relevance is not dependent on whether the gossip is true, the evidence of reputation is not hearsay.[3] Similarly, family tradition is hearsay when its relevance depends upon the tradition being true, which is almost always the case. The reputation and family tradition hearsay exceptions, which are preserved in civil proceedings by s.7 of the 1995 Act, relate to:

(1) general reputation as to character;
(2) family tradition as to pedigree;
(3) general reputation or family tradition as to marriage;
(4) general reputation or family tradition as to public or general rights;
(5) general reputation or family tradition as to the identity of any person or thing;

The remaining hearsay exceptions that have survived the 1995 Act are concerned with various forms of public information:

(6) published works dealing with matters of a public nature;
(7) public documents.

[126]

Evidence admitted under the seven common law exceptions mentioned above still matter because they are not subject to the notice and weighing provisions of the Civil Evidence Act 1995.[4]

[1] Defined in s.18(1) of the Civil Evidence Act 1995.

[2] See Ch.29.

[3] cf. C. Frank, "Gossip, hearsay and the character exception in Victorian law and literature" (2015) 9 *Law & Humanities* 172–202.

[4] Civil Evidence Act 1995 ss.2, 4.

6.   BANKERS' BOOKS

(a)   Bankers' books

(ii)   Inspection of bankers' books

Replace the first paragraph with:

Under s.7,[573] if legal proceedings are in existence, a court or judge[574] has a discre-   **32-112** tion, on the application of any party to legal proceedings, to inspect and take copies of entries in the accounts either of parties, their spouses[575] or strangers, provided such entries would have been admissible in evidence prior to the Act,[576] but the power will only be exercised in respect of a third party to the proceedings with great caution.[577] Section 7 has been exercised in respect of banks in Scotland and, in the 19th century, in Ireland[578] for the purpose of legal proceedings taking place in England.[579] Although the Bankers' Book Evidence Act 1879 has no express territorial limitation, it is well-established that to order a third party based outside the jurisdiction to disclose documents is an excess of extraterritorial jurisdiction and the same holds for foreign banks with branches in England.[580] In *Meng v HSBC Plc*[581] the High Court said that s.7 applies to:

(1)   legal proceedings that are taking place within the UK; he pointed out that to extend s.7 to foreign proceedings would subvert the existing framework for obtaining aid for foreign proceedings;[582] and

(2)   actual transactional banking records, which means that records maintained for the purpose of regulatory compliance are excluded.[583]

"What a court can readily, and reliably, get from the banker's book or record is prima facie evidence of whether a banking transaction took place: when, in what amount, involving whose account, at what branch, and so on."[584]

In *Meng* Fordham J indicated that had he held that s.7 applied to regulatory compliance documents required for proceedings taking place abroad, he would not have exercised his discretion to require disclosure in *Meng* because it was not the business of an English court to ensure that extradition proceedings in Canada are conducted fairly.[585] Prior to *Meng*, the Court of Appeal allowed an appeal against an order for the inspection of the bank account of a non-party who was a customer of a branch of a bank located in the Isle of Man (and therefore subject to Manx law) even though this bank used an English bank as its clearing house for cheques.[586]

[573] As to requirements for valid orders under s.7 see *Blanchfield v Hartnett* [2002] I.E.S.C. 39, per Fennelly J, Supreme Court of Ireland.

[574] Or stipendiary magistrate, *R. v Kinghorn* [1908] 2 K.B. 949; though quaere the Lord Mayor, *R. v Bradlaugh* (1883) 15 Cox 217, 222n.

[575] *R. v Andover Justices Ex p. Rhodes* [1980] Crim. L.R. 644.

576 *Howard v Beall* (1889) 23 Q.B.D. 1; *South Staffordshire Co v Ebsmith* [1895] 2 Q.B. 669; *M'Gorman v Kierans* (1901) 35 I.L.T.R. 84; *Marshfield, Re* (1886) 32 Ch. D. 499; *Lister v Varley* (1890) 89 L.T. 232; *Ironmonger v Dyne* (1828) 44 T.L.R. 579.

577 *Pollock v Garle* [1898] 1 Ch. 1, in which the Court of Appeal refused to make such an order in the case of third persons who were neither actual nor constructive parties to the case, e.g. as to the bank balance of a company, in an action against one of its directors for inducing a purchase of its shares by alleged misrepresentation as to such balance; and cf. *L'Amie v Wilson* [1907] 2 I.R. 130; *Anselm v Anselm* unreported 15 December 1999, Neuberger J.

578 *Kissam v Link* [1896] 1 Q.B. 574.

579 *Parnell v Wood* [1892] P. 137; *Fitzpatrick v M'Donald* (1891) 30 L.R.Ir. 249; *Perry v Phosphor Co* (1894) 71 L.T. 854.

580 *Mackinnon v Donaldson Lufkin & Jenrette Securities Corp* [1986] Ch. 482.

581 *Meng v HSBC Bank Plc* [2021] EWHC 342 (QB). The claimant, the CFO of a telecommunications company, sought disclosure of documents relevant in proceedings in Canada to obtain her extradition to the US in connection with a breach of US sanctions against Iran.

582 *Meng v HSBC Bank Plc* [2021] EWHC 342 (QB) at [17]. Thus, in civil litigation an order for disclosure against a Swiss bank can only be obtained via a letter of request issued by the High Court to the designated Swiss Central Authority pursuant to RSC Ord 39, FPR 2010 r.24.12 and the Hague Convention of 18 March 1970 on the Taking of Evidence Abroad in Civil or Commercial Matters.

583 *Meng v HSBC Bank Plc* [2021] EWHC 342 (QB) at [28].

584 *Meng v HSBC Bank Plc* [2021] EWHC 342 (QB) at [24], per Fordham J.

585 *Meng v HSBC Bank Plc* [2021] EWHC 342 (QB) at [32]. Moreover, an order under s.7 would have circumvented statutory provisions applicable to foreign extradition proceedings that prohibited disclosure.

586 *R. v Grossman* (1981) 72 Cr. App. R. 302; [1981] Crim. L.R. 396.

CHAPTER 33

OPINION AND EXPERT EVIDENCE

5. EXPERT EVIDENCE IN CIVIL PROCEEDINGS

(b) System under CPR summarised

Replace footnote 211 with:

[211] *R. (AB) v Chief Constable of Hampshire* [2019] EWHC 3461 (Admin) at [16]–[20]; *R. (Banks* **33-23**
Renewables Ltd) v Secretary of State for Business, Energy & Industrial Strategy [2020] EWHC 436
(Admin); *R. (Law Society) v Lord Chancellor* [2020] EWHC 2094 (Admin); *Circle Nottingham Ltd v
NHS Rushcliffe Clinical Commissioning Group* [2019] EWHC 3635 (TCC) (expert evidence in public
procurement challenge); *The Good Law Project Ltd v Minister for the Cabinet Office* [2021] EWHC
2091 (TCC) For a useful summary of the relevant principles for admission of expert evidence in judicial
review proceedings, see *Siemens Mobility Ltd v High Speed Two (HS2) Ltd* [2022] EWHC 2190 (TCC);
[2022] B.L.R. 576 at [14]–[20]; *R. (Fridman) v HM Treasury* [2023] EWHC 2657 (Admin) at [70]–
[71]. As regards the practice of the Competition Appeal Tribunal, where dealing with judicial review
cases, see *Dye and Durham Ltd v Competition and Markets Authority* [2023] CAT 32 at [24]–[29].

(ii) Expert's duty to the court

Duties and independence

Replace paragraph with:

  Where an expert has a material or significant conflict of interest, the court may **33-32**
well decline to act on his evidence or even refuse permission for it to be adduced.
In any event, the expert must disclose any potential conflict of interest.[255] The courts
are particularly critical of experts who fail to disclose a conflict of interest or other
matter which goes to their independence from the parties.[256] It is contrary to the

public interest for a party and an expert to contract that the expert will not act for the other party.[257] Even where an expert has been approached by one party and given confidential information, it does not necessarily follow that the expert is precluded from being retained by another party. Where the expert has not been shown to have used confidential or privileged material and where it is not likely that he might do so in the future, the court may refuse an injunction restraining him from acting.[258] However, the court may grant an injunction restraining a person from acting as an expert where it is likely that he would be unable to act without having resort to privileged material. An injunction may be granted restraining an expert from acting for another party against the original party; if the expert can be shown to have owed fiduciary duties to the original party, on the basis of a conflict of interest.[259]

[255] *Toth v Jarman* [2006] EWCA Civ 1028; [2006] 4 All E.R. 1276; see also *Guidance*, para.16e.

[256] *Rowley v Dunlop* [2014] EWHC 1995 (Ch) (conflict of interest not disclosed, evidence not excluded, but a matter for cross-examination); *EXP v Barker* [2015] EWHC 1289 (QB) (failure by medical expert to disclose connection with defendant medical practitioner; evidence not excluded, but connection went to weight); *Bux v General Medical Council* [2021] EWHC 762 (Admin); [2021] Med. L.R. 350 (disclosure of conflict of interest); *Royal Mail Group Ltd v DAF Grucks Ltd* [2023] CAT 6; [2023] 5 C.M.L.R. 6 at [235]–[257] (failure to disclose dealings with party).

[257] *Lilly ICOS Ltd v Pfizer Ltd (No.2)* [2002] EWCA Civ 2; [2002] 1 W.L.R. 2253.

[258] *A Lloyd's Syndicate v X* [2011] EWHC 2487 (Comm); [2012] 1 Lloyd's Rep. 123; *Wheeldon Bros Waste Ltd v Millenium Insurance Co Ltd* [2017] EWHC 218 (TCC); [2017] B.L.R. 234 (defendant permitted to use expert even though expert had advised claimant on a potential claim against a third party).

[259] *A Company v X* [2020] EWHC 809 (TCC); [2020] B.L.R. 433.

Replace footnote 261 with:

33-33 [261] *Bank of Ireland UK Plc v Watts Group Plc* [2017] EWHC 16 (TCC) (bank's expert found not to be independent as bank provided most of his work). Where an expert from another jurisdiction is giving expert evidence as to the law in which he practices, but at the same time he is acting in related proceedings in his jurisdiction for the same client, he may find his independence questioned and the weight given to his evidence reduced, even if such relationship does not operate as a bar to him giving expert evidence: *Hulley Enterprises Ltd v The Russian Federation* [2023] EWHC 2704 (Comm) at [68]–[71].

(iii) Experts' reports

Contents of experts' reports

In the second paragaph, after ", or if those facts are not proved.", add new footnote 295a:

33-37 [295a] *Dana UK Axle Ltd v Freudenberg FST GmbH* [2021] EWHC 1413 (TCC); [2021] B.L.R. 500 (expert evidence excluded where reports failed to identify the documents, data and other information relied upon to reach conclusions); *R. (Good Law Project) v Secretary of State for Health and Social Care* [2021] EWHC 2595 (TCC).

Replace footnote 301 with:

[301] *Kennedy v Cordia (Services) LLP* [2016] UKSC 6; [2016] 1 W.L.R. 597 at [40]; *De Sena v Notaro* [2020] EWHC 1031 (Ch); [2021] 1 B.C.L.C. 366 at [151]; *Declan Coglan Music Ltd v UMG Recordings Inc* [2023] EWHC 4 (Ch).

Expert evidence falling below acceptable standards

Replace the second paragraph with:

33-39 An expert who verifies a document containing a false statement without an honest belief in its truth may be subject to contempt proceedings.[314] Furthermore, an expert may become personally liable for costs if he causes costs to be incurred through his evidence given in breach of his duties to the court.[315] An expert who fails to comply with the CPR or court order or causes excessive delay, may find the party who instructed him penalised in costs and even his evidence excluded.[316] In addition, an expert whose evidence falls significantly below an acceptable standard may find himself subject to disciplinary proceedings before his own professional body.[317] Formerly the position was that an expert could not be sued in respect of his report and evidence in court, and in general there is little room for an opposing party to sue the other side's expert.[317a] However, the Supreme Court, overturning earlier authority, has held that an expert may be sued for breach of a duty of care or tort by the party who had instructed him.[318] Further an expert's report may be made publicly available if the expert is called at trial and thus opens up the report to public scrutiny.[319] Experts are generally professionals and in particular fields are repeatedly instructed to provide expert reports and evidence. Thus their reputation is important to them and anyone considering using them. Judges are able to and indeed not infrequently do criticise experts who fail to give reliable and objective evidence, act like advocates for the party instructing them, or fail to comply with their duties.[320] Where there are opposing experts weaknesses and inaccuracies can easily be laid bare. The possibility of judicial criticism and public exposure is an important check on experts and their evidence. Fortunately standards of expert evidence has generally improved both in civil and criminal cases in recent years as the procedure rules, statements of truth and guidance reinforce the need for high standards and professionalism.

[314] CPR r.32.14; CPR Pt 35 PD para.3.3; *Guidance*, para.92(a)–(b) (contempt and perjury); *Liverpool Victoria Insurance Company Ltd v Zafar* [2019] EWCA Civ 392; [2019] 1 W.L.R. 2833 (6 months prison sentence for medical expert who had changed opinion at solicitor's suggestion found to be unduly lenient as conduct dishonest and reckless).

[315] *Phillips v Symes (A Bankrupt)* [2004] EWHC 2330 (Ch); [2005] 4 All E.R. 513.

[316] *Guidance*, para.91; *Balmoral Group Ltd v Borealis (UK) Ltd* [2006] EWHC 2531 (Comm), where indemnity costs awarded against party whose expert evidence was seriously deficient.

[317] *Guidance*, para.90; *Meadow v General Medical Council* [2006] EWCA Civ 1390; [2007] Q.B. 462 (disciplinary proceedings may be brought even where a judge has not referred the expert's conduct to his professional body); *Pearce v Ove Arup Partnership Ltd (Copying)* (2002) 25(2) I.P.D. 25011 (judge may refer expert's conduct to his professional body); *Hussein v William Hill Group* [2004] EWHC 208 (QB) (reference to General Medical Council). See also D. Dwyer, "Legal remedies for the negligent expert" (2008) 12 E. & P. 93; *Bux v General Medical Council* [2021] EWHC 762 (Admin) (doctor erased from medical register by GMC who had produced medico-legal reports on an industrial scale, failed to comply with CPR Pt 35 and did not disclose conflicts of interest).

[317a] In *WWRT Ltd v Tyshchenko* [2023] EWHC 2043 (Ch), Bacon J granted a final anti-suit injunction to restrain the defendants from suing the claimant's Ukraine law expert in the Ukraine courts. The aim of the proceedings was to put pressure on the expert to change the evidence being given in the English proceedings.

[318] *Jones v Kaney* [2011] UKSC 13; [2011] 2 W.L.R. 823; overruling *Stanton v Callaghan* [2000] Q.B. 75 CA. Where on appeal it is sought to adduce fresh evidence, one factor against allowing this is if the party has the possibility of redress against the experts: *Ridgeland Properties Ltd v Bristol City Council* [2011] EWCA Civ 649. See also *Guidance*, para.92(c); see also *Hersk & Co Solicitors v Lord Chancellor* [2018] EWHC 946 (QB) at [95]; *Radia v Marks* [2022] EWHC 145 (QB); [2022] Med. L.R. 210 at [61] (experts duty does not extend to protect a party from adverse credibility findings).

[319] *X (Children) (Morgan Intervening), Re* [2011] EWHC 1147 (Fam); [2012] 1 W.L.R. 182.

[320] *Bank of Ireland UK Plc v Watts Group Plc* [2017] EWHC 1667 (TCC) (expert not independent as bank provided most of his work and acted like an advocate); *Gee v DePuy International Ltd* [2018] EWHC 1208 (QB) (lacked impartiality and balance, acted like advocate).

(iv)   Court's general control of expert evidence

Introduction

At the end of the paragraph, add:

33-40   Expert evidence is also dealt with in the various courts guides.[322a]

[322a] *Chancery Guide* (2022), para.9; *King's Bench Guide* (2022), paras 10.40–10.55; *Commercial Court Guide* (2022), paras H2–H3 and Appendix 8; *Technology and Construction Court Guide* (2022), para.13; *Administrative Court Judicial Review Guide* (2022), para.23.2.

Replace paragraph with:

33-42   One issue which arises in practice is whether CPR r.35.4 applies in relation to expert evidence deployed for interlocutory applications whether in the form of a free-standing expert report or a report exhibited to a factual witness statement in support of or in opposition to an application. In principle permission should be required and sought to deploy any expert evidence at whatever stage in proceedings, at interlocutory stages just as much as for trial. CPR r.35.4 applies to all expert evidence and that follows the aim of placing all expert evidence under judicial control. The courts have not followed a consistent practice in respect of whether permission is required to rely on expert evidence for an interlocutory application. It is clear that a party may not circumvent CPR Pt 35 by exhibiting expert evidence to a factual witness statement.[331] Expert evidence is often deployed in security for costs applications, and in that context in some cases the court has permitted a party to rely on expert evidence without CPR Pt 35 being complied with.[332] This is not ideal. In one case it was held that permission was not required in relation to an expert report exhibited to a witness statement in opposition to a summary judgment and strike out application.[333] The admission of such evidence was explicable in that case, however it would have been preferable to have held permission as was required and granted permission. In jurisdiction challenges evidence on foreign law is routinely deployed and in that context permission of the court should be sought under CPR r.35.4.[334] In practice a party can file with his jurisdiction application or challenge an application for permission for expert evidence and request the court to deal with it initially. In many cases the court can deal with the application for permission to rely on expert evidence on paper in advance of the main hearing on the application.

[331] *New Media Distribution Company v Kagolovsky* [2018] EWHC 2742 (Ch).

[332] *Pipia v Bgeo Group Ltd* [2019] EWHC 325 (Comm) (expert evidence exhibited to factual witness statement admitted).

[333] *Ross v Attanta Ltd* [2021] EWHC 503 (Comm); [2021] P.N.L.R. 18.

[334] *Deutsche Bank AG v Commune Di Savona* [2018] EWCA Civ 1740; [2018] 4 W.L.R. 151 at [16]; *BB Energy (Gulf) DMCC v Al Moudi* [2018] EWHC 2595 (Comm) at [49]–[50]; *Gulf International Bank BSC v Aldwood* [2019] EWHC 1666 (QB) at [9]; [2020] 1 All E.R. (Comm) 334; *Chancery Guide* (2022), para.9.55.

Replace footnote 335 with:

33-43   [335] *Barings Plc v Coopers & Lybrand (No.2)* [2001] Lloyd's Rep. Bank 85; see also *LHS Holdings v Laporte* [2001] EWCA Civ 278; [2001] 2 All E.R. (Comm) 563; *Kennedy v Cordia (Services) Ltd* [2016] UKSC 6; [2016] 1 W.L.R. 597 at [44] (listing considerations governing the admissibility of expert evidence).

In the list, at the end of item (4)(a), add new footnote 342a:

342a *Declan Colgan Music Ltd v UMG Recordings Inc* [2023] EWHC 4 (Ch) at [150]–[164] (even if expert evidence may be of assistance, cost not proportionate).

Replace footnote 344 with:

344 *R. (Law Society) v Lord Chancellor* [2018] EWHC 2094 (Admin); [2019] 1 W.L.R. 1649 at [36].   **33-44**

Replace footnote 355 with:

355 *Calenti v North Middlesex NHS Trust* unreported 2 March 2001 QBD, Buckley J (permission refused   **33-46**
weeks before trial where no excuse for not seeking earlier); *Dew Pitchmastic Plc v Birse Construction Ltd*, 78 Con. L.R. 162 QBD (TCC); *Guntrip v Cheney Coaches Ltd* [2012] EWCA Civ 392 (permission for new expert refused at late stage, after experts had already served reports and met); *Charles Terrence Estates Ltd v The Cornwall Council* [2011] EWHC 1683 (QB) (application four weeks before trial refused); *ICI v Merit Merrell Technology Ltd* [2018] EWHC 1577 (TCC) (permission to rely on further expert report provided at trial refused); *TQ Delta LLC v ZyXEL* [2019] EWHC 1597 (Pat) (late application refused); *L'Oreal (UK) Ltd v Liqwd Inc* [2019] EWCA Civ 1943 (expert evidence after judgment refused); *Correia v Williams* [2022] EWHC 2824 (KB) (expert evidence application issued one week before trial, no good reason for delay and judge entitled to refuse application which had it been granted would have led to adjournment of trial to the prejudice of the respondent).

Replace footnote 362 with:

362 *King's Bench Guide* (2022), para.10.51; *Chancery Guide* (2022), para.9.20.*Hajigeorgiou v Vasilou*   **33-47**
[2005] EWCA Civ 236; [2005] 3 All E.R. 17 CA. This may even apply to a report obtained before proceedings were started, but whilst the parties were acting under a pre-action protocol: *Edwards-Tubb v JD Wetherspoon Plc* [2011] EWCA Civ 136; [2011] 1 W.L.R. 1373 CA. It does not always follow that such a condition will be imposed, especially where there is no question of expert shopping: *Vilca v Xstrata Ltd* [2017] EWHC 1582 (QB). See also *BMG (Mansfield) Ltd v Galliford Try Construction Ltd* [2013] EWHC 3183 (TCC), where the court permitted a party to change its architectural expert witness, finding that the circumstances did not point to the claimants expert shopping. While the claimants needed the court's permission to call an expert witness under CPR Pt 35, it was appropriate for them to call a different expert as their current expert had indicated (at the age of 70) that he no longer wished to continue with the instruction. *Allen Tod Architecture Ltd v Capita Property* [2016] EWHC 2171 (TCC) (no order for disclosure of documents such as notes of discussion with first expert in absence of evidence of expert shopping). In *Murray v Devenish* [2017] EWCA Civ 1016, the claimant had instructed three experts. The first he did not rely upon. The second he relied upon and disclosed. He sought permission to call a third expert, having lost confidence in the second expert. Permission was refused, largely because the application was too close to trial. The decision was upheld on appeal, but as the trial date had already been lost, the Court of Appeal granted permission but subject to a condition that the first expert's report be disclosed. *University of Manchester v John McAslan & Partner* [2022] EWHC 2750 (TCC); [2023] T.C.L.R. 2; *Avantage (Cheshire) Ltd v GB Building Solutions Ltd* [2023] EWHC 802 (TCC) at [17] (expert ill, new expert permitted without imposing condition that reports of first expert be disclosed, but source material and notes ordered to be disclosed on basis contained primary evidence otherwise not available. However in respect of substituting another expert, where had lost confidence in initial expert, condition that earlier expert's report be disclosed).

Procedure at trial

At the end of the third paragraph, after "… where he may require the most assistance.", add:

It also enables each expert to respond immediately to the other on those issues   **33-54**
which the court considers to be the most important and contentious.437a

437a *Royal Mail Group Ltd v DAF Trucks Ltd* [2023] CAT 6; [2023] 5 C.M.L.R. 6 at [234].

(v) Restriction and control of expert evidence

Limitation of the scope of disputes relating to expert evidence

Discussions

Replace footnote 471 with:

33-58 [471] *BDW Trading Ltd v Integral Geotechnique (Wales) Ltd* [2018] EWHC 1915 (Ch); [2018] P.N.L.R. 34 at [16]–[21]; *Andrews v Kronospan Ltd* [2022] EWHC 479 (QB) (permission to rely on expert's evidence revoked where inappropriate contact with solicitors); *Pickett v Balkind* [2022] EWHC 2226 (TCC); [2022] 4 W.L.R. 88.

(vi) Acceptance of expert evidence at trial

Replace footnote 514 with:

33-66 [514] *Griffiths v TUI UK Ltd* [2021] EWCA Civ 1442; *Volpi v Volpi* [2022] EWCA Civ 464; [2022] 4 W.L.R. 48 at [4].

7. EXPERT EVIDENCE AS TO COMPETENCY, RELIABILITY AND CREDIT

Replace the eighth paragraph with:

33-78 Though the expert must be "skilled", by special study or experience, the fact that he has not acquired his knowledge professionally goes merely to weight and not to admissibility.[578] Likewise the fact that the proponent of a particular form of expertise adopts an approach which would be unacceptable to the majority of experts in that field does not mean that he is incapable of giving expert evidence about the topic, provided he can demonstrate that his approach is based on rational considerations, backed up by adequate intelligence, study and relevant formal qualifications.[579] However merely because one is qualified as an accountant or lawyer does not mean the person is sufficiently experienced or competent to be an expert in a particular field that he has not specialised or practiced in.[580] Further, to have studied a subject academically does not necessarily mean that a person is sufficiently qualified to give expert evidence.[581] Equally, one can acquire expert knowledge in a particular sphere through repeated contact with it in the course of one's work, notwithstanding that the expertise is derived from experience and not from formal training.[582] Police officers habitually give evidence relating to matters about which they have acquired in depth knowledge in the course of their duties, such as the values of prohibited drugs and the paraphernalia associated with using or with dealing with drugs.[583] Police officers can give expert evidence as to the practices of gangs as well.[584] Police officers with specialist training in the investigation and reconstruction of road traffic accidents, routinely give evidence in both criminal and civil trials. A person can be so involved with a particular transaction that expertise is acquired in relation to it, as where a policeman studied a video tape about 40 times, examining it frame by frame and replaying it as often as he needed to do so for the purpose of giving evidence to the jury that the persons seen on the video were those accused of the offences recorded there.[585] This has been called making the witness an "ad hoc expert".[586] Where a police officer is called as an expert, whether by training or experience or both, he comes under the same duties to the court as any other expert. Compliance with these duties can be difficult for a police officer who is effectively combining the duties of active investigator and those of independent expert.[587] As to who are experts in science, art, foreign law, etc. see paras 33-88 to 33-105.

578 *R. v Silverlock* [1894] 2 Q.B. 766; *R. v Somers* [1963] 3 All E.R. 808; *McCaughan v Secretary of State for Northern Ireland* [2009] N.I.Q.B. 65 at [15]–[21] (citing this passage in the 16th edition of Phipson, and finding a loss adjuster to be a suitable expert); and cf. *R. v Davies* [1962] 3 All E.R. 97.

579 *R. v Robb* (1991) 93 Cr. App. R. 161 CA.

580 *De Sena v Notario* [2020] EWHC 1031 (Ch) at [154]–[157] (forensic account in sufficient experience in demergers). The expert must have the relevant expertise prior to being engaged as the expert in the case, as opposed to acquiring such expertise as part of his engagement for the proceedings: *Sycurio Ltd v PCI-Pal Plc* [2023] EWHC 2361 (Pat) at [11]–[12].

581 *R. v Brecani* [2021] EWCA Crim 731; [2021] 2 Cr. App. R 12 at [70] (expert had studied slavery but insufficient knowledge of modern slavery).

582 *R. v Oakley* [1979] R.T.R. 417 CA; *R. v Murphy* (1980) 71 Cr. App. R. 33 CA. cf. *Nickisson v R.* [1963] W.A.R. 114; *R. v Davies* [1962] 3 All E.R. 97; *R. v Brecani* [2021] EWCA Crim 731; [2021] 2 Cr. App. R. 12 at [52]–[54] (case workers in the Single Competent Authority established by Home Office to consider whether persons are victims of slavery are not experts).

583 *R. v Hill* (1992) 96 Cr. App. R. 456 CA; *R. v Jeffries* [1997] Crim. L.R. 819 CA (though the detective constable in this latter case was not entitled to give evidence that lists of figures written on pieces of paper found at the accused's address represented records of drug transactions); *R. v Hodges* [2003] EWCA Crim 290; [2003] 2 Cr. App. R. 15 (police officer's expert evidence on usual method of supply and value of heroin; whether amount found would have been for personal use); *Myers v The Queen (Bermuda)* [2015] UKPC 40; [2016] A.C. 314 at [57], [61].

584 *Myers v The Queen (Bermuda)* [2015] UKPC 40; [2016] A.C. 314 at [57]; A. Ward and S. Fouladvand, "Bodies of Knowledge and Robes of Expertise: Expert Evidence about Drugs, Gangs and Human Trafficking" [2021] Criminal Law Review 442–460; *R. v Heslop* [2022] EWCA Crim 897; [2022] 2 Cr. App. R. 20 (police officer evidence as to how gangs operated and gang-related activity and culture).

585 *R. v Clare and Peach* [1995] 2 Cr. App. R. 333 CA; *Att.-Gen.'s Reference (No.2 of 2002)* [2002] EWCA Crim 2373; [2003] 1 Cr. App. R. 21.

586 See Munday, "Videotape Evidence and the Advent of the Expert ad hoc" (1995) 159 J.P. 547.

587 *Myers v The Queen (Bermuda)* [2015] UKPC 40; [2016] AC 314 at [60].

10.   SUBJECTS OF EXPERT EVIDENCE

(b)   Science and art

Replace footnote 669 with:

669 *R. v George (Dwaine)* [2014] EWCA Crim 2507; [2015] 1 Cr. App. R. 15 CA; *Hewey v The Queen (Bermuda)* [2022] UKPC 12.   **33-88**

(c)   Trade: market value: "materiality" in policies, etc.

At the end of the paragraph add:

In *Fenty v Arcadia Group Brands Ltd*[704a] Birss J summaried the case law and   **33-89**
principles in relation to trade evidence:

(1)   Trade witnesses may give evidence of "the circumstances of the trade" and "nature and circumstances of [the] market", even including expressions of opinion as to the likely behaviour of market participants, without this amounting to expert evidence under CPR Part 35.[704b]

(2)   This is so even though such witnesses will explain and rely on their experience in the trade "in order to justify their evidence and add credibility to it".[704c]

(3)   Deciding whether evidence given by a trade witness amounts to expert

evidence "cannot be done" without close examination of the evidence itself in the context of the issues in the proceedings (and in that case, Birss J had the benefit of the statements already being in evidence).[704d]

In *Kent v Apple Inc*[704e] and *Coll v Alphabet Inc*[704f] permission was granted to adduce expert evidence from an App industry expert.

[704a] *Fenty v Arcadia Group Brands Ltd* [2013] EWHC 1945 (Ch); [2013] Bus. L.R. 1165.

[704b] See *Fenty v Arcadia Group Brands Ltd* [2013] EWHC 1945 (Ch); [2013] Bus. L.R. 1165 at [35] and [39]–[40].

[704c] See *Fenty v Arcadia Group Brands Ltd* [2013] EWHC 1945 (Ch); [2013] Bus. L.R. 1165 at [35].

[704d] See *Fenty v Arcadia Group Brands Ltd* [2013] EWHC 1945 (Ch); [2013] Bus. L.R. 1165 at [40] and following.

[704e] *Kent v Apple Inc* [2023] CAT 22.

[704f] *Coll v Alphabet Inc* [2023] CAT 47.

(f)   Foreign law

Replace footnote 728 with:

33-95   [728] *King v Reinsurance Co* [2005] EWCA Civ 235; [2005] 1 Lloyd's Rep. 655 at [68]. *Kyrgyz Republic v Stans Energy Corp* [2017] EWHC 2539 (Comm) at [44]–[65]; *Alhamrani v Alhamrani* [2014] UKPC 37 at [18]–[20]; *Deutsche Bank AG v Commune Di Savona* [2018] EWCA Civ 1740; [2018] 4 W.L.R. 151 at [15] (construction of jurisdiction clause in contract); *BNP Paribas SA v Trattamento Rifiuti Metropolitani SpA* [2019] EWCA Civ 768; [2019] 2 Lloyd's Rep. 1 at [45]–[49]; *National Iranian Oil Company v Crescent Petroleum Co International Ltd* [2023] EWCA Civ 826 at [77]–[78].

At the end of the paragraph, after ", was not specially conversant with such law.[757]*", add:*

33-98   It is not unusual for the purposes of interlocutory applications for a party to rely on expert evidence of a foreign lawyer who is acting for the same party in related proceedings in the jurisdiction of such expert. However at least when it comes to trial, the expert's independence may be questioned in cross examination and the court may decide to give less weight to such evidence.[757a]

[757a] *Hulley Enterprises Ltd v The Russian Federation* [2023] EWHC 2704 (Comm) at [68]–[71].

After the first paragraph, add new paragraph:

33-99   Based on a review of the authorities, Calver J distilled the following principles as to the proper approach as to expert evidence of foreign law:[759a]

(1)   The court is not entitled to construe a foreign code itself; it is the function of the expert witness to interpret its legal effect.

(2)   The task for the English court is to evaluate the expert evidence of foreign law and to predict the likely decision of the highest court in the relevant foreign system of law, rather than imposing his/her personal views as to what the foreign law should be, or allowing the expert to press upon the English judge his personal views of what the foreign law might be.

(3)   This court may decide what conclusion a foreign court would reach on a developing area of law but it is not, however, seeking to make findings which go beyond the present state of foreign law and to anticipate a rational development of it.

(4)   The more senior the court which gives the relevant court decision, or the greater the number of foreign court decisions to a particular effect, the more difficult it will be for the English court to conclude that, nonetheless, those decisions do not reflect the law of the relevant jurisdiction.

(5) If there is a clear decision of the highest foreign court on the issue of foreign law, other evidence will carry little weight against it. That is generally so even if the decisions are unworkable in commercial practice or their reasoning illogical or inconsistent. When it falls to an English court to ascertain the content of foreign law, that means the law with whatever imperfections, policy-orientated determinations and impracticalities it manifests.

[759a] *Suppipat v Narongdej* [2023] EWHC 1988 (Comm) at [908].

12. Opinions of Non-experts

(a) Introduction

At the end of the final paragraph, after "… opinion of non-experts accordingly remains inadmissible.", add new footnote 824a:

[824a] The paragraph was cited with approval in *D (A Child), Re (Abduction: Child's Objections: Representation of Child Party) (Rev1)* [2023] EWCA Civ 1047. **33-112**

CHAPTER 34

STATISTICAL AND SURVEY EVIDENCE

2. CLASSICAL STATISTICS

(a) Data collection

(i) Study design

At the end of the first paragraph, after ", and can be misleading.", add new footnote 14a:

34-04   [14a] *Kerseviciene v Quadri* [2022] EWHC 2951 (KB) provides a good illustration of the difficulties involved in assessing the utility of figures without a comparator: the case involved a defendant seeking to support a case that several road traffic personal injury claims were dishonest by proving that the claimants were represented by a specific firm of solicitors that had represented claimants in 372 other similar claims and that in a significant proportion of these the claimants were alleged to have suffered psychological injuries with a recovery period (with treatment) in excess of two years; Freedman J upheld the decision that the defendant should not be debarred from relying on the witness statement, despite the lack of evidence as to the general prevalence of such injuries in road accidents, noting that the figures might cohere with other evidence that emerged in the case, such as evidence of a particular method of inflating claims.

(b) Drawing inferences

(i) Reference classes and base rates

Replace the second paragraph with:

34-11   If we want to know the likelihood that it was the defendant's trainers, rather than anyone else's, that had made marks found at a crime scene, the likelihood produced will vary depending on whether we compare the defendant's shoe against a database made up of shoe prints that had come into forensic science laboratories, particularly from crime scenes, or a database consisting of frequencies of distribution of all shoes by manufacturers.[24] The former database will be representative of the sort of shoes worn by people commonly associated with crime scenes, while the latter database is representative of the population as a whole, most of whom are not associated with crime scenes. The choice of reference class can therefore significantly affect the calculation of the likelihood ratio.[25]

[24] *R. v T* [2010] EWCA Crim 2439; [2011] 1 Cr. App. R. 85, particularly at [42]–[43]. The current databases appear to be the "National Footwear database" and the "National Footwear Reference Collection".

[25] In *R. v T* [2010] EWCA Crim 2439, the Bayesian likelihood ratio was derived from the probability that the marks discovered at the scene would have been observed if the trainers owned by the appellant had made the marks, divided by the probability that the marks would have been observed if those trainers had not made the marks. The case involved marks made by a size 11 Nike trainer (or a fake version) produced since 1995; clearly the second probability (and hence the likelihood ratio) would be different depending on whether we used a reference class of "all sports shoes produced since 1995" or "all sports shoes produced in adult male sizes since 1995" or "all sports shoes in adult male sizes associated with crime scenes". See para.34-40.

3.   PROBABILITY AND PROOF

(d)   Calculations of future loss and support

Replace footnote 106 with:

[106] *Actuarial Tables with Explanatory Notes for Use in Personal Injury and Fatal Accident Cases*, 8th edn (updated) (Government Actuary's Department, 2020 (updated August 2022), *https://www.gov.uk/government/publications/ogden-tables-actuarial-compensation-tables-for-injury-and-death* [Accessed 1 August 2023], "Explanatory Notes to the Eighth Edition" paras [7]–[8] (explaining mortality assumptions); para.121 (an example of a situation where specialist actuarial advice may be required); paras [131]–[133] (an example of use of a simplified approach).

34-37

Replace footnote 107 with:

[107] The "Duxbury tables" are found in a publication that is revised annually and published on behalf of the Family Law Bar Association: *At A Glance 2023-2024: Essential Court Tables for Financial Remedies* (London: Class Legal, 2023). In *Tattersall v Tattersall* [2018] EWCA Civ 1978; [2019] 1 F.L.R. 470 at [42], the Court of Appeal held that in calculating an appropriate financial remedy in a family case a judge ought to use the Duxbury tables rather than the Ogden tables, but that it would not be an error of law to use the latter: "Although I would expect judges typically to use Duxbury, a judge can decide to use a method of calculation other than Duxbury", per Moylan LJ. One important difference, is the assumption that the Duxbury Tables make as to income yield and capital growth: for a judicial discussion of some of the assumptions see *JL v SL (No.3)* [2015] EWHC 555 (Fam); [2015] 2 F.L.R. 1220. See also *ND (by her litigation friend KW) v GD* [2021] EWFC 53 at [24]–[29] for a judicial caution (from Peel J) against commissioning expert financial advisors to make calculations using assumptions other than those in the Duxbury model.

34-38

5.   SURVEY EVIDENCE

(b)   Survey methodology

After the third paragraph, add new paragraph:

In *Lidl Great Britain Ltd v Tesco Stores Ltd*[150a] Joanna Smith J allowed a claimant to adduce survey evidence despite the fact that prior permission to conduct the survey had not been obtained and no pilot survey had been conducted. It was significant that the cost of producing the survey in the case was relatively modest (£7,750), because the questions concerned could be asked online, rather than requiring street interviews; moreover, there was no significant dispute as to the value of conducting a survey to investigate the issue whether a mark was regarded by "grocery shoppers" as designating the origin of goods. Joanna Smith J opined that neither the absence of prior permission nor the absence of any pilot was a reason

34-45

in itself for excluding evidence derived from a survey.[150b] In the circumstances, the points raised against the way in which the survey questions were phrased were marginal and did not undermine the survey's extrinsic value. Moreover, she held that when considering the important question of whether the value of the survey would be sufficient to justify its cost (or, the cost disproportionate to any likely benefit), it was not appropriate to include the costs of the application to adduce the evidence and it would be appropriate to consider the cost—if the survey was excluded—of generating alternative evidence to address the same point.[150c]

[150a] *Lidl Great Britain Ltd v Tesco Stores Ltd* [2022] EWHC 1434 (Ch); [2022] E.T.M.R. 39. The Court of Appeal allowed an appeal against a different aspect of the judgement: [2022] EWCA Civ 1433; [2023] E.T.M.R. 6. The claimants succeeded at trial, with the survey evidence treated as providing strong support for the proposition that the claimant's wordless mark had acquired the capacity to demonstrate exclusive origin: [2023] EWHC 873 (Ch) at [211].

[150b] *Lidl Great Britain Ltd v Tesco Stores Ltd* [2022] EWHC 1434 (Ch); [2022] E.T.M.R. 39 at [152].

[150c] *Lidl Great Britain Ltd v Tesco Stores Ltd* [2022] EWHC 1434 (Ch); [2022] E.T.M.R. 39 at [203].

(c)   The value of survey evidence

Replace footnote 163 with:

34-48   [163] Competition and Markets Authority, "Good practice in the design and presentation of customer survey evidence in merger cases" (CMA78) (revised, May 2018) *https://www.gov.uk/government/publ ications/mergers-consumer-survey-evidence-design-and-presentation/good-practice-in-the-design-an d-presentation-of-customer-survey-evidence-in-merger-cases* [Accessed 9 August 2023].

CHAPTER 35

RESTRICTIONS ON THE RIGHT TO SILENCE

3. PRE-TRIAL SILENCE

Replace footnote 17 with: "See Mirfield, *Silence, Confessions and Improper Evidence* (London: Clarendon, 1997), 246; Pattenden [1995] Crim. L.R. 602; R. Leng (2001) 5 E. & P. 240; Dennis [2002] Crim. L.R. 25. For a critical evaluation of the development of English law on drawing adverse inferences from silence at the investigative stage see E. Cape and M. Hardcastle, "Recent cases on inferences from 'silence': what is left of the right to silence?" [2022] Crim. L.R. 796."

(a) Reliance upon a fact

After the third paragraph, add new paragraph:

The approach adopted in *Green* was endorsed and further developed in the **35-08** important Court of Appeal decision of *R. v Harewood*.[79a] After their arrest both appellants had submitted prepared statements and gave "no comment" interviews. At their trial a s.34 direction was given in relation to various unmentioned facts despite the appellants' submission that the prosecution had failed to establish that they had ever been asked specific questions, and therefore that they had not failed to answer questions, about these matters. No evidence had been adduced as to what questions were posed during their interviews. Nevertheless, Popplewell LJ concluded at [40]–[41]:

"The jury are entitled to infer that if the interviews lasted a considerable period, the questions are likely to have descended to a commensurate level of detail. The jury are entitled to infer that if an accused has provided a prepared statement, such questions will at least in part have been directed to the contents of that statement. This is so even if, as in this case, the jury have not had identified for them in the course of cross-examination the specific questioning which the Crown says gave rise to the particular opportunity to mention the facts. ... [N]or was it necessary to establish that the unmentioned facts which were

[141]

included in the adverse inference direction were central to the account at trial of either Harewood or Rehman. The question was solely whether a jury could properly conclude that in all the circumstances each applicant could reasonably have been expected to mention the facts in question".

[79a] *R. v Harewood* [2021] EWCA Crim 1936; [2022] Crim. L.R. 767.

6.   SCOPE OF SECTION 35

Replace footnote 149 with: "Criminal Justice and Public Order Act 1994 s.35 applies only to a trial for a criminal offence and does not apply to civil contempt: *Royal & Sun Alliance Insurance Plc v Maharouf Fahed* [2015] EWHC 1092 (QB); *Wildin v Forest of Dean DC* [2021] EWCA Civ 1610."

7.   "PROPER" INFERENCES OF GUILT

After the second paragraph, add new paragraph:

35-20   In *R. v Hamer*[176a] the trial judge, after consulting with counsel, gave an unusual s.35 direction which identified particular topics on which the defendant might have been cross-examined if he had given evidence. In contrast to s.34, that approach is not referred to in the Crown Court Compendium, but the Court of Appeal confirmed that there was no absolute prohibition on the judge doing so; it depended on the facts of the particular case. Here the judge felt that the extensive common ground on the facts made it was appropriate to identify the relatively narrow range of issues in relation to which any question of drawing an adverse inference might arise.

[176a] *R. v Hamer* [2021] EWCA Crim 861.

CHAPTER 36

CONFESSIONS

1.   MEANING OF CONFESSION

Replace the second paragraph with:

For the purposes of the Police and Criminal Evidence Act 1984 (PACE) "confession" includes "any statement wholly or partly adverse to the person who made it,   **36-01** whether made to a person in authority or not and whether made in words or otherwise".[5] Whether a statement amounts to a confession must be considered, not in the abstract, but in the light of what is in issue in any particular case. This exercise may reveal that rather than being adverse, a statement is wholly exculpatory.[5a] Whether a statement has to be adverse at the time it was made in order to qualify as a confession has been the subject of recent debate. The Court of Appeal,[6] which was later reversed, stated that the test was to be applied at the time when the statement was tendered in evidence.[7] It adopted a broad view of self-incrimination[8] which was influenced by the decision of the European Court of Human Rights in *Saunders v United Kingdom*[9] that art.6 extended to a statement obtained under compulsion which had become adverse by the time it was sought to use it in evidence. The House of Lords[10] concluded that there was no need to adopt a strained interpretation of s.82(1), given that the s.78 discretion could be used to exclude a purely exculpatory statement obtained by oppression. Moreover, the Court of Appeal's reliance upon Saunders had been misplaced.

[5] PACE s.82(1). For an example of conduct as an admission, see *Preece v Parry* [1983] Crim. L.R. 170.

[5a] *R. v Beqa* [2022] EWCA Crim 1661 at [16].

[6] sub nom. *R. v Z* [2003] EWCA Crim 191; [2003] 2 Cr. App. R. 12.

[7] Disapproving *R. v Sat-Bhambra* (1989) 88 Cr. App. R. 55 in which the view was expressed, in obiter, that statements which are apparently exculpatory at the time they are made are not "wholly or partly" adverse to the person who made it under s.82(1) of the Act. In *Sat-Bhambra* it was observed that the words of s.82(1) did seem prima facie to be speaking of statements adverse on the face of them. See also *R. v Park* (1994) Cr. App. R. 270 at 274.

[8] This is consistent with the views expressed by the United States Supreme Court in *Miranda v Arizona* (1966) 384 U.S. 436, 477; and the Supreme Court of Canada in *Piché v R.* [1971] 1 S.C.R. 23.

[9] *Saunders v United Kingdom* (1997) 23 E.H.R.R. 313 at [71].

[10] *R. v Hasan* [2005] UKHL 22; [2005] 2 W.L.R. 709, their lordships agreeing with the views expressed by Lord Steyn at [43] et seq.

4. ADMISSIBILITY BEFORE THE POLICE AND CRIMINAL EVIDENCE ACT 1984

Replace the fourth paragraph with:

36-04 A less technical version of the voluntariness test still operates in Ireland,[30] Australia,[31] New Zealand[32] and some other Commonwealth countries.[33] It was recently reviewed by the Supreme Court of Canada in *R. v Tessier*[33a] which, in a 7-2 split decision, held that the absence of a police caution, although relevant, was not determinative of the existence of voluntariness. If the person being questioned was a suspect, the absence of a police caution was prima facie evidence of an unfair denial of the choice to speak to the police. This placed a heavy burden on the Crown but if it could "prove that the suspect maintained their ability to exercise a free choice because there were no signs of threats or inducements, oppression, lack of an operating mind or police trickery, that will be sufficient to discharge the Crown's burden that the statement was voluntary".[33b] The common law retains some significance in England with old convictions based on earlier police practices being referred to the Criminal Cases Review Committee. In *R. v Steel*,[34] which applied *R. v King*,[35] the appellant adduced new evidence of his vulnerability to suggestion by reason of low intelligence which raised doubts as to the voluntariness of his confession.

[30] *The People v Doyle* [2017] IESC 1 at [32].

[31] *Sinclair v R.* (1947) 73 C.L.R. 316; *McDermott v R.* (1948) 76 C.L.R. 501; *Murphy v R.* (1989) 167 C.L.R. 94.

[32] *R. v Cooney* [1994] 1 N.Z.L.R. 38.

[33] Such as Seychelles: *Roble v Republic* [2015] SCCA 24; [2016] 1 LRC 1 at [59]; Bahamas: *McPhee v R* [2016] UKPC 29 and Trinidad and Tobago: *Pitman v State* [2017] 3 LRC 407; [2017] UKPC 6 at [20].

[33a] *R. v Tessier* 2022 SCC 35.

[33b] *R. v Tessier* 2022 SCC 35 at [89] per Kasirer J for the majority.

[34] *R. v Steel* [2003] EWCA Crim 1640.

[35] *R. v King* [2002] 2 Cr. App. R. 391.

5. ADMISSIBILITY UNDER THE POLICE AND CRIMINAL EVIDENCE ACT 1984 SECTION 76

After "… (whether or not amounting to", replace "torture," with:
torture),   **36-06**

15. CONFESSIONS OF CO-DEFENDANTS AND OTHERS

After the fourth paragraph, add new paragraph:
A confession which has been ruled to be admissible under s.76A must still, pursu- **36-28**
ant to s.133 of the Criminal Justice Act 2003, be laid before the jury. In *R. v Dirie*[238a]
a written confession was obtained by a co-accused in unusual circumstances. O
produced a signed "defence case statement" containing three admissions that were
helpful to his case at a *voir dire* and gave evidence that during the trial, while he
was in the custody area at court, his co-accused, D, had handed the document to
him. D did not testify and in the absence of any other witness who could produce
the document, the trial judge ruled that D's confession could not go before the jury
unless O himself was willing to go into the witness box, which he was not. The
Court of Appeal confirmed that this was correct and said that there was no unfairness in this situation.

[238a] *R. v Dirie* [2023] EWCA Crim 341.

21. LIES OF THE ACCUSED

Replace footnote 319 with:

[319] i.e. a lie concerning a something not directly relevant to the issue in the case. On this point see *R. v* **36-38**
Harron [1996] 2 Cr. App. R. 457; *R. v Burge & Pegg* [1996] 1 Cr. App. R. 163; (1995) 139 S.J.L.B. 99;
R. v Yousaf [2009] EWCA Crim 435 at [22]; *R. v Murray* [2016] EWCA Crim 1051; *R. v Pierre* [2023]
UKPC 15 (Bahamas); and the New Zealand case of *R. v Dehar* [1969] N.Z.L.R. 763 at 765. Cases held
not to fall within the so-called *Dehar* exception include *R. v Wood* [1995] Crim. L.R. 154; *R. v Gordon*
[1995] Crim. L.R. 306; *R. v Holman* [1995] Crim. L.R. 80; *R. v Genus* [1996] Crim. L.R. 502; and *R. v*
Rodrigues [2001] EWCA Crim 444.

Replace footnote 328 with:

[328] *R. v RG* [2015] EWCA Crim 715; *R. v Taskaya* [2017] EWCA Crim 632; *R. v Spottiswood* [2019]
EWCA Crim 949; *R. v Wainwright* [2021] EWCA Crim 122; *R. v Dabycharun* [2021] EWCA Crim
1923; [2022] R.T.R. 25 at [35].

CHAPTER 37

STATEMENTS IN THE PRESENCE, AND DOCUMENTS IN THE POSSESSION, OF A PARTY

2. STATEMENTS

(a) Reply, denial, silence

Replace the second paragraph with:

37-07   Clearly, there is some conflict as to whether *Hall* or *Christie* is to be preferred, and as to what constitutes "even terms". The Court of Appeal asserts on the one hand that the presence of a solicitor puts a man accused of crime in a police station on equal terms with an experienced police officer interrogating him. On the other hand, the Privy Council points to the fact in *Parkes* that the accusation was not made "by or in the presence of a police officer or any other person in authority or charged with the investigation of crime" when holding that the mother was on equal terms with the appellant. In *R. v Horne*,[31] the victim made a spontaneous accusation in the presence of the defendant and the police but not a solicitor. The trial judge suggested that some reply could have been expected but did not give the jury further directions. This failure was not fatal as the prosecution's case was strong and the Court of Appeal did not decide whether the parties were on equal terms. In *Western Australia v Stanton*[31a] the court endorsed the principles on the admissibility of implied admissions set out in *Western Australia v McBride*,[31b] including the notion of speaking on "even terms" set out in *R. v Mitchell* and *Parkes v R*.[31c]

[31] *R. v Horne* [1990] Crim. L.R. 188.

[31a] *Western Australia v Stanton* [2023] WADC 19 at [45].

[31b] *Western Australia v McBride* [2015] WASC 275.

[31c] *R. v Mitchell* (1892) 17 Cox C.C. 508; and *Parkes v R.* [1976] 1 W.L.R. 1251; (1977) 64 Cr. App. R. 25. See also *Stern v R.* [2023] VSCA 57.

CHAPTER 38

AGENCY, PARTNERSHIP, COMPANIES, COMMON PURPOSE,
ACTING IN A CAPACITY

2. PARTNERS, TRUSTEES, EXECUTORS

(a) Partners

Replace footnote 30 with:

[30] See *Lindley & Banks on Partnership*, 20th edn (London: Sweet & Maxwell, 2020), Ch.12. See now **38-05**
Lindley & Banks on Partnership, 21st edn (London: Sweet & Maxwell, 2022).

3. CORPORATIONS

(a) Criminal liability

Replace footnote 44 with: "See generally the Law Commission's Discussion
Paper on *Corporate Criminal Liability* (June 2021)*https://s3-eu-west-2.amazona
ws.com/lawcom-prod-storage-11jsxou24uy7q/uploads/2021/06/Corporate-Crimi
nal-Liability-Discussion-Paper.pdf* [Accessed 11 October 2021]. See now the
Law Commission's Options Paper on *Corporate Criminal Liability* (June 2022),
available at *https://s3-eu-west-2.amazonaws.com/lawcom-prod-storage-11jsxou
24uy7q/uploads/2022/06/Corporate-Criminal-Liability-Options-Paper_LC.pdf*."

Replace footnote 46 with:

[46] See Smith, Hogan, and Ormerod's *Criminal Law*, 15th edn (Oxford: Oxford University Press, 2018), **38-08**
p.601. See now Smith, Hogan and Ormerod's *Criminal Law*, 16th edn (Oxford: Oxford University Press,
2021), p.633.

Replace footnote 56 with:

[56] *Meridian Global Funds v Management Asia Ltd* [1995] 2 A.C. 500 at 507. In the civil case of *Jetivia* **38-09**
SA v Bilta (UK) Ltd (in liquidation) [2015] UKSC 23; [2016] A.C. 1 the Supreme Court adopted and
applied the attribution rules devised by Lord Hoffmann in the context of a discussion of the scope of
the illegality defence. The principles established in *Jetivia SA Bilta* [2015] UKSC 23; [2016] A.C. 1 were
again applied by the Supreme Court in *Crown Prosecution Service v Aquila Advisory Ltd* [2021] UKSC
49; [2021] 1 W.L.R. 5666, in which it declined to create an exception to the rules of attribution where

[147]

the director's conduct in breach of fiduciary duty was intended to or did in fact secure a financial benefit to the company. This unwarranted distinction would undermine the clarity and simplicity of the law in relation to attribution. Therefore, the dishonest state of mind of a director could not be attributed to the company so as to afford an illegality defence to the director against company's claim for breach of fiduciary duty.

CHAPTER 39

JUDICIAL DISCRETION TO ADMIT OR EXCLUDE EVIDENCE

4. POLICE AND CRIMINAL EVIDENCE ACT 1984 s.78

(c) The meaning of s.78(1)

Replace the first paragraph with:

In short, there is no definitive authority on the scope of s.78. However, there are **39-13** three stages in its application. First, the court must have regard to "all the circumstances, including the circumstances in which the evidence was obtained". Second, the court must consider whether it appears that the admission of the evidence "would have such an adverse effect on the fairness of the proceedings that the court ought not to admit it". Third, if the court reaches that conclusion, it "may" exclude the evidence. On a strict reading of the wording of the section, the second stage involves the making of a judgment rather than the exercise of a discretion, while the third stage involves the exercise of the court's discretion. However, the words "the court ought not to admit it" import a discretionary flavour into the second stage of the exercise.[51] In any event, the court would hardly reach the conclusion that it ought not to admit the evidence and then exercise its discretion to admit it.[52] In *R. v Chalkley and Jeffries*,[53] the Court of Appeal expressed the view that strictly a decision under s.78(1) is not the exercise of a discretion. It is said that this position was reinforced by the introduction of the Human Rights Act 1998. The right to a fair trial is enshrined in art.6 of the European Convention on Human Rights. Section 6(1) of the Human Rights Act 1998 makes it unlawful for any public authority (which includes the court[53a]) to act in a way which is incompatible with

[149]

a convention right. In circumstances, therefore, where there would be an unfair trial that is unlawful pursuant to s.6(1) of the Human Rights Act 1998, it may not be appropriate to refer to there being a "discretion" since it is not possible, in law, to admit evidence which would render a trial unfair.[53b]

[51] In *R. v Samuel* [1988] Q.B. 615; (1988) 87 Cr. App. R. 232 at 245, the Court of Appeal treated the matter as one of discretion.

[52] In *R. v Hughes* [1988] Crim. L.R. 519, the Court of Appeal concentrated entirely on the first two stages. cf. *R. v O'Leary* (1988) 87 Cr. App. R. 387 at 391; [1988] Crim. L.R. 827.

[53] *R. v Chalkley and Jeffries* [1998] Q.B. 848; [1998] 2 Cr. App. R. 79 at 105. See also *R. v Twigg (Christopher)* [2019] EWCA Crim 1553; [2019] 1 W.L.R. 6533 at [42].

[53a] Human Rights Act 1998 s.6(3)(a).

[53b] *R. v Twigg (Christopher)* [2019] EWCA Crim 1553; [2019] 1 W.L.R. 6533 at [43]. See also *R. v LT* [2019] EWCA Crim 58; [2019] 4 W.L.R. 51 at [36], where the Court of Appeal acknowledged the debate as to whether the court is exercising a discretion or a judgment but stated:

"If it is a *discretion* it is a broad discretion, and if it is a judgement it is the judgement which the Court of Appeal recognises is primarily a matter for the judge in the Crown Court. In either case, this court is reluctant to interfere with such decisions in relation to these matters."

10. OTHER ASPECTS OF S.78

(b) Procedure

In the second paragraph, after "… just before the evidence is to be called.", add new footnote 149a:

39-23 [149a] Ultimately, the trial judge has a discretion as to the procedure to be adopted in dealing with the issue: see, for example, *R. v Wright (Carlos)* [2022] EWCA Crim 1722 at [14]–[15].

(d) Burden of proof

Replace footnote 164 with:

39-25 [164] *R. v Governor of Brixton Prison, Ex p. Saifi* [2001] 1 W.L.R. 1134; *R. v Shinn (Paul)* [2023] EWCA Crim 493 at [52].

(i) Other examples

Replace footnote 207 with:

39-30 [207] *R. (Ibrahim) v Crown Prosecution Service* [2016] EWHC 1750 (Admin).

CHAPTER 40

AUTHORSHIP AND EXECUTION, ATTESTATION, ANCIENT DOCUMENTS, CONNECTED AND INCORPORATED DOCUMENTS, ALTERATIONS AND BLANKS, REGISTRATION, STAMPS, ETC.

TABLE OF CONTENTS

(c)   PRESUMPTION IN FAVOUR OF AUTHENTICITY

Replace paragraph with:

Under CPR r.32.19(1), a party to civil litigation "shall be deemed to admit the   **40-04**
authenticity of a document disclosed to him under Pt 31 of the Rules (disclosure
and inspection of documents) unless he serves notice that he wishes the document
to be proved at trial".[7] There may be circumstances in which a party's failure to
serve a notice under CPR r.32.19 will not be a barrier to challenging the authenticity of a document.[8] Under CPR r.32.19(2), a notice to prove a document must be
served by the latest date for serving witness statements, or within seven days of
disclosure of the document, whichever is the later.[8a] Requiring a party to "prove"
a document means that the party relying upon the document must lead apparently
credible evidence of sufficient weight that the document is what it purports to be.[9]
If a party bears the legal onus of proof, the service by that party on the other party
of a notice to prove the authenticity of a document pursuant to CPR r.32.19 cannot
operate to shift the legal burden.[9a] The approach taken by the court to the question
of "proof" of documents which have been challenged by way of notice pursuant to
CPR r.32.19 is an evaluative, fact-sensitive approach.

[7] *Jones v Oven* [2017] EWHC 1647 (Ch) at [14]. See also *McGann v Bisping* [2017] EWHC 2951
(Comm) at [18]; *Redstone Mortgages Ltd v B Legal Ltd* [2014] EWHC 3398 (Ch); and *Nageh v David
Game College Ltd* [2013] EWCA Civ 1340.

[8] See *McGann v Bisping* [2017] EWHC 2951 (Comm) at [17]–[26], where the court found that the
justice of the case required a different result in circumstances where the defendant had failed to serve a
notice under CPR r.32.19, but where the parties had been preparing for trial on the shared assumption
that the authenticity of the document was in issue. The court exercised its power under CPR r.3.10(2)
by making an order to remedy an error of procedure and thereby dispensing with the need for service

of a notice under CPR r.32.19. See also *Eco3 Capital Ltd v Lusdin Overseas Ltd* [2013] EWCA Civ 413 at [100]–[111] where the Court of Appeal found that it was inappropriate on the last day of a trial to invite the trial judge to ignore parts of the evidence on the basis it was shut out by a deemed admission due to a failure to serve a notice under CPR r.32.19, in circumstances where the genuineness and accuracy of the document had been fully explored in evidence without objection.

[8a] Where, due to the late disclosure of a document, it or its contents of character cannot practicably be challenged within the time limits prescribed, the document may only be relied on by the party disclosing it with the permission of the court and having regard to the overriding objective in CPR r.1.1: see the Commercial Court Guide, 11th edn (2022), para.E4.1.

[9] *Redstone Mortgages Ltd v B Legal Ltd* [2014] EWHC 3398 (Ch) at [57]; *Mitchell v Al Jaber* [2023] EWHC 364 (Ch) at [179]–[181].

[9a] *Mitchell v Al Jaber* [2023] EWHC 364 (Ch) at [179](iv).

CHAPTER 41

DOCUMENTS AND DOCUMENTARY EVIDENCE; HOW
DOCUMENTARY EVIDENCE IS PROVED; CATEGORIES OF
DOCUMENTARY EVIDENCE: PUBLIC, JUDICIAL, PRIVATE

1. DOCUMENTS AND DOCUMENTARY EVIDENCE

(a) Document defined

Replace paragraph with:

In *Victor Chandler International Ltd v Customs & Excise Commissioners*[1] Sir **41-01** Richard Scott VC agreed with Lord Milligan in *Rollo v HM Advocate*[2] that the "essence of a document is that it is something containing recorded information of some sort".[3] Until the late nineteenth century, a document tended to mean something physical[4] inscribed with writing, markings or symbols which a qualified person could interpret. All of the following were accepted as documents: Exchequer tallies, wooden scores used by milkmen and bakers, and inscriptions upon walls,[5] coffin-plates,[6] and rings.[7] Drawings, plans, charts and maps were also regarded as documents. A taximeter was treated as an "account" under the Falsification of Accounts Act 1875.[8] In the Identity Cards Act 2006,[9] the term "document" "includes a stamp or label". With technological progress, it has come to be accepted that a document includes a photograph,[10] an audio[11] or visual[12] recording, fax,[13] and also microdots[14] and computer files[15] (including text messages[16] and, by extension, social media conversations, including with chatbots, and the texts of websites) but not an image such as the image produced on the screen of a Speedman speed trap computer.[17] As these examples illustrate, it makes no difference that "to be meaningful, the information requires to be processed in some way, such as ... decoding or electronic retrieval".[18] In *Grant v Southwestern & County Properties Ltd*[19] Walton J said that "the mere interposition of necessity of an instrument for deciphering the information cannot make any difference in principle". Is an electronic transfer of funds a document? It seems not. "The intention [is] not to create a document of transmission [which can be inspected and copied] but to effect a funds transfer, by the creation of corresponding credit and debit accounts."[20] Labels on decanters,[21] parcels[22] or exhibits[23] are not documents but part of the objects they identify. Markings or writing on flags and placards put on public display are the equivalent of speech.[24] In *Jones v Tarleton*,[25] Parke B stated that the evidence in the former case was received as res gestae; but in *Butler v Mountgarret*[26] he considered the better ground to be the inconvenience or impossibility of procuring the banners.

[1] *Victor Chandler International Ltd v Customs & Excise Commissioners* [2000] 1 W.L.R. 1296 at 1302.

[2] *Rollo v HM Advocate*, 1997 J.C. 23 at 26.

[3] cf. CPR r.31.4: "anything in which information of any description is recorded", Civil Evidence Act 1995 s.13 as to which see *R. v Duffy (Paula) (No.1)* [1999] Q.B. 919, Road Traffic Offenders Act 1988 s.13(3). Contrast *Grant v Southwestern and County Properties* [1975] Ch. 185 at 197: "a document is primarily something that instructs", per Walton J. On meaning of document for purposes of disclosure in civil proceedings, see Matthews and Malek, *Disclosure*, 5th edn (London: Sweet & Maxwell, 2016), paras 5.02 to 5.07.

[4] "[I]t is a document no matter upon what material it be", *R. v Daye* [1908] 2 K.B. 333, per Darling J.

[5] *Ruscoe v Grounsell* (1903) 20 T.L.R. 5.

[6] *R. v Edge* (1842) Wills, Cir. Ev., 6th edn, pp.309, 340.

[7] *R. v Farr* (1864) 4 F. & F. 336.

[8] *R. v Solomons* [1909] 2 K.B. 980.

[9] See s.41(1).

[10] *Lyell v Kennedy (No.3)* (1884) 50 L.T. 730. "A document which conveys thought does so directly. A document which bears actual representations still conveys thought, only indirectly" says Yock Lin Tan "Making Sense of Documentary Evidence" [1993] Singapore J Legal Studies 504, 510; citing Gulson, *Philosophy of Proof* (1905).

[11] *R. v Stevenson* [1971] 1 W.L.R. 1; *R. v Robson* [1972] 1 W.L.R. 651; *Grant v Southwestern and County Properties* [1975] Ch. 185. See also Iron and Steel Act 1967 (Schedule); cf. *Beneficial Finance v Conway* [1976] V.R. 321; *R. v Matthews* [1972] V.R. 3. In *R. v Mills* [1962] 3 All E.R. 298 at 301, Winn J. pointed out that the tape-recording machine was performing a function "which would otherwise have been performed by a pen or pencil in his own hand". In *Butera v DPP* (1987) 164 C.L.R. 180 the High Court of Australia held that if of good quality, a tape-recording should normally be played in court but, if not, it may be presented in the form of a transcript.

[12] *Senior v Holdsworth, Ex p. Independent Television News Ltd* [1976] Q.B. 23. In *Glyn v Weston Feature Film Co* [1916] 1 Ch. 36; 85 L.J. Ch. 261 a cinema film was held not to be a document, but it is unlikely that that decision would now be followed.

[13] *Hastie and Jenkerson v McMahon* [1990] 1 W.L.R. 1575.

[14] *Hastie and Jenkerson v McMahon* [1990] 1 W.L.R. 1575 at 196–197.

[15] *Derby v Weldon (No.9)* [1991] 1 W.L.R. 652; in Canada, a file which had been deleted but which could be retrieved has been held to be a document: *Prism Hospital Software Ltd v Hospital Medical Research Institute* [1992] 2 W.W.R. 157. See also, *Electronic Disclosure: A report of a working party chaired by the Honourable Mr Justice Cresswell* dated 6 October 2004; *Marlton v Textronix UK Holdings* [2003] EWHC 382 (Ch) (order for inspection of computer hard drive by expert); *Sony Music Entertainment (Australia) Ltd v University of Tasmania* [2003] F.C.A. 532; (2003) 198 A.L.R. 367 Fed Ct of Aus (disclosure of CD-ROMs and back-up tapes as documents). No distinction has been made between a webpage and a printout of a computer file for the purposes of authentication: *R. v Skinner* [2005] EWCA Crim 1439.

[16] e.g. *Price v Powell* [2013] EWHC 1325 (QB).

[17] *Darby v DPP* (1995) 159 J.P. 533.

[18] *Rollo v HM Advocate*, 1997 J.C. 23 at 26.

[19] *Grant v Southwestern & County Properties Ltd* [1975] Ch. 185 at 197.

[20] Yock Lin Tan, "Making Sense of Documentary Evidence" [1993] Singapore J Legal Studies 504, 508.

[21] *Commonwealth v Blood* (1858) 77 Mass. 74.

[22] *Burrell v North* (1847) 2 C. & K. 680 at 682; contra, *R. v Fenton*, cited C.B. 760 and 13 Q.B. 260, per Parke B; *R. v Hinley* (1843) 1 Cox 12 at 13, per Maule J.

[23] *Commissioner for Railways (NSW) v Young* (1962) 106 C.L.R. 535. cp. *Taylor v DPP* [2009] EWHC 2824 (Admin).

[24] *R. v Hunt* (1820) 3 B. & Ald. 566; contra, *R. v Hinley* (1843) 1 Cox 12.

[25] *Jones v Tarleton*, 9 M. & W. 676.

[26] *Butler v Mountgarret*, 7 H.L.C. 639.

CHAPTER 42

ADMISSIBILITY OF EXTRINSIC EVIDENCE

1.   INTRODUCTION

Replace paragraph with:

42-02   The rule is frequently and interchangeably referred to as the "parol evidence rule", although it is not limited to the oral testimony of witnesses. It applies to all forms of evidence outside the document itself, such as early drafts of the written document,[2] preliminary agreements[3] and written communications exchanged as part of negotiations,[4] etc. The admissibility of extrinsic evidence is most commonly considered in contractual disputes,[5] although it is not limited to this area of law and has been considered in other areas such as planning disputes[6] and even defamation cases.[7] In contractual disputes, the issues are usually two-fold: (1) whether it is permissible to adduce evidence of terms other than those expressly embodied in the written document; and (2) whether extrinsic evidence may be admitted to explain or interpret the words in the document.

[2] *National Bank of Australasia v Falkingham & Sons* [1902] A.C. 585.

[3] *Henderson v Arthur* [1907] 1 K.B. 10; *Hitchings & Coulthurst Co v Northern Leather Co of America and Doushkess* [1914] 3 K.B. 907; *Hutton v Watling* [1948] Ch. 398; *Youell v Bland Welch & Co Ltd* [1992] 2 Lloyd's Rep. 127. cf. *HIH Casualty and General Insurance Ltd v New Hampshire Insurance Co* [2001] EWCA Civ 735; [2001] 2 Lloyd's Rep. 161 at [83], where Rix LJ stated that: "it is always admissible to look at a prior contract as part of the matrix or surrounding circumstances of a later contract. I do not see how the parol evidence rule can exclude prior contracts, as distinct from mere negotiations" but that "a cautious and sceptical approach to finding any assistance in the earlier contract seems to me to be a sound principle. What I doubt, however, is that such a principle can be elevated into a conclusive rule of law." Rix LJ's statement was adopted by the court in *Medenta Finance Ltd v Hitachi Capital (UK) Plc* [2019] EWHC 516 (Comm) at [49].

[4] *Mercantile Bank of Sydney v Taylor* [1893] A.C. 317.

[5] A more detailed examination concerning the admissibility of extrinsic evidence in the context of contractual disputes can be found in *Chitty on Contracts*, 34th edn (London: Sweet & Maxwell, 2021), paras 15-022 to 15-046. See also *Smith v Gregory* [2022] EWHC 910 (Ch); [2022] B.P.I.R. 1298 at [31]–[36].

[6] See, for example, University of *Leicester v Secretary of State for Communities and Local Government, Oadby & Wigston Borough Council* [2016] EWHC 476 (Admin); *R. (on the application of Gallagher Ventures Ltd) v Secretary of State for Housing, Communities and Local Government* [2021]

EWHC 3007 (Admin); [2023] 1 P. & C.R. 11; *Patel v Secretary of State for Housing, Communities and Local Government* [2021] EWHC 2115 (Admin); [2022] J.P.L. 505 at [61]–[62].

[7] In *Riley v Murray* [2020] EWHC 977 (QB) at [10], Niklin J stated that in respect of defamatory posts on social media, there is "a creeping tendency, under the guise of alleged 'context', to attempt to adduce evidence extrinsic to the words complained of on the issue of the natural and ordinary meaning."

4. EVIDENCE TO CONTRADICT, VARY, SUBSTITUTE, ADD OR SUBTRACT

(a) Principle

After ", particularly with the inclusion of an 'entire agreement' clause.[95]", add:

The effect of an "entire agreement" clause will depend on its wording. Such **42-20** clauses may prevent the use of extrinsic evidence to establish additional terms and collateral agreements, or claims based on warranties and misrepresentations; however, they do not prevent the use of extrinsic evidence to ascertain the meaning of an express term in the contract.[95a]

[95a] *Buckinghamshire Council v FCC Buckinghamshire Ltd* [2021] EWHC 2867 (TCC) at [121]–[125].

(b) Forms of extrinsic of parol evidence

Replace footnote 108 with:

[108] See *Marley v Rawlings* [2014] UKSC 2; [2015] A.C. 129 at [24]–[26], where Lord Neuberger stated **42-23** that where s.21 applied to a will, extrinsic evidence, including evidence of a testator's actual intention, may be admissible as an aid to interpretation; see also *Bathurst v Chantler* [2018] EWHC 21 (Ch); *Lattimer v Karamanoli* [2023] EWHC 1524 (Ch) at [45]–[46].

5. EXCEPTIONS

(d) True nature and operation of the transaction and relationship of parties

(i) Sale or mortgage: merger

After "… a loan on security[203]; a conveyance", add new footnote 203a:

[203a] *Dunlop v Romanoff* [2023] UKUT 200 (LC). **42-40**

CHAPTER 43

JUDGMENTS

1. JUDGMENTS AS EVIDENCE OF THEIR EXISTENCE, CONTENTS AND

2. JUDGMENTS AS GIVING RISE TO ESTOPPELS IN SUBSEQUENT PROCEEDINGS

(a) All judgments are impeachable on certain grounds

(iv) Obtained by fraud or collusion

Replace footnote 64 with:

43-08 ⁶⁴ *Takhar v Gracefield Developments Ltd* [2019] UKSC 13; [2019] 2 W.L.R. 984 at [55]. See *Elu v Floorweald Ltd* [2020] EWHC 1222 (QB); [2020] 1 W.L.R. 4369 at [146]; *Finzi v Jamaican Redevelopment Foundation Inc* [2023] UKPC 29 at [72]–[76].

After the fifth paragraph, add new paragraph:
    A claim to set aside a judgment for fraud may be barred by a party's election not to pursue such a claim at an earlier stage.⁸⁴ᵃ

⁸⁴ᵃ *Bhandal v Revenue and Customs Commissioners* [2023] EWHC 1498 (Ch).

(d) Judgments in civil cases as affecting parties and privies

(iii) Res judicata estoppels

Central principle

Replace footnote 194 with:

43-23 ¹⁹⁴ *Fidelitas Shipping Co v V/O Exportschleb* [1966] 1 Q.B. 630 CA; *Test Claimants in the Franked Investment Income Group Litigation v Revenue and Customs Commissioners* [2021] UKSC 31 at [64], [76]. This may include later stages of the same arbitration: *Union of India v Reliance Industries Ltd* [2022] EWHC 1407 (Comm); [2022] 2 Lloyd's Rep. 201.

Scope of the rule

Replace the first paragraph with:

43-24   The principle that estoppels arise from a judgment in previous litigation between the same parties applies in general to all civil litigation, including arbitrations,¹⁹⁶ civil proceedings in courts of summary jurisdiction[197] and public law proceedings.[198] A cause of action estoppel operates to prevent a party relitigating a claim he has lost, even if he is now able to show that the earlier decision was wrong.[199] But an order of a court of summary jurisdiction will not operate as an estoppel as to any matter which that court had no authority to adjudicate directly and immediately between the parties; nor as to any matter incidentally coming in question as to which a finding if held conclusive between the parties would operate in prejudice of the rights of others not parties to the proceedings; nor as to any incidental matter not otherwise determined than as having been the particular ground on which the court dismissed a charge or complaint.[200] Under certain statutes no estoppel arises: e.g. awards under the Workmen's Compensation Act 1925[201] did not estop.[202] The dismissal of a bankruptcy petition is no bar to a second notice and petition for the same debt, though vexatious reapplications will be checked.[203] So, the Registrar's decision as to the validity of a debt for the purpose of granting a receiving order,[204] or his provisional decision on a question of title for the purpose of ordering an account,[205] does not estop. Moreover, in bankruptcy, the consideration for a judgment may, on account of the danger of fraud, always be inquired into, at the instance either of the trustee or of the debtor themselves[206] and the file of proceedings creates no estoppel.[207] So, neither a winding-up order,[208] nor a balance order under the Companies Act,[209] was res judicata. Nor do decisions in ecclesiastical cases, when not affecting rights or property, estop.[210] Res judicata cannot be relied on so as to give a jurisdiction which the relevant statute says that court is not to have[211] nor to deprive it of a discretion conferred by statute.[212] It cannot be relied on where the result would be to compel the court to give a judgment contrary to the relevant statute.[213] The General Medical Council is a statutory body, not bound by the strict rules of evidence, and their statutory duty was inconsistent with their accepting a finding of adultery by the Divorce Court as conclusive. It merely constituted a strong prima facie case.[214] The dismissal of a claimant's interim application for judgment on admissions (not involving trial of a preliminary issue) does not create a cause of action estoppel preventing the substantive trial of the same issues in the claim.[214a]

---

[196] *Eastwood v Studer* (1926) 31 Com. Cas. 251; *Alexander Brothers Ltd (Hong Kong SAR) v Alstom Transport SA* [2020] EWHC 1584 (Comm) at [104]–[105]; [2020] Bus. L.R. 2197 (Cockerill J holding that there where an arbitral tribunal had jurisdiction to determine an issue of illegality and had determined there was no illegality on the facts, there was almost no scope for the court to re-open that issue on enforcement of the award; in any event, where an allegation of bribery issue could with reasonable diligence have been brought before the arbitral tribunal and therefore was no explanation for why that was not done, this was prima facie an abuse of process and there were no special circumstances which would make it unjust for the defendant to be debarred from raising the point on enforcement); *PJSC National Bank Trust v Mints* [2022] EWHC 871 (Comm); [2022] 1 W.L.R. 3099; *Union of India v Reliance Industries Ltd* [2022] EWHC 1407 (Comm); [2022] 2 Lloyd's Rep. 201; *National Iranian Oil Co v Crescent Petroleum Co International Ltd* [2022] EWHC 1645 (Comm); [2023] 1 All E.R. (Comm) 549.

[197] *Wright v LGO Co*, 2 Q.B.D. 271; *R. v Miles* (1890) 24 Q.B.D. 423 (applied in *R. v Campbell, Ex p. Hoy* [1953] 1 Q.B. 585 DC; *Ribble Joint Committee v Croston* [1897] 1 Q.B. 251).

[198] See *Konodyba v Royal Borough of Kensington and Chelsea* [2012] EWCA Civ 982 where Longmore LJ stated: " … I see no reason why this general approach should not apply as much in public as in private law with the possible qualification that a public body with statutory obligations to provide, for example, housing assistance or a home from, no doubt, scarce housing stock should not be over-protected from addressing points which are truly new, even if they arise on facts which have already been subject to a determination." (at [16]).

[199] See also para.43-15. *Marriott v Hampton* (1797) 7 T.R. 269 is an early and clear illustration of this principle. But see *Arnold v National Westminster Bank Plc* [1991] 2 A.C. 93; and see further, para.43-43.

[200] *R. v Hutchins* (1878) 6 Q.B.D. 300 at 304; *Att.-Gen. v Eriché* [1893] A.C. 518; *Wakefield v Cooke* [1904] A.C. 31; *Dover v Child* (1876) 1 Ex. D. 172; *Midland Ry v Martin* [1893] 2 Q.B. 172.

[201] Repealed by the National Insurance (Industrial Industries) Act 1946.

[202] *Radcliffe v Pacific Co* [1910] 1 K.B. 685.

[203] *Victoria* [1894] 2 Q.B. 387; *King v Henderson* [1898] A.C. 720 at 730; *Prince Marwaha v Entertainment One Ltd* [2023] EWHC 480 (Ch) at [42]–[43] (noting that the principle in *Henderson v Henderson* [1843-60] All E.R. Rep. 378; 67 E.R. 313 may be applied in cases of presentation of a bankruptcy petition).

[204] *Victoria* [1894] 2 Q.B. 387; *King v Henderson* [1898] A.C. 720 at 730.

[205] *Cronmire* [1894] 2 Q.B. 246.

[206] See para.43-83.

[207] *Ex p. Bacon* (1881) 17 Ch. D. 447.

[208] *Bowling* [1895] 1 Ch. 663.

[209] *Westmoreland Co v Fielden* [1891] 3 Ch. 15.

[210] *Read v Lincoln (Bishop)* [1892] A.C. 644 at 655.

[211] *Stone v Levitt* [1947] A.C. 209 at 216.

[212] *State of Norway's Application (No.2)* [1990] A.C. 723 CA. The point was not considered on appeal to the House of Lords.

[213] *Griffith v Davies* [1943] K.B. 618.

[214] *GMC v Spackman* [1943] A.C. 627; see also *Towuaghantse v General Medical Council* [2021] EWHC 681 (Admin).

[214a] *Valley View Health Centre v NHS Property Services Ltd* [2022] EWHC 1393 (Ch) at [562]–[587].

Same parties or their privies

Privies

After the third paragraph, add new paragraph:

43-28   Res judicata estoppel can be found against a sovereign state and the State Immunity Act 1978 does not preclude such a finding.[273a]

[273a] *Hulley Enterprises Ltd v The Russian Federation* [2023] EWHC 2704 (Comm) at [30]–[55], applying *Dallah Real Estate & Tourism Holding Co v Pakistan* [2010] UKSC 46; [2011] 1 A.C. 763 and *Diag Human SE v Czech Republic* [2014] EWHC 1639 (Comm); [2014] 2 Lloyd's Rep. 283.

Privity of interest

Replace the first paragraph with:

43-29   In *Carl-Zeiss Stiftung v Rayner and Keeler Ltd (No.2)*[274] Lord Reid suggested that a person who was employed by a former litigant to perform some act calculated to provoke litigation which would re-open a matter previously adjudicated on against the employer, for instance a servant sent to assert a right to fish in order to provoke a trespass writ, might be treated as a privy of his employer.[275] In *Gleeson v J Wippell & Co*,[276] Megarry VC considered the question of whether any relationship short of this would suffice to establish privity of interest. He stated that a mere curiosity or concern in the outcome of the previous litigation would be insufficient, and suggested a purposive approach: asking whether in the circumstances it would be fair to prevent a person from litigating the matter for a second time, and whether the answer would be equally clear if the original decision had been the opposite of what it in fact was.[277] In *Kirin-Amgen Inc v Boehringer Mannheim GmBH*,[278] Aldous LJ built on Megarry VC's approach and held that the mere fact that a company's commercial success or failure was linked to the outcome of litigation involving another company did not make the companies privies, and nor did the fact that the company which was not a party to the previous litigation had supplied witnesses.[279] Guidance was given by the Court of Appeal, in *Resolution Chemicals Ltd v H Lundbeck A/S*,[280] where it was stated that a court which has the task of assessing whether there is privity of interest between a new party and a party to previous proceedings needs to examine: (a) the extent to which the new party had an interest in the subject-matter of the previous action; (b) the extent to which the new party can be said to be, in reality, the party to the original proceedings by reason of his relationship with that party; and (c) against this background to ask whether it is just that the new party should be bound by the outcome of the previous litigation. The scope of issue estoppel arising from an arbitration award is not confined to contractual privies, although the contractual source of the arbitral tribunal's jurisdiction is a highly relevant factor in assessing whether findings in an arbitral award bind a non-party to the arbitration.[280a]

[274] *Carl-Zeiss Stiftung v Rayner and Keeler Ltd (No.2)* [1967] 1 A.C. 853 HL.

[275] If the employee was privy then the former judgment would be conclusive. Thus Lord Reid's proposal conflicted to some extent with *Kinnersley v Orpe* (1780) 2 Dougl. K.B. 517.

[276] *Gleeson v J Wippell & Co* [1977] 1 W.L.R. 510 Ch D. See generally, *Johnson v Gore Wood (No.1)* [2002] 2 A.C. 1 HL. *House of Spring Gardens Ltd v Waite (No.2)* [1991] 1 Q.B. 241; [1990] 3 W.L.R. 347; *Resolution Chemicals Ltd v H Lundbeck A/S* [2013] EWCA Civ 924; [2014] R.P.C. 5 and *Ward v Savill* [2021] EWCA Civ 1378. The High Court in *PJSC National Bank Trust v Mints* [2022] EWHC 871 (Comm); [2022] 1 W.L.R. 3099 at [28]–[31] declined to consider the correctness of the decision in *Gleeson*.

[277] This approach was approved by the Court of Appeal in *Kirin-Amgen Inc v Boehringer Mannheim GmBH* [1997] F.S.R. 289 CA.

[278] *Kirin-Amgen Inc v Boehringer Mannheim GmBH* [1997] F.S.R. 289 CA.

[279] See *Resolution Chemicals Ltd v H. Lundbeck A/S* [2013] EWCA Civ 924; 29 July 2013 where Floyd LJ stated: "… in in my judgment a court which has the task of assessing whether there is privity of interest between a new party and a party to previous proceedings needs to examine (a) the extent to which the new party had an interest in the subject matter of the previous action; (b) the extent to which the new party can be said to be, in reality, the party to the original proceedings by reason of his relationship with that party, and (c) against this background to ask whether it is just that the new party should be bound by the outcome of the previous litigation" (at [32]).

[280] *Resolution Chemicals Ltd v H Lundbeck A/S* [2013] EWCA Civ 924.

[280a] *Golden Ocean Group Ltd v Humpuss Intermoda Transportasi Tbk Ltd* [2013] EWHC 1240 (Comm); [2013] 2 Lloyd's Rep. 421 at [33]; *Vale SA v Steinmetz* [2021] EWCA Civ 1087; [2021] 2 Lloyd's Rep. 601 at [31]; *PJSC National Bank Trust v Mints* [2022] EWHC 871 (Comm); [2022] 1 W.L.R. 3099 at [17]–[27].

Issue estoppel

Arbitrations

Replace the first paragraph with:

It is clear that the issue estoppel doctrine applies to arbitrations.[349] Although these **43-42** decisions concern English arbitrations, it is thought that the principle applies equally to awards in arbitrations conducted abroad. The Court of Appeal has confirmed that a prior arbitration award can be the basis for an argument that subsequent litigation is an abuse of process, albeit the courts will be cautious where a strike-out application is founded on a prior arbitration award and it may be a "rare" (or perhaps "very rare") case where court proceedings against a non-party to an arbitration will be an abuse of process.[350]

[349] *Fidelitas Shipping Co Ltd v V/O Exportchleb* [1966] 1 Q.B. 630; [1965] 2 W.L.R. 1059; *Qatar Petroleum v Shell* [1983] 2 Lloyd's Rep. 35 CA; *Northern Regional Health Authority v Crouch* [1984] Q.B. 644; *PJSC National Bank Trust v Mints* [2022] EWHC 871 (Comm); [2022] 1 W.L.R. 3099 at [13]; *Union of India v Reliance Industries Ltd* [2022] EWHC 1407 (Comm); [2022] 2 Lloyd's Rep. 201.

[350] *Michael Wilson & Partners Ltd v Sinclair* [2017] EWCA Civ 3; [2017] 1 W.L.R. 2646 at [67]–[68].

Fresh evidence and other special circumstances

Replace footnote 354 with:

43-43 [354] *Takhar v Gracefield Developments Ltd* [2019] UKSC 13; [2020] A.C. 450; *Bhandal v Revenue and Customs Commissioners* [2023] EWHC 1498 (Ch). See para.43-08.

In the fifth paragraph, after "... of process does not arise, and the", replace "Phosphate Sewage" with:
Phosphate Sewage

Abuse of process

Claims which could and should have been brought previously

After the ninth paragraph, add new paragraph:

43-46 There is no third category of claims that were "raised but not brought", falling between the doctrine of res judicata and the wider doctrine of abuse of process. The latter doctrine applies where a party has raised the matter in question even if they have not formally brought a claim based on it (for example because, at the time of compromise of the claim, the court had not granted permission for amendment of the party's statement of case in order to raise the issue).[386a]

[386a] *Warburton v Chief Constable of Avon and Somerset* [2023] EWCA Civ 209; [2023] 3 W.L.R. 371 at [48]–[56].

Should have been litigated in earlier proceedings

Replace paragraph with:

43-49 This form of abuse of process is usually relied on between the parties to previous litigation (or arbitration[400a]). As such it operates as, in effect, an extension of the doctrine of merger and cause of action estoppel: although the subsequent litigation does not rely on the identical cause of action, the argument is that because the second claim "covers issues of facts which are so clearly part of the subject-matter of the litigation and so clearly could have been raised that it would be an abuse of the process of the court to allow a new proceeding to be started in respect of them".[401] In *MCC Proceeds Inc v Lehman Brothers International*,[402] Mummery LJ treated it as critical that "the essential factual basis of the claims is the same in both cases" and that joinder of the defendant in the second action as a defendant in the first would not have "overloaded, or introduced complexity into, the first action".[403] A party would be unlikely to be able successfully to allege that a claim "could and should" have been litigated in previous proceedings if in all likelihood the judge in the previous proceedings would have directed that it should be held over to await the conclusion of the previous claim.[404]

[400a] *Union of India v Reliance Industries Ltd* [2022] EWHC 1407 (Comm); [2022] 2 Lloyd's Rep. 201 (where Sir Ross Cranston held that issues of res judicata and abuse of process, arising in a London-seated arbitration, were rightly decided by the tribunal according to English law, whatever the governing law of the contract).

[401] *Greenhalgh v Mallard* [1947] 2 All E.R. 255 CA at 257, per Somervell LJ.

[402] *MCC Proceeds Inc v Lehman Brothers International* [1998] 4 All E.R. 675 CA at 693.

[403] *MCC Proceeds Inc v Lehman Brothers International* [1998] 4 All E.R. 675 CA at 694.

[404] *Barrow v Bankside Members Agency* [1996] 1 Lloyd's Rep. 278 CA. But note that this is opposed by the importance attached to defendants knowing their total possible liability at an early stage so they could negotiate on that basis. See, e.g. Stuart-Smith LJ in *Talbot v Berkshire CC* [1994] Q.B. 290 CA.

Previous litigation ending in compromise

Replace footnote 407 with:

[407] *Johnson v Gore Wood (No.1)* [2002] 2 A.C. 1 HL; applied in *Warburton v Chief Constable of Avon and Somerset* [2023] EWCA Civ 209; [2023] 3 W.L.R. 371 at [48]–[56].   **43-51**

Application of abuse of process beyond the parties

After "… refused to hold that a girl with Down's", add:
syndrome   **43-57**

Effects beyond the parties

Replace paragraph with:

The Hunter doctrine of abusive collateral attack played a central role in the deci-   **43-59**
sion of the House of Lords in *Arthur JS Hall & Co v Simons*[433] to remove the advocate's immunity from suit. The operation of the rule in *Hunter* was regarded by the majority of their Lordships as providing the necessary safeguards to prevent litigants using an action against their former advocate as a means of launching a collateral challenge against previous criminal convictions. Lord Hoffmann gave the most extensive analysis of the purpose of the *Hunter* doctrine. In criminal cases, public policy demands that there not be conflicting decisions, since this would bring the system for the administration of justice into disrepute (this is subject to the rare exceptional cases where the existence of conflicting decisions would not, because of special circumstances, have this effect). In the case of a previous conviction, the rule in *Hunter* is sufficient to prevent a litigant bringing an action for negligence against a former legal adviser which might result in two different courts coming to conflicting decisions on the litigant's guilt. A separate rule of advocate's immunity is therefore otiose. However, in civil cases, the issues are normally only of interest to the parties involved. "There is no public interest objection to a subsequent finding that, but for the negligence of his lawyers, the losing party would have won."[434] It is not clear from the speech of Lord Hoffmann whether he regarded the *Hunter* doctrine as having any role to play in preventing challenges to previous civil judgments. From his exposition of the public policy rationale behind *Hunter*, it would seem that the doctrine is confined to challenges to earlier convictions. Both Lord Steyn[435] and Lord Browne-Wilkinson[436] conceived that there might be some residual role for the *Hunter* doctrine in cases of challenge to earlier civil judgments, but their Lordships did not expand upon these observations. The Court of

Appeal in *Allsop v Banner Jones Ltd*[437] concluded that a clear distinction had to be drawn between collateral challenge to previous criminal decisions and collateral challenges to previous civil (including family law) decisions. Thus, if a subsequent action challenges the factual findings and conclusions of a prior civil decision, there will only be an abuse of process if "(a) it would be manifestly unfair to a party to the later proceedings that the same issues should be re-litigated; or (b) to permit such relitigation would bring the administration of justice into disrepute".[438] A close "merits based" analysis of the underlying facts of the particular case (including the procedural history) is required in order to determine whether success on the second claim would involve re-litigating the "very same issues" as in the first claim and the court reaching different conclusions on those issues on the same evidence.[438a] However, relitigating the very same issues does not alone give rise to abuse of process, and either limb (a) or (b) above must be satisfied. Thus, it will only be in very rare or exceptional cases that a second set of proceedings will be an abuse of process where the parties are not the same as in the first set of proceedings.[438b]

[433] *Arthur JS Hall & Co v Simons* [2002] 1 A.C. 615 HL (applied by the Court of Appeal in *Secretary of State for Trade & Industry v Bairstow (No.1)* [2004] Ch. 1; and by the House of Lords in *Moy v Pettman Smith (A Firm)* [2005] UKHL 7; [2005] 1 W.L.R. 581).

[434] Per Lord Hoffmann, *Arthur JS Hall & Co v Simons* [2002] 1 A.C. 615 HL at 706.

[435] *Arthur JS Hall & Co v Simons* [2002] 1 A.C. 615 HL at 679.

[436] *Arthur JS Hall & Co v Simons* [2002] 1 A.C. 615 HL at 685.

[437] *Allsop v Banner Jones Ltd (t/as Banner Jones Solicitors)* [2021] EWCA Civ 7; [2021] P.N.L.R. 17 at [44]–[45].

[438] *Hunter v Chief Constable of West Midlands Police* [1982] A.C. 529 HL at 536 (Lord Diplock); *Arthur JS Hall & Co v Simons* [2002] 1 A.C. 615, 685 (Lord Browne-Wilkinson) at 702–703 (Lord Hoffman); *Secretary of State for Trade and Industry v Bairstow* [2003] EWCA Civ 321; [2004] Ch. 1 at [38] (Sir Andrew Morritt V-C); *Michael Wilson & Partners Ltd v Sinclair* [2017] EWCA Civ 3; [2017] 1 W.L.R. 2646 at [65]; *Kamoka v Security Service* [2017] EWCA Civ 1665; *Allsop v Banner Jones Ltd (t/as Banner Jones Solicitors)* [2021] EWCA Civ 7; [2021] P.N.L.R. 17 at [45].

[438a] *Laing v Taylor Walton (A Firm)* [2007] EWCA Civ 1146; [2008] B.L.R. 65; *Arts & Antiques Ltd v Richards* [2013] EWHC 3361 (Comm); [2014] Lloyd's Rep. I.R. 219; *Michael Wilson & Partners Ltd v Sinclair* [2017] EWCA Civ 3; [2017] 1 W.L.R. 2646 at [48]; *PricewaterhouseCoopers LLP v BTI 2014 LLC* [2021] EWCA Civ 9 at [27].

[438b] *Bragg v Oceanus Mutual Underwriting Association (Bermuda) Ltd* [1982] 2 Lloyd's Rep. 132 at [138]–[139]; *Michael Wilson & Partners Ltd v Sinclair* [2017] EWCA Civ 3; [2017] 1 W.L.R. 2646 at [48]; *Norris, Re* [2001] UKHL 34; [2001] 1 W.L.R. 1388; *PricewaterhouseCoopers LLP v BTI 2014 LLC* [2021] EWCA Civ 9 at [86]–[89]. For example, it may be "manifestly unfair" for the sole director of a company to relitigate matters already determined in previous litigation involving the company, where the director had control of the earlier litigation on behalf of the company: *Wilson v Mehta* [2023] EWHC 1214 (Ch) at [13]–[17].

The nature and effect of the earlier judgment

Varieties of judgments

Replace paragraph with:

43-61   In *Arthur JS Hall v Simons*,[443] the Court of Appeal held that in deciding whether a subsequent case was an illegitimate collateral attack different weights could be given to different categories of previous judgments. The scale that the court proposed accorded the greatest weight to criminal convictions, particularly those upheld on appeal, and did not distinguish between convictions following guilty pleas and by juries. Second in importance were civil judgments following fully contested hearings. Interlocutory/interim judgments, judgments approving compromises and consent orders for ancillary relief, were accorded less weight, but a litigant mounting a collateral challenge to such a judgment would still be expected to explain why steps had not been taken to challenge or set aside the judgment. Although not a question of issue estoppel, the general principle is that a party cannot fight again an interlocutory battle that has already been fought unless there has been a significant change of circumstances or the party has become aware of facts that they could not reasonably have known or discovered in time for the first decision.[444]

[443] As to the outcome in the House of Lords, see para.43-59.

[444] *Chanel Ltd v FW Woolworth & Co Ltd* [1981] 1 W.L.R. 485; followed in *Kea Investments Ltd v Watson* [2020] EWHC 472 (Ch) at [42]–[50]. *Laemthong International Lines Co Ltd v Artis (The Laemthong Glory) (No.1)* [2004] EWHC 2226 (Comm); [2004] 2 All E.R. (Comm) 797 at [24]; *Valley View Health Centre v NHS Property Services Ltd* [2022] EWHC 1393 (Ch); cf. *Morina v McAleavey* [2023] EWHC 1234 (Ch) at [178]–[197] (where the judge's ruling on an issue during an interim application, whilst unnecessary to that decision, was held to be in effect a ruling on a preliminary issue)

3. JUDGMENTS AS EVIDENCE AGAINST STRANGERS

(b) At common law

Replace footnote 525 with:

[525] *Hollington v F Hewthorn & Co Ltd* [1943] K.B. 587. The rule in *Hollington* is about the admissibility in English proceedings of findings and decisions of courts and tribunals in proceedings between different parties; it has no application as between different stages of proceedings between the same parties: *Crypto Open Patent Alliance v Wright* [2021] EWHC 3440 (Ch); *Bailey v Bailey* [2022] EWFC 5; [2022] 2 F.L.R. 829 at [17].   **43-77**

(d) Under the Civil Evidence Act 1968

Replace footnote 585 with: "There are certain other statutory exceptions to the rule in *Hollington v Hewthorn*: see, e.g. Medical Act 1983; Dentists Act 1984; Army Act 1955 s.200; Air Force Act 1955 s.200; Proceeds of Crime Act 2002 ss.240–241 (*Director of the Assets Recovery Agency v Virtosu* [2008] EWHC 149 (QB); [2009] 1 W.L.R. 2808). The rules of most professional bodies provide that previous judgments and findings may be admitted in evidence (see e.g. the General Medical Council (Fitness to Practise) Rules Order of Council 2004 r.34(1)), which puts beyond doubt the fact that the rule in *Hollington v Hewthorn* does not apply in inquisitorial or regulatory proceedings; *Towuaghantse v General Medical Council* [2021] EWHC 681 (Admin) at [31]."

(i) Previous convictions in subsequent civil cases (other than defamation)

Replace the first paragraph with:
Broadly,[588] s.11(1) provides that any subsisting conviction by a UK court (or a court-martial[589]) is admissible in subsequent "civil proceedings",[590] to prove that the offence was committed by the person convicted, whenever it is relevant to do so. A "subsisting" conviction for these purposes is one which has not been quashed on appeal[591] but if an appeal is pending, the court may adjourn the civil proceedings so that the issue of the admissibility of the conviction may abide the outcome.[592] Convictions which lead to probation or discharge are admissible.[593] By contrast,   **43-87**

convictions by a foreign court are not rendered admissible by the Civil Evidence Act 1968 and remain inadmissible either as evidence of the guilt of the defendant or any fact found as part of the basis for the conviction.[593a]

[588] Subject to the provisions of s.13 (which relate to defamation actions): see s.11(3).

[589] Defined in s.11(6) of the Act (as amended).

[590] Defined in s.18(1) of the Act.

[591] *Raphael* [1973] 1 W.L.R. 998. For another view, see A. Zuckerman (1971) 87 L.Q.R. 21; but cf. the wording of s.13(3) of the Act.

[592] *Raphael* [1973] 1 W.L.R. 998.

[593] See s.11(5) of the Act.

[593a] *Daley v Bakiyev* [2016] EWHC 1972 (QB); *Benyatov v Credit Suisse Securities (Europe) Ltd* [2022] EWHC 135 (QB); [2022] 4 W.L.R. 54 at [239], [352]–[356] (there was no appeal on this point to the Court of Appeal: [2023] EWCA Civ 140 at [23]); In *W-A (Children: Foreign Conviction), Re* [2022] EWCA Civ 1118; [2022] 3 W.L.R. 1235 (notwithstanding obiter dicta of Peter Jackson LJ at [35]).

(e) Under the Police and Criminal Evidence Act 1984 sections 73–75

Replace footnote 644 with:

43-92   [644] *R. v Mauricia* [2002] EWCA Crim 676; [2002] 2 Cr. App. R. 27 CA; *W-A (Children: Foreign Conviction), Re* [2022] EWCA Civ 1118; [2022] 3 W.L.R. 1235.

Replace footnote 660 with:

43-95   [660] This view is expressed in Sir J.C. Smith, *Criminal Evidence* (1995), p.126. See also, *Cross and Tapper on Evidence*, 13th edn (London: Butterworths, 2018) at p.119: "… s.74(3) which deals with previous convictions of the accused, is concerned exclusively with the means of proof, and does not furnish an independent route to admissibility" (citing *R. v Harris* unreported 19 April 2000 CA at [21]).

CHAPTER 44

EVIDENCE IN ARBITRATION

2. LIMITS TO THE TRIBUNAL'S POWERS OVER EVIDENTIAL MATTERS

Replace "Sonatrach v Staoil" with:
Sonatrach v Statoil   **44-03**

Replace the fourth paragraph with:
In *P v D* the court upheld a challenge to an award on the basis that the arbitrators had reached a decision on a core issue without it being put to the losing party's witness.[17] The losing party in the arbitration successfully argued that there was a violation of s.33 of the 1996 Act because the tribunal did not adhere to the following rule based on *Browne v Dunne*[18]:

> "where there is a challenge to a witness on a core issue as to credibility, it ought to be put in cross-examination to that witness, or the party not so challenging may be precluded from relying on his case not so put".

[17] *P v D* [2019] EWHC 1277.

[18] *P v D* [2019] EWHC 1277 at [27(i)].

After the fourth paragraph, add new paragraphs:
In contrast, and more recently, a challenge to an award based on *Browne v Dunne* did not succeed in *BPY v MXX*.[18a] Butcher J. in the Commercial Court distinguished *P v D* on the basis that the facts of that case were "considerably removed" from the situation in *BPY v MXX*. In *P v D*[18b]—

> "there was no cross-examination at all on the core issue in circumstances where the tribunal had itself suggested that such cross-examination would be appropriate ([15], [34]); where the issue was one of the credibility of conflicting accounts of what had been said; and where, though Mr E's evidence was not found unreliable, it was analysed by the tribunal in an unexpected way. In the present case, by contrast, the core issue of whether

the PSAs were intended to create payment obligations was extensively cross-examined upon; BPY's relevant witnesses were found to be unreliable; and the Arbitrator had indicated that she was not constrained if a particular point was not challenged in cross-examination. Accordingly, I agree with MXV's submission that *P v D* is distinguishable."

Observing that the rule in *Browne v Dunn* is applied flexibly even in court cases, Butcher J. went on to hold that[18c]:

"In arbitration proceedings, subject to any specific agreement between the parties otherwise, the tribunal is likely to have a wide discretion as to how to conduct proceedings. The LCIA Rules expressly provide for this. Subject to compliance with the general duties enshrined in s. 33 AA a tribunal may adopt a procedure which does not involve oral cross-examination of witnesses, whether on a particular point or at all. This includes in a case in which it is said that a witness is not telling the truth, although in some cases fairness will necessitate cross-examination."

[18a] *BPY v MXX* [2023] EWHC 82 (Comm); [2023] 2 All E.R. (Comm) 523.

[18b] *BPY v MXX* [2023] EWHC 82 (Comm); [2023] 2 All E.R. (Comm) 523 at [42].

[18c] *BPY v MXX* [2023] EWHC 82 (Comm); [2023] 2 All E.R. (Comm) 523 at [35].

These cases raise the interesting question of whether the rule in *Browne v Dunn*, with its exceptions, constitutes a minimum mandatory rule of evidence for England seated international arbitrations. Both cases are unlikely to be the final word on the issue as they are relatively recent. Butcher's emphasis on the "wide discretion" a tribunal enjoys to even adopt a process without cross examination reflects closely the practice in international arbitration.

Legally, imposing such a rule does not sit easily with the "complete" power the tribunal enjoys under the 1996 Act over matters of evidence including a right to disregard strict rules of evidence that may otherwise apply in the English courts. This power cannot trump the general duty of fairness. In that context it is noteworthy that while the rule is tied to the question of trial fairness in common law jurisdictions, it is not a rule that would be recognised by a party from a civil law jurisdiction or seen by it as crucial to making the proceedings fairer.[19] This tension may explain why practically such a rule is not usually followed in arbitrations, whether seated in England or elsewhere. The different legal traditions involved in an arbitration mean that not all parties see the rule as enhancing fairness. The commonly used IBA Rules do not contain such a rule and writers have suggested the rule does not apply to international arbitration.[20] Indeed the tribunal in *P v D* recognised that the issue had not been put to the witness and yet did not insist on it, precisely because it did not believe the rule in *Browne v Dunn* applied. There is also the reality that unlike court proceedings arbitrations are usually conducted to a far more compressed timetable, meaning there is less time to test all key aspects of witness testimony in cross examination. This is why it is common for parties to agree procedural orders that state that a failure to cross examine a party's witness on certain points does not mean that those points are accepted; and that, further, such points (which have not been cross examined) may still be contradicted through documents and other evidence.

[19] "To a businessman from a civil law country, concepts like the parol evidence rule, the hearsay rule, common law discovery or the rule in *Browne v Dunn* (1893) 6 R 67 do not make much sense": *BQP v BQQ* [2018] 4 SLR 1364 at [126].

[20] J. Waincymer, *Procedure and Evidence in International Arbitration* (2012), p.917 (fn.99).

7. RES JUDICATA ESTOPPELS

In the third paragraph, after ", although there is a debate", delete "in the arbitra-   **44-10**
tion community".

Add new paragraph:

Jurisdictional challenge versus issue estoppel   Under s.67 of the 1996 Act, par-   **44-11A**
ties are permitted to challenge an arbitral award on the basis that the tribunal did
not have substantive jurisdiction. Although the question does not arise very often,
what if the challenge to the jurisdiction involves a challenge to the merits finding?
The handful of cases that have addressed this question have all adopted the sensible
and unanimous view that on the basis of issue estoppel, a jurisdictional challenge
under s.67 will not be permitted to the extent that it also contradicts and undermines
a final merits (non-jurisdictional) finding in an award.[70a]

[70a] *Westland Helicopters Ltd v Al-Hejailan* [2004] EWHC 1625 (Comm); [2004] 2 Lloyd's Rep. 523
at [37]; *C v D1* [2015] EWHC 2126 (Comm) at [85]–[86]; and more recently in *National Iranian Oil
Co v Crescent Petroleum Co International Ltd* [2022] EWHC 2641 (Comm); [2023] Bus. L.R. 235 at
[45]–[50].

8. PRIVACY & CONFIDENTIALITY

(b) Confidentiality

Replace the third paragraph with:
The extent and effect of the confidentiality obligation on use of arbitration docu-   **44-15**
ments was considered by the Court of Appeal in *Michael Wilson & Partners Ltd v
Emmott*.[85] Lawrence Collins LJ identified the circumstances in which a litigant
might seek disclosure or use of arbitration documents. First, a party to litigation in
the courts might seek disclosure of documents generated in an arbitration.[86]
Secondly, a party to an arbitration may seek the assistance of the court to obtain
through a witness summons material deployed in another arbitration,[87] although the
court will take into account the strong policy in favour of confidentiality in
arbitration. Thirdly, issues may arise about the disclosure of documents on the court
file relating to an arbitration[88] or whether the judgment of a court given in relation
to an arbitration should be published,[89] where the privacy of arbitration will be
important but not decisive. Fourthly, a party to an arbitration may have an interest
in disclosing documents generated in an arbitration, or the award, to another party
or in another arbitration,[90] a situation where the other party to the arbitration may
seek to restrain disclosure by injunction.

[85] *Michael Wilson & Partners Ltd v Emmott* [2008] EWCA Civ 184; [2008] 2 All E.R. (Comm) 193.

[86] *Dolling-Baker* [1990] 1 W.L.R. 1205 CA; *Science Research Council v Nasse* [1980] A.C. 1028 HL.

[87] *London and Leeds Estates Ltd v Paribas Ltd (No.2)* [1995] 1 E.G.L.R. 102 (Mance J); *South Tyneside
MBC v Wickes Building Suppliers Ltd* [2004] EWHC 2428 (Comm) (Gross J).

[88] *Glidepath BV v Thompson* [2005] EWHC 818 (Comm); [2005] 2 Lloyd's Rep. 349 (Colman J).

[89] *Economic Department of City of Moscow v Bankers Trust Co* [2004] EWCA Civ 314; [2005] Q.B.
207.

[90] *Hassneh Insurance Co of Israel v Mew* [1993] 2 Lloyd's Rep. 243, Insurance Co v Lloyds Syndicate
[1995] 1 Lloyd's Rep. 272 (Colman J); *Ali Shipping v Trogir* [1999] 1 W.L.R. 314; *Associated Electric
and Gas Insurance Services v European Reinsurance of Zurich* [2003] UKPC 11; [2003] 1 W.L.R. 1041.

Replace footnote 91 with:

[91] *Michael Wilson & Partners Ltd v Emmott* [2008] EWCA Civ 184; [2008] 2 All E.R. (Comm) 193 at [81].

CHAPTER 45

FACT FINDING AND THE ASSESSMENT OF EVIDENCE

1. THE JUDGE AND HIS TASK

Replace the second paragraph with:

In England a judge can be proactive in the way he conducts a trial and can state **45-05** that he wants the parties and the evidence to focus on the key factual issues in dispute. Judges take a more interventional approach than in the past, however excessive judicial intervention during the evidence may undermine the fairness of the process.[5a] Where one or both parties are litigants in person, as so frequently occurs in the county court given the cost of legal representation and lack of legal aid, a judge may need to take a proactive role at trial by probing matters of fact and asking questions of the parties and witnesses.[6] No doubt most trial judges have faced the situation where a litigant in person (sometimes with limited English or conversational skills) is told it is his turn to ask questions of witnesses, simply looks lost, not knowing what to ask, let alone how. However, a judge conducting the questioning of witnesses and cross-examination in lieu of the litigant has its shortfalls and dangers, and in general a judge should not place himself in the position of an advocate.[7] In a civilian law and middle east legal systems primarily it is the judge who asks the questions of witnesses not the parties or their advocates. Whether one is dealing with a common law or civilian law system, the object is the same, which is to find the truth within the constraints of the legal system and the evidence before the court. There is much to be learned from how cases and evidence are dealt with in different legal systems.

[5a] *Southwark LBC v Kofi-Adu* [2006] EWCA Civ 281; [2006] H.L.R. 33 at [146]; *K (Children: Fairness of Hearing), Re* [2023] EWCA Civ 686; [2023] 4 W.L.R. 61 at [25]–[29]; see also *Yuill v Yuill* [1945] P. 15 at 20 (Lord Greene MR).

[6] There are limits as to how far a judge should go in being proactive during a trial and he should bear in mind the overall fairness of the proceedings: *Serafin v Malkiewicz* [2020] UKSC 23 at [40]–[46]. An unrepresented party will often need some assistance with the trial process.

[7] *PS v BP* [2018] EWHC 1987 (Fam), the judge refused to allow a father to cross-examine a mother where the allegations were that he had abused her, but the judge questioned the mother. At the end of the day there are situations where it does fall to the judge to conduct the questioning of a witness, but the matter needs to be handled very carefully: *K and H (Children)* [2015] EWCA Civ 543 at [52]–[62].

After the second paragraph, add new paragraph:

A trial judge should not decide a case in one party's favour on the basis of a theory not relied upon by either party either in the pleadings or in argument.[7a]

[7a] *Al-Medenni v Mars UK Ltd* [2005] EWCA Civ 1041 at [21]; *Satyam Enterprises Ltd v Burton* [2021] EWCA Civ 287; [2021] B.C.C. 640 at [35]–[38]; *Ali v Dinc* [2022] EWCA Civ 34.

2. ASSESSING THE EVIDENCE OVERALL

After "… each item of evidence against the rest of the evidence.", add new footnote 12a:

45-09   [12a] Evidence should not be evaluated and assessed in separate compartments, a matter which has been stressed in a number of cases relating to the welfare of children: *T (Children) (Abuse: Standard of Proof), Re* [2004] EWCA Civ 558; [2004] 2 F.L.R. 838 at [33]; *S (A Child: Adequacy of Reasoning), Re* [2019] EWCA Civ 1845; [2020] 1 F.C.R. 396 at [33]; *Re B (A Child) (Fact-finding), Re* [2023] EWCA Civ 905 at [50]–[59] (where the trial judge had failed to take into account some material factors; looked at the evidence in compartments and did not have regard to each piece of evidence in the context of the totality of the evidence).

Replace the second paragraph with:

As has been observed, the nature of the evidence that the fact-finding tribunal may consider in deciding whether or not to draw an inference is almost limitless.[14] Criminal cases, civil disputes involving conspiracies and fraud often are inferential cases where circumstantial evidence needs to be drawn together and considered. In such cases the fact-finding process involves the assessment of various strands of evidence. As reflected in Pollock CB's direction, the nature of circumstantial evidence is that its effect is cumulative, and the existence of a successful case based on circumstantial evidence is that the whole is stronger than the individual parts.[15] Calver J has summarised the following principles as to inferring fraud or dishonest conduct generally[15a]:

> "a. It is not open to the Court to infer dishonesty from facts which are consistent with honesty or negligence, there must be some fact which tilts the balance and justifies an inference of dishonesty, and this fact must be both pleaded and proved: *Three Rivers District Council v Bank of England* [2001] UKHL 16; [2003] 2 AC 1, [55]-[56] per Lord Hope and [184]-[186] per Lord Millett.
>
> b. The requirement for a claimant in proving fraud is that the primary facts proved give rise to an inference of dishonesty or fraud which is more probable than one of innocence or negligence: *JSC Bank of Moscow v Kekhman* [2015] EWHC 3073 (Comm) at [20] per Bryan J; *Surkis & Ors v Poroshenko & Anr* [2021] EWHC 2512 (Comm) at [169(iv)] per Calver J
>
> c. Although not strictly a requirement for such a claim, motive 'is a vital ingredient of any rational assessment' of dishonesty: *Bank of Toyo-Mitsubishi UFJ Ltd v Baskan Sanayi Ve Pazarlama AS* [2009] EWHC 1276 (Ch) at [858] per Briggs J. By and large dishonest people are dishonest for a reason; while establishing a motive for conspiracy is not a legal requirement, the less likely the motive, the less likely the intention to conspire unlawfully: *Group Seven Ltd v Nasir* [2017] EWHC 2466 (Ch) at [440] per Morgan J.
>
> d. Assessing a party's motive to participate in a fraud also requires taking into account the disincentives to participation in the fraud; this includes the disinclination to behave immorally or dishonestly, but also the damage to reputation (both for the individual and, where applicable, the business) and the potential risk to the 'liberty of the individuals involved' in case they are found out: *Bank of Tokyo-Mitsubishi UFJ Ltd v Baskan Sanayi Ve Pazarlama AS* [2009] EWHC 1276 (Ch) at [858], [865] per Briggs J."

[14] *Fortune v Wiltshire Council* [2012] EWCA Civ 334; [2013] 1 W.L.R. 808 at [22], per Lewison LJ, citing Pollock CB's famous direction.

[15] *Lakatamia Shipping Co Ltd v Su* [2021] EWHC 1907 (Comm) at [63]–[65]; citing *JSC BTA Bank v Ablyazov* [2012] EWCA Civ 1411 at [52], per Rix LJ.

[15a] *Suppipat v Narongdej* [2023] EWHC 1988 (Comm) at [904].

Replace footnote 18 with:

[18] *Kogan v Martin* [2019] EWCA Civ 1645 at [88]–[89]; *B-M (Children: Findings of Fact)* [2021] EWCA Civ 1371 at [23]–[25]; *Barrow v Merrett* [2022] EWCA Civ 1241; [2023] R.T.R. 1 at [19]–[21], [97] (road traffic case where eyewitness accounts critical). **45-10**

After the second paragraph, add new paragraph:

Cotter J in *Muvepa v Ministry of Defence*[19a] set out his approach to the fact finding exercise both in terms of assessing witness evidence and documentary evidence and the relation between the two. He stressed the importance of contemporaneous documents in *Aspinalls Club Ltd v Lester Hui Chun Mo*.[19b]

[19a] *Muvepa v Ministry of Defence* [2022] EWHC 2648 (KB); [2023] Crim. L.R. 235 at [10]–[21].

[19b] *Aspinalls Club Ltd v Lester Hui Chun Mo* [2023] EWHC 2036 (KB) at [136].

Replace footnote 20 with:

[20] *Group Seven Ltd v Notable Services LLP* [2019] EWCA Civ 614 at [21]–[23]; *Volcafe Ltd v Cia Sud Americana de Vapores SA* [2018] UKSC 61; [2018] 3 W.L.R. 2087 at [41]; *B-M (Children: Findings of Fact)* [2021] EWCA Civ 1371 at [25]; *Natwest Markets Plc v Bilta (UK) Ltd* [2021] EWCA Civ 680 at [48]–[51]; *Barrow v Merrett* [2022] EWCA Civ 1241; [2023] R.T.R. 1 at [19]–[21], [89], [97]. **45-11**

After the first paragraph, add new paragraphs:

In the context of a medical negligence action, Dexter Dias KC (sitting as a Deputy High Court Judge) set out what he described as 13 axioms of fact finding[22a]:

"(1) The burden of proof rests exclusively on the person making the claim (she or he who asserts must prove), who must prove the claim to the conventional civil standard of a balance of probabilities;

(2) Findings of fact must be based on evidence, including inferences that can properly (fairly and safely) be drawn from the evidence, but not mere speculation (*Re A (A child) (Fact Finding Hearing: Speculation)* [2011] EWCA Civ 12, per Munby LJ);

(3) The court must survey the 'wide canvas' of the evidence (*Re U, Re B (Serious injuries: Standard of Proof)* [2004] EWCA Civ 567 at [26] per Dame Elizabeth Butler-Sloss P (as then was)); the factual determination 'must be based on all available materials' (*A County Council v A Mother and others* [2005] EWHC Fam 31 at [44], per Ryder J (as then was));

(4) Evidence must not be evaluated 'in separate compartments' (*Re T* [2004] EWCA Civ 558 at [33], per Dame Elizabeth Butler-Sloss P), but must 'consider each piece of evidence in the context of all the other evidence' (*Devon County Council v EB & Ors.* [2013] EWHC Fam 968 at [57], per Baker J (as then was)); such 'context' includes an assessment of (a) inherent coherence, (b) internal consistency, (c) historical consistency, (d) external consistency/validity - testing it against 'known and probable facts' (*Natwest Markets Plc v Bilta (UK) Ltd* [2021] EWCA Civ 680 at [49], per Asplin, Andrews and Birss LJJ, jointly), since it is prudent 'to test [witnesses'] veracity by reference to the objective facts proved independently of their testimony, in particular by reference to the documents in the case' (*The Ocean Frost* [1985] 1 Lloyd's Rep 1 at p.57, per Robert Goff LJ) [2];

(5) The process must be iterative, considering all the evidence recursively before reaching any final conclusion, but the court must start somewhere (*Re A (A Child)* [2022] EWCA Civ 1652 at [34], per Peter Jackson J (as then was)):

'... the judge had to start somewhere and that was how the case had been pleaded. However, it should be acknowledged that she could equally have taken the allegations in a different order, perhaps chronological. What mattered was that she sufficiently analysed the evidence overall and correlated the main elements with each other before coming to her final conclusion.'

(6) The court must decide whether the fact to be proved happened or not. Fencesitting is not permitted (*In re B* [2008] UKSC 35 at [32], per Lady Hale);

(7) The law invokes a binary system of truth values (*In re B* at [2], per Lord Hoffmann):

'If a legal rule requires a fact to be proved (a "fact in issue"), a judge or jury must decide whether or not it happened. There is no room for a finding that it might have happened. The law operates a binary system in which the only values are 0 and 1. The fact either happened or it did not. If the tribunal is left in doubt, the doubt is resolved by a rule that one party or the other carries the burden of proof. If the party who bears the burden of proof fails to discharge it, a value of 0 is returned and the fact is treated as not having happened. If he does discharge it, a value of 1 is returned and the fact is treated as having happened.'

(8) There are important and recognised limits on the reliability of human memory: (a) our memory is a notoriously imperfect and fallible recording device; (b) the more confident a witness appears does not necessarily translate to a correspondingly more accurate recollection; (c) the process of civil litigation subjects the memory to 'powerful biases', particularly where a witness has a 'tie of loyalty' to a party (*Gestmin SCPS S.A. v Credit Suisse (UK) Ltd EWHC 3560 (Comm)* at [15]-[22], per Leggatt J (as then was)); and the court should be wary of 'story-creep', as memory fades and accounts are repeated over steadily elapsing time (*Lancashire County Council v C, M and F (Children - Factfinding)* [2014] EWFC 3 at [9], per Peter Jackson J); [3]

(9) The court 'takes account of any inherent probability or improbability of an event having occurred as part of the natural process of reasoning' (*Re BR (Proof of Facts)* [2015] EWFC 41 at [7], per Peter Jackson J); 'Common sense, not law, requires that ... regard should be had, to whatever extent appropriate, to inherent probabilities' (*In re B* at [15], per Lord Hoffmann);

(10) Contemporary documents are 'always of the utmost importance' (*Onassis v Vergottis* [1968] 2 Lloyd's Rep. 403 at 431, per Lord Pearce), [4] but in their absence, greater weight will be placed on inherent probability or improbability of witness's accounts:

'It is necessary to bear in mind, however, that this is not one of those cases in which the accounts given by the witnesses can be tested by reference to a body of contemporaneous documents. As a result the judge was forced to rely heavily on his assessment of the witnesses and the inherent plausibility or implausibility of their accounts. (*Jafari-Fini v Skillglass Ltd* [2007] EWCA Civ 261 at [80], per Moore-Bick LJ);'

And to same effect:

'Faced with documentary lacunae of this nature, the judge has little choice but to fall back on considerations such as the overall plausibility of the evidence (*Natwest Markets* at [50]).'

(11) The judge can use findings or provisional findings affecting the credibility of a witness on one issue in respect of another (*Bank St Petersburg PJSC v Arkhangelsky* [2020] EWCA Civ 408). [5]

(12) However, the court must be vigilant to avoid the fallacy that adverse credibility conclusions/findings on one issue are determinative of another and/or render the witness's evidence worthless. They are simply relevant:

'If a court concludes that a witness has lied about a matter, it does not follow that he has lied about everything. (*R v Lucas* [1981] QB 720, per Lord Lane CJ);'

Similarly, Charles J:

'a conclusion that a person is lying or telling the truth about point A does not mean that he is lying or telling the truth about point B... (*A Local Authority v K, D and L* [2005] EWHC 144 (Fam) at [28]).'

What is necessary is (a) a self-direction about possible 'innocent' reasons/explanations for the lies (if that they be); and (b) a recognition that a witness may lie about some things and yet be truthful 'on the essentials ... the underlying realities' (*Re A (A Child) (No.2)* [2011] EWCA Civ 12 at [104], per Munby LJ).

(13) Decisions should not be based 'solely' on demeanour (*Re M (Children)* [2013] EWCA Civ 1147 at [12], per Macur LJ); but demeanour, fairly assessed in context, retains a place in the overall evaluation of credibility: see *Re B-M (Children: Findings of Fact)* [2021] EWCA Civ 1371, per Ryder LJ:

'a witness's demeanour may offer important information to the court about what sort of a person the witness truly is, and consequently whether an account of past events or future intentions is likely to be reliable (at [23]);'

so long as

'due allowance [is] made for the pressures that may arise from the process of giving evidence (at [25]).'

But ultimately, demeanour alone is rarely likely to be decisive. Atkin LJ said it almost 100 years ago (*Societe d'Avances Commerciales (SA Egyptienne) v Merchans' Marine Insurance Co (The 'Palitana')* (1924) 20 Ll. L. Rep. 140 at 152):

'... an ounce of intrinsic merit or demerit in the evidence, that is to say, the value of the comparison of evidence with known facts, is worth pounds of demeanour.'"

[22a] *Powell v University Hospitals Sussex NHS Foundation Trust* [2023] EWHC 736 (KB) at [25].

Where there is a paucity of evidence, the fact-finding task of a judge can pose significant problems. In the context of a road traffic accident where there may be a lack of live evidence from witnesses and little to go on, a judge should be wary of falling into the trap of making unwarranted precise findings. [22b]

[22b] *Lambert v Clayton* [2009] EWCA Civ 237; [2010] R.T.R. 3 at [35]–[39]; *Zanatta v Metroline Travel Ltd* [2023] EWCA Civ 224; [2023] R.T.R. 26 at [31]–[35].

3. TYPES OF EVIDENCE

(a) Factual witnesses

In the second paragraph, after "... or that of the party calling him.", add:

It is not an uncommon feature of litigation that witnesses who have a consider- **45-15** able amount to gain if their recollection of events is accepted by the court are biased in their recollections towards the outcome they seek, and the witness may unconsciously reconstruct these events.[29a]

[29a] *Bannister v Freemans Plc* [2020] EWHC 1256 (QB); *Jackman v Harold Firth and Son Ltd* [2021] EWHC 1461 (QB); *Goyal v BGF Investment Management Ltd* [2023] EWHC 1180 (Comm); [2023] 4 W.L.R. 65 at [77]; *A v B* [2022] EWHC 3089 (Fam); [2023] 1 W.L.R. 677 at [49]; *Seneschall v Trisant Foods Ltd* [2023] EWHC 1029 (Ch) at [110].

(c) Documentary evidence

Replace footnote 59 with:

[59] *Simetra Global Assets Ltd v Ikon Finance Ltd* [2019] EWCA Civ 1413 at [48]; see also *Aspinalls Club* **45-30** *Ltd v Lester Hui Chun Mo* [2023] EWHC 2036 (KB) at [137]; *Watchstone Group Plc v Pricewater-houseCoopers LLP* [2023] EWHC 1133 (Comm) at [155]–[160].

Replace footnote 60 with:

[60] R. *(Dutta) v General Medical Council* [2020] EWHC 1974 (Admin) at [39]; *Hay v Cresswell* [2023] EWHC 882 (KB); [2023] E.M.L.R. 17 at [39]–[42] (testing recollection of witnesses against the contemporary documentation)..

After the first paragraph, add new paragraph:

45-31 That not all contemporaneous documents carry the same weight is obvious. As noted by Cotter J in *Aspinalls Club Ltd v Lester Hui Chun Mo*[62a]:

"137. The events in this case took place over seven years ago. Given the inevitable deterioration in recollections over such a long period, significant assistance is obviously likely to be gained from the contemporaneous documents, together with inferences drawn from those documents. An obvious example of a document establishing a baseline of facts against which recollections can be judged is the automatically produced records of the time and amount of any bet placed on the evening in question (and other earlier occasions). However, not all contemporaneous documentation carries the same weight and it is necessary to treat with caution documentation which may have been self-serving at the time of creation and to consider carefully whether the document can be taken at face value."

[62a] *Aspinalls Club Ltd v Lester Hui Chun Mo* [2023] EWHC 2036 (KB) at [137].

CHAPTER 46

APPENDIX: MISCELLANEOUS STATUTES, RULES, ETC.

TABLE OF CONTENTS

Note

Replace "[Accessed 22 October 2021]" with:
  [Accessed 22 September 2023]

the considerable body of new case law that has emerged since the previous edition. Students and practitioners will find comprehensive and practical case law illustrations in relation to every point and an unparalleled analysis of Convention authority. The new edition has been revised to reflect recent statutory developments such as coming into force of Protocols 15 and 16 and case law concerning issues such as surrogacy, migrants' rights, privacy of email, racial profiling, age assessment of migrants, euthanasia, bulk interception of communications, cyberbullying and internet at work (among other things).

Gatley on Libel and Slander, 13th Edition

Richard Parkes KC, Godwin Busuttil, Professor David Rolph, Professor Alastair Mullis, Dr Andrew Scott, Tom Blackburn SC

978-0-414-09970-8
May 2022
Hardback/Westlaw UK/ProView eBook

Part of the prestigious Common Law Library, *Gatley on Libel and Slander* has established itself as the definitive work on defamation law and practice. The work has been comprehensively updated and restructured throughout to provide a thorough examination of the English law of defamation and other media and communications claims, including malicious falsehood, privacy, data protection and harassment—both substantive and procedural. The 13th edition also contains new chapters on serious harm and the defences of truth, honest opinion and publication on a matter of public interest.

Documentary Evidence, 14th Edition

Charles Hollander KC

978-0-414-09203-7
September 2021
Hardback/Westlaw UK/ProView eBook

Documentary Evidence is a comprehensive guide to the legal obligations of disclosure. Logically presented and lucidly written, it provides detailed analysis and sensible practical advice. Following a chronological structure, it shows when and how a practitioner should take action in relation to the obligation to disclose. It is a standard work that is often cited in court judgments. The 14th edition includes a rewritten and revised Chapters 6 (Access to Court Documents), 7 (Disclosure under CPR 31), 8 (The Disclosure Pilot) and 9 (Disclosure Principles). It also includes detailed coverage of new case law including *Dring v Cape Intermediate Holdings Ltd, Arcelormittal USA LLC v Essar Global Funds Ltd, Volaw Trust & Corporate Services Ltd v Office of Comptroller of Taxes (Jersey), WH Holdings Ltd v E20 Stadium LLP, Glencore International AG v Commissioners of Tax for Australia* and *PJSC Tatneft v Bogolyubov.*